BEYOND THE GREEN ECONOMY

The world needs a new economy. In spite of tremendous and growing material prosperity, inequality is on the rise and the current organization of the Earth's natural resources has failed to address the basic human needs of billions of people. This book exposes the bottlenecks of the present path of economic growth and discusses the main path to alternatives.

In spite of undeniable advances, all evidence points towards the growing depletion of the very ecosystems that societies depend on. By placing ethics squarely in the middle of economic life, this book demonstrates the need for a new economy, one that fosters unity between society, nature, economics and ethics. It questions the most important scientific and political pillar that forms the basis for evaluating social resource use: economic growth.

Written in a non-specialist language, this book is an introduction to the main issues involving sustainable development. It will be essential reading for both students and professionals working in the field of socioenvironmental responsibility.

Ricardo Abramovay is Professor in the Department of Economics, University of São Paulo, Brazil.

BEYOND THE GREEN ECONOMY

Ricardo Abramovay

Routledge
Taylor & Francis Group

LONDON AND NEW YORK

First published 2016
by Routledge
2 Park Square, Milton Park, Abingdon, Oxon OX14 4RN

and by Routledge
711 Third Avenue, New York, NY 10017

Routledge is an imprint of the Taylor & Francis Group, an informa business

British Library Cataloguing in Publication Data
A catalogue record for this book is available from the British Library

Library of Congress Cataloging in Publication Data
Abramovay, Ricardo.
[Muito alem da economia verde. English]
Beyond the green economy / Ricardo Abramovay.
Revised and translated edition of Muito alem da economia verde.
Includes bibliographical references and index.
1. Sustainable development. 2. Sustainable development—Brazil.
3. Economic development—Social aspects. 4. Environmental
economics. 5. Environmental economics—Brazil. 6. Agriculture—
Economic aspects. 7. Agriculture—Economic aspects—Brazil. I. Title.
HC79.E5A25513 2015
338.9'27—dc23
2015012990

ISBN: 978-1-138-93885-4 (hbk)
ISBN: 978-1-138-93886-1 (pbk)
ISBN: 978-1-315-67539-8 (ebk)

Typeset in Bembo
by Book Now Ltd, London

Printed and bound in Great Britain by
TJ International Ltd, Padstow, Cornwall

To Ignacy Sachs, who teaches us, always, to look for the third bank of the river.

CONTENTS

ILLUSTRATIONS

Figures

Tables

Boxes

FUNDACIÓN AVINA – PRESENTATION

As a Latin American foundation, a commitment to sustainable development in Latin America is at the heart of the mission of Fundación Avina. While our region has advanced on a number of fronts over the past decades, still there is a growing perception that this progress is not always balanced or sustainable. Is the economic growth we have seen in recent years sustainable? What levels of consumption can our natural resource base withstand?

Instead of paralysing us, these questions and concerns constantly challenge us to find new roads and better solutions with potential relevance not only for our own region but for others as well. That is why Avina has supported and pushed for social change in Latin America over the past 20 years through hundreds of actions and initiatives. One such action was to team up with Professor Ricardo Abramovay to produce the research and ideas that are contained in this publication.

This book is the result of a process of open debate led by Ricardo with a working group created and coordinated by Avina in Brazil in 2011. Our objective was, and continues to be, to extend conceptual and practical knowledge, exploring the opportunities and the challenges of creating an economy compatible with sustainability. We hope in this way to make our current and future action strategies more effective.

In recognition of the value of this text for a number of regional and global discussions, our intention from the beginning was to share the products of this debate. We are very pleased with the response thus far to the Portuguese and Spanish releases and hope that the English-speaking audience will be similarly engaged.

This book is an invitation to join in building a new economy, one in which business and market practices incorporate ethical considerations, where innovation is the norm and where incentives favour real value creation for people and the planet. We hope this publication can serve as an inspiration for other individuals and organizations that are, like us, committed to promoting and working for the common good.

Sean McKaughan
Board Chair of Fundación Avina

FOREWORD

Marina Silva –

> Brazilian environmentalist and politician; Former Minister of the Environment; Former Senator; recipient of the Sophie Prize (2009) and Goldman Environmental Prize (2007); named one of the 'Champions of the Earth' by the United Nations Environment Programme (2007) and 'Woman of the Year' by the *Financial Times* (2014).

What lies beyond a green economy? That question seems – to me – to be a good way to start this foreword to Ricardo Abramovay's excellent work. And why is that? Another question; but such questions are essential, and the author presents them throughout the work in a daring but unpretentious manner. Indeed, unpretentiousness itself is one of our main forms of daring. Among the questions he poses are:

> *A new economy to what end? What kind of life do we want to lead? What is the significance and the sense of economic life? Poor in what way? How much is enough? Does inequality really matter? Is more always worth more? If economic growth is not the main route to greater happiness, what is?*

Raising question after question, the author weaves the fabric of his ideas and reveals his understanding in regard to social and economic relations. He presents complex concepts in an instructive way and, above all, objectively and consistently addresses each one of the questions he raises.

The reasoning is constructed pebble by pebble – each one carefully set in a good, thick mortar of data, information and examples – just like those solid, sophisticated buildings made of rough unshaped stones in which the setting of each one calls for much more than the minimal amounts of cement used in standard stone setting.

One question in particular caught my attention: could capitalism ever show consideration for the world at large? First the author shows us how capitalism, in the way it operates today, fails to take the world into consideration. To do so he has recourse to the conceptual bases of the market-based economy proposed by Friedrich von Hayek, winner of the Nobel Prize for Economics, whereby individual decisions – taking prices as their main choice parameter – ensure the best possible allocation of the economy's overall resources. Abramovay synthesizes Hayek's thinking in the following way:

> *What actually foster coordination, human cooperation, are not the actions specifically aimed at achieving it. It is a system that no one has control over and which transmits the information needed to all decision makers: the market, through the medium of prices.*

And so he goes on, showing us in an educational way that the markets are social structures that can, and must urgently, incorporate environmental and ethical values. Furthermore, the counterpoint to individual decisions as the market-organizing element is not planning but, instead, the cooperation provided by the new communication structures. Therein lies, *in my view, and with all due poetic licence, the old but utterly up-to-date Shakespearean dilemma moulding the questions posed in the book: the individual and the collective – behold, the inseparable dual.* How can the essential mediation of individual and collective interests be conducted in such a way as to avoid widening the gap that separates the latter from the productive, creative and free motivation of individuals, without which the necessary support for human affairs could never exist?

As the author observes, such processes are still merely incipient but they are by no means irrelevant. For that very reason he stimulates his readers by presenting a long list of innovative initiatives that includes everything from free software, new ways of remunerating intellectual property or cultural production rights, innovative business in the world of fashion, and distributed energy production, to systems for hiring vehicles that break away from the individual ownership of goods, and many other examples.

It is society occupying new spheres of governance in a new social metabolism, as the book defines it. Instruments such as tracking and certification systems are already being created, an important example of how the market is increasingly taking other values into account besides those of the market. Another example presented in the book is the description of the agreement that was drawn up between the socioenvironmental organizations and the major soy producers in 2006 to reduce deforestation. In that case, the ethical embarrassment caused by the government authorities' real-time publication of information on deforestation was a strong motivating factor for the signing of the agreement to take place. In other words, the free circulation of information is capable of inducing fundamental processes for the emergence of a new economy based on ethical values.

Not to bypass a single one of the more inconvenient questions: is there really any space in today's world for ethical values? Yes, there is, when humanity faces up to its greatest challenge, one that could make its very survival as a species unfeasible – the limits set by the ecosystems' capacity to regenerate themselves. As the author puts it in the first lines of the introduction, our unsustainable way of being and doing has already destroyed or severely threatened the existence of 16 of the 24 major fundamental services that ecosystems provide for the maintenance of our economic activities and of life itself.

We find it difficult to accept the idea of limitations because it obliges us to make difficult choices. So, if we really intend to maintain our ethical intent to constantly expand substantive individual freedoms as proposed by Amartya Sen, another winner of the Nobel Prize for Economics quoted by Abramovay, then we do need a new economy.

And what would that new economy be like? Given that the author uses questions as the main basis and fuel to stimulate readers to pose their own questions, I would offer another quote:

> *Increasing efficiency and reducing inequality in the use of resources are the strategic objectives of a new economy which has ethics at the heart of its decision-making processes and supports itself on a social metabolism capable of guaranteeing the healthy reproduction of human societies.*

This quotation carries an outstanding message: reducing inequality is not just desirable, it is the necessary way forward, and the author helps us to choose it by presenting deliberately extensive data that reveal the tremendous inequality that exists in the use of natural resources such as energy – including the use of fossil fuels – as well as minerals and other material resources extracted from the Earth.

And to address the double challenge of reducing carbon emissions and reducing inequalities, gains in the efficiency of productive processes are essential, but, at the same time, they are insufficient on their own. We need to reinvent ourselves and reconnect with one another and with Nature. We need a new relationship that redefines happiness and places collective well-being in first place.

A new economy calls for a new culture and that involves a certain discontinuity in the values passed on by a high consumption society *"that fails to take the world at large into consideration"*. It calls for fair, sustainable forms of consumption, supported by a vision of the world that sees sustainability as a way of being, a life ideal for now and for the future – one that is capable of providing the conditions to foster a healthier relationship with time, a drawing closer to Nature and the overcoming of any fears of relating to it, and to foster our own reenchantment with people and with ourselves.

To become amenable to making such changes, we need to understand the meaning of what really motivates us. Ricardo Abramovay's work helps us to achieve that understanding and that fact is the driving force that sustains his highly relevant contribution.

ACKNOWLEDGEMENTS

In June 2011 I had the privilege of being approached by the Fundación Avina with a request to help towards promoting a reflection on 'new economy' without the meaning of the term being very narrowly defined. Much more important, however, than any eventual clearly pre-established conceptual reference framework are the parameters on which Avina bases its own performance. The ethics of caring, an expression widely used by Leonardo Boff and Bernardo Toro, is at the very root of Avina's own culture.[1] Far from being restricted to a set of rigid orders, the ethics of caring or the care paradigm is a general orientation whereby the fight against various forms of injustice and in favour of sustainable development first has to go through the stages in which each individual conquers, above all else, the capacity to be the protagonist of his or her own emancipation. In that sense then, well-being is not fundamentally a result that can be expressed by measuring what people receive or possess. It is a process of construction in which their victories are presumed to be associated with personal growth, strengthening of community identities and bonds, and, at the same time, strengthening of their ability to respond to the challenges of innovation and contact with social groups that are not part of their universe. It is very close, as will be seen in Chapter 1, to the thinking of Amartya Sen and Martha Nussbaum. My task was to think on what is possibly the most emblematic theme (economy and society) of sociological thinking in the light of the ethic or paradigm of caring. To that end, contact with various Avina Foundation members and others that Avina works with was decisive.

Thus I must mention Neylar Lins, Valdemar de Oliveira Neto, Telma Rocha, Anna Romanelli, Paulo Rocha, Paula Ellinger, Cynthia Loria, Rafael Luna, Ramiro Fernandez, Carlos Miller, Carlos March, Cecilia Baria, Sean McKaughan, Federico Bellone, Guyaana Páez Acosta, Oscar Fergutz, Juliana Strobel and Pedro Tarak.

In addition to the interaction with the Fundación Avina, the detailed criticisms and suggestions I received from José Eli da Veiga, Roberto Smeraldi, Anamaria

Schindler, Nelmara Arbex, Jacques Marcovitch, Thiago Morello Silva, Ronaldo Lemos, Márcio Vasconcellos and Rachel Biderman were of fundamental importance.

In December 2011 a group of friends and colleagues met in São Paulo, at the FEA/USP, to discuss the work which eventually transformed into this book. I need hardly state how pleased and honoured I felt by the suggestions and criticisms I received, albeit the text that the reader now has in his or her hands is certainly of a lesser quality than the observations made in that and other discussions by Marina Silva, Bazileu Alves Margarido Neto, Paulo Itacarambi, Tasso Azevedo, Nelmara Arbex, Roberto S. Waack, Anamaria Schindler, Fabio Feldmann, Maria Alice Setubal, Eduardo Viola, José Eli da Veiga, Carlos Antonio Rocha Vicente, Rubens Born and Carolina Evangelista. The assistance given by Quico Meirelles and Thiago Morello Silva on the occasion of the seminar was also invaluable.

Let me also mention the team that stimulated the publication of the first version of this book in Portuguese and organized its launch at the Rio+20. They belong to Planeta Sustentável, an open platform dedicated to sustainable development issues.[2] Many thanks to Caco de Paula, Matthew Shirts, Gabriela Moya and Mônica Nunes. I am also grateful to my translator, Martin Charles Nicholl, and to Maria Bitarello who has worked with me on the revision of the first edition of this book.

Notes

1 'The ethics of caring' is a fundamental expression in the thinking of Leonardo Boff (http://leonardoboff.com, consulted on 19 March 2012). There is an interesting confe-rence given by Bernardo Toro on the 'Paradigm of Care' (https://www.youtube.com/watch?v=5nivihNqbXk, consulted on 24 June 2015). His definition of the paradigm is inspiring: it is like spectacles, not before our eyes but in our very brains.
2 See http://planetasustentavel.abril.com.br (consulted on 25 June 2015).

INTRODUCTION: PUTTING THE ECONOMY TO WORK FOR DEVELOPMENT

The world needs a new economy. In spite of the tremendous and growing material prosperity, the current organization of the use of resources that are essential to social reproduction fails to adequately address the proposal to foster the permanent expansion of substantive human freedoms.[1] The destruction or, at the very least, the serious threats to no less than 16 of the 24 services that ecosystems provide to society show that all that apparent vigour has feet of clay.[2] The chances of keeping the rise in temperatures down to two degrees in the course of the twenty-first century are now minimal, and the catastrophic perspective of a four-degree rise is increasingly present in the scenarios examined in internationally renowned journals and reviews.[3] Despite the impressive reduction in poverty levels in developing countries, billions of people still do not have even the most precarious access to the means for meeting their most basic needs. Almost everywhere inequalities are on the rise: in incomes, in energy consumption, in emissions, in consumption, in health and in education – all at the same time that production is expanding. Corporate and civil society leaders and multilateral development organizations are increasingly converging on the idea that 'business as usual' is actually the quickest way to end up in dire straits. There may be disagreement as to what the term stands for, but the affirmation that any progress in the development process must necessarily involve the emergence of a 'new economy' is almost indisputable. But a new economy to what end?

The response of the overwhelming majority of private sector leaders, government authorities and multilateral bodies, and even a significant portion of trade union leaders, is that the basic mission of a new economy is to increase goods and services supply. In that line of thinking, increased consumption is what will make it possible to address the basic needs of those billions of people who still live in conditions of extreme material deprivation, and economic growth will foster social cohesion, insofar as it will create jobs, increase tax revenues and make it possible to further expand the supply of public and private goods and services. As an example of that kind of response, national and international authorities of countries affected by the 2008 crisis are unanimous in declaring their belief that the core objective of policies designed to attenuate its effects must be to regain economic growth. There are two basic flaws to that argument, and they reveal how urgent it is to review the parameters currently used to analyse the relations between society and its economic life.

First, the idea of continual growth of production and consumption conflicts with the limitations imposed by the ecosystems on the expansion of the production systems. The second problem is that, up until now, the effective capability of the functioning production systems to create social cohesion and make a positive contribution to eradicating poverty has been extremely limited. Furthermore, any link between the expansion of goods and services production and gains in the form of the well-being of people, communities and their territories, facilitated by a certain level of abundance, is increasingly difficult to detect. Even though the production of material goods has reached an impressive level, there have never been so many people living in extreme poverty, albeit representing a smaller proportion of the general population than at any other time in modern history. Even in the planet's richest countries, there is now an abundance of studies showing that increases in the availability of material goods and income are far from bearing any proportional relationship to a generalized feeling of improved quality of life.

In these conditions, what is the point of incessantly expanding the economic system even in those places where access to goods and services necessary for a decent social life has already been almost universally guaranteed? One of the greatest challenges faced by a reflection of this nature is that formulating objectives for an economic system that does not fundamentally depend on its own permanent expansion also means formulating objectives for companies that will alter the meaning of corporate activity and the measurements of its efficiency. At the same time, as Peter Victor has shown so clearly, it means assessing the worth of people's personal objectives: "for people to be happy living in a no growth (steady state) economy there needs to be a reassessment of what is important in life ... growth would no longer be the most important thing but, instead, having more free time and a better social life with stronger communities", which brings us back to questioning the importance and value of consumption in people's lives.[4] As Victor points out, the real question is, what kind of a life do we want to lead? The fact that the use of social resources depends on the initiative of economic agents acting in a decentralized manner makes it unfeasible to set those objectives in a hierarchy stemming from the power of a central authority. Thus, considering that the process in question is evolutionary, the transition that is the subject of this book is expressed in the emergence of new forms of corporate organization and new individual aspirations that are beginning to have decisive weight in private management and in the way individuals relate to the world of consumption. The decisive point of this evolution is the growing influence that public policies and, above all, a variety of social forces have on it, interfering more and more explicitly in companies' management systems and their value chains. That is what makes it feasible to imprint a strategic orientation on this evolutionary process.

The alternative strategy for the transition to a new economy (one whose meaning no longer lies in the phenomenon of its own growth fuelled, in turn, by an incessant expansion in consumption) is guided by two decisive changes. The first concerns the relations between *society* and *nature*, and the essence of these changes can be best expressed in two key words, the most important one being *limits*. The best possibilities for the development process lie in the recognition of the limits of the ecosystems, and an important group of corporations is already headed in that direction. The prevailing idea in twentieth-century economics – that human talent and ingenuity would always be able to substitute exhausted resources and repair the damage caused by production and consumption – has revealed itself to be tragically mistaken, and climate change is the most resounding expression of that error. Limits are also apparent in the fact that crude oil is not alone in having already passed the peak of its production levels but is accompanied by a vast set of other raw materials whose extraction costs, in terms of energy consumption, are soaring at an alarming rate. Not even the extraordinary progress achieved with renewable energy sources, the chemical and biological advances in handling plants and soils or the technological achievements in recycling and reusing residues will be capable of providing humanity with any kind of energy and material cornucopia that would make the idea of limits redundant.[5]

The second important word in the sphere of changing the relations between society and nature is *innovation*. It is fundamental that limitations and innovation go hand in hand. Innovation however must not be generically mistaken for increased productivity – how to produce more and more with less and less work or capital. Today, more than ever, innovation means improving the transformation of energy, materials and biodiversity itself into products and services in ways that are useful to society. It is in that sense that the discussion today revolves around the need for *sustainability-oriented innovation systems* – in other words, directed at reducing the current dependency of the economic system on the increasing use of material and energetic resources. Twentieth-century innovation systems concentrated on increasing capital and labour's productivity, which are considered to be relatively scarce factors in comparison with natural resources whose prices, overall, went steadily down and nowadays are imbued with an impressive volatility.[6] While the world population increased fourfold in the course of the century, the global GDP increased 20-fold (with obvious impacts stemming from the increased demand for energy and materials), and the index that measures commodity prices fell by almost half. That latter decline was interrupted in the first decade of the twenty-first century and prices have become three times more volatile, fluctuating around values 50% higher than those that had typified their behaviour from the 1980s onwards. As one of the papers of the 2011 McKinsey global consultancy states, the consequence is that companies need to concentrate their "strategic and operational focus on resource productivity".

A new economy has precisely the function of underscoring the finite nature of those resources while, at the same time, stimulating creativity in the processes for obtaining goods and services based on the increasingly intelligent, efficient and parsimonious use of materials, energy and biodiversity. The most emblematic expression of this challenge is the need to cut global greenhouse gas emissions by something in the range of 50% to 80% by 2050, while, at the same time, making sure that doing so does not prevent billions of individuals from achieving living standards that ensure that they are not deprived of those basic freedoms that are indispensable to a dignified existence.[7] Such emissions are vastly unequal (in 2004, the United States emitted 155 times more greenhouse gases than Bangladesh, and 74 times more if the calculation is made on a per capita basis).[8] That means limitations and innovation can only be approached in the light of a global effort against inequality in the use of wealth.

A document produced by the UN Department of Economic and Social Affairs in 2011 went so far as to advocate that a per capita limit on energy consumption should be established – 70 gigajoules a year – which would mean that an average European would have to cut his energy consumption by half and an average North American by three-quarters.[9] Indian citizens on the other hand would have plenty of space to expand their primary consumption, which currently stands at around 15 gigajoules. That proposed limit, however, only refers to primary energy consumption (the energy corresponding to a barrel of oil, for example), and it could be amply compensated for by innovation, that is to say, by increasing energy use efficiency at all stages prior to the actual service provision or goods production it will be used for.[10]

In a similar vein, inequality in the very use of material resources on which economic life is actually based needs to be drastically reduced. Global extraction of resources (considering only the physical weight of biomass, fossil fuels, ores and industrial minerals and construction materials) increased no less than eightfold over the course of the twentieth century.[11] In 1980 it stood at 35 billion tons a year and by 2005 it was up to 60 billion tons. That means an annual average of around 9 tons a year per inhabitant. What that fails to show is that a person born in India today will only be using 4 tons a year, while a Canadian citizen uses 25 tons a year throughout his lifetime. In coal alone, a US citizen consumes an average 3.4 tons a year.[12] In the preface of the UN Environment Programme (UNEP) report for 2011, which addresses this question, Achim Steiner does not hesitate to declare that in the coming decades the amount of resources used by each inhabitant of the earth will have to drop to somewhere around 6 tons per capita and that can only be done by uniting limitations and innovation.

The secret of the new economy lies in the emergence of a special *social metabolism* capable of ensuring the permanence and regeneration of the services that the ecosystems provide to society. To be more precise, the new economy should be supported by an *industrial metabolism* that drastically reduces the use of carbon in its material and energy bases while at the same time offering possibilities for the basic needs of human beings to be met within the limits of the ecosystems' capabilities.[13] That presupposes a drastic reduction in inequality and, at the same time, expanding material and energy productivity of the production processes by means of innovation. A new social metabolism supports itself on the basis of a revision of the objectives of the economic system itself. It is incompatible with the currently prevailing tenet whereby the economy's purpose is to foster the incessant growth of production and consumption.

That in turn leads to another change, just as important as the first, and without which the significance of the *limits/innovation* duality would be seriously jeopardized. It is the relationship between *economics* and *ethics*. The transition to a new economy presumes that ethics (i.e. questions involving good, justice and virtue) will occupy a central position in decisions on the use of material and energy resources and in the organization of people's work itself. The central question here is one that most of the social sciences consider unfounded: produce and consume, but to what end? That is not a mere pious or traditionalist utterance or an expression of the vain wish of those who fail to understand the real logic of the way business is organized. Quite the contrary; placing ethics squarely in the middle of economic life (and that means insisting on the human finalities of production and the use of wealth) is the core theme of some of the most important currents of contemporary social thinking. Indeed, nowadays, corporate administration itself can no longer measure its efficiency merely by referring to the accounting balance; it has been increasingly incorporating into its sets of evaluation parameters the immediate effects it has on the lives of individuals, families, territories and the ecosystems. That goes far beyond what has been referred to in the debate so far as 'corporate socioenvironmental responsibility' and it is also not restricted to minimizing the eventual negative impacts stemming from the very existence of the corporation. Instead it means situating the economic activity as part of a process that regenerates the social and environmental fabric. As an example, the North American organization Benefit Corporation explicitly proposes to use the power of business to solve social and environmental problems.[14]

As another example, it makes less and less sense for the foodstuffs industry to treat the global epidemic of obesity as an issue that has nothing to do with it. The logic that consists of producing goods whose daily consumption is largely responsible for widespread obesity and at the same time building sports courts or stimulating the recycling of water used to produce soft drinks is fatally flawed in its origin, as has been clearly revealed in an important work published in the *Harvard Business Review* in 2011 by Michael Porter and Mark Kramer. It fails to take into account that the creation of value on the part of the company cannot be decently reconciled with the effects of consuming its products (however much the manufacturers may have improved their production methods in comparison with former methods) leads to socially negative results.

Another highly emblematic example is the automobile industry; it is shocking that it still sets an increase in the number of individual vehicles as its corporate horizon in the face of the glaring inadequacy of such vehicles in addressing the problems of urban and metropolitan mobility. The issue involved transcends the question of corporate socioenvironmental responsibility and strikes at the very heart of business itself. It is the micro-dimension of the macro-challenge that consists of making economic growth a means and not an intransigent end, unyielding to anything other than itself.

The hardest argument to get across concerning the emergence of a new economy is that this challenge needs to be faced, not by means of any state monopoly over entrepreneurial decisions, or by abolishing the markets, but rather in the sphere of a decentralized economy in which the markets play a decisive but obviously not exclusive role.

One gleam of hope in addressing this issue is that social participation in public life, resulting from a considerable strengthening of civil society, now has a tremendous and largely unexploited potential for interfering in the most important corporate decisions. The advent of the information networks society at the end of the twentieth century opened up revolutionary possibilities for the advancement of unprecedented forms of cooperation as the basis for the functioning of the economic world. A new economy's mission is to expand the participation of individuals and various kinds of communities in innovation processes and the creation of wealth. Far from being a mere vague desire, such expansion is based on the power to recombine, mix and bring into contact social, cognitive, material and financial worlds, which, up until a short time ago, functioned in an entirely segmented way. The new economy is much more than the mere result of certain communication and information techniques; at its heart lies the possibility of organizing society on the basis of relatively cheap instruments, working in networks readily accessible to individuals and in which the potential for social participation in public life and business is greater than ever before. Information, culture and knowledge come under the aegis of a single form of logic whereby the boundaries (so typical of an industrial society) between production, distribution and consumption become fainter and fainter. Far from the image of an inert consumer sitting in front of a television screen that spews out contents in his direction (typical of the old culture industry), the dynamics of the new digital culture are eminently participative, and that alters the social hierarchy itself, in the production and diffusion of culture.

However, far from treating information, culture and knowledge as a separate domain, the digital media open the way that enables social cooperation to take on the organization and supply of goods and services in the most diverse domains, ranging from the decentralized production of energy to sharing the use of automobiles and even of buildings, as will be shown in the course of this book. The digital media go well beyond being simply a simple new technology and open up a pathway to what Jeremy Rifkin calls 'lateral power', that is, an economic organization based on widespread, large-scale social cooperation that is capable of attaining allocative efficiency based on shared use and decentralization of resources.[15]

It is in that sense that Michel Bauwens insists on doing away with the idea of the rigid separation of market, government and civil society – a separation that is strongly imprinted on the very formation of the social sciences themselves.[16] According to such separation the market is inevitably a blind sphere incapable of providing society with those goods and services that would improve people's lives.

Bauwens' work shows that civil society is the foundation of the markets, of the common goods supply (the air, public spaces) and of the government itself.

The consequences of this new reality are decisive, not only in defining conventional property rights over the innovations but also because it opens up unprecedented prospects for social interaction in corporate management. That is particularly important in regard to knowledge and innovation. The open and, in many cases, voluntary models (often functioning based on ethical and community precepts) compete with forms that marked technological progress in the industrial economy. What is most interesting and promising in that respect is that it is not only the alternative and relatively marginalized communities but also some large companies that adopt new open models of innovation. Tesla, for instance, opened up its patents on its battery and energy storage in 2014 under the motto "all our patents belong to you",[17] and Patagonia did the same with its guayule rubber wetsuits.[18] At the same time, the digital media confer unprecedented potential on grassroots economic initiatives based on direct forms of social cooperation that can range from water resource management through waste pickers' cooperatives to micro-credit and other modalities of inclusive markets.

The main philosophical foundation for economics as it came to be consolidated at the end of the nineteenth century has been the idea that people and economic units (firms) act strictly in their own interests, and that the less they explicitly or intentionally coordinate their actions, the better the social results of whatever they do will be. In that light, the great virtue of the modern economy would lie in its power to surpass and emancipate social life from the communitarian and parochial restrictions with which tradition had always bound it. Thus human cooperation would only depend on material incentives to stimulate individuals separately, inducing them to offer on the market that for which they sought the highest possible remuneration and, in turn, seek to satisfy their desires there for the lowest possible price. From that standpoint, cooperation would be seen as always indirect, ephemeral and sporadic, and the cost of constructing personalized confidence, reputation and solid relationship ties is substituted by the mobility facilitated by the market. Thus the minimal, negligible nature of ethical norms in the workings of the market would be seen as a necessary condition to ensure its fluidity. That has been the decisive philosophical basis for the social organization of the world ever since the Industrial Revolution and it is on that foundation that the world has constructed its impressive material prosperity.

The importance of ethics in economic life is not just a new and far-reaching, alternative, philosophical aspiration but, rather, a decisive trait in social life which the information networks society values to an unprecedented extent. The means of producing wealth that is not based on private ownership or individual remuneration are multiplying. Collaborative communities with a shared ethic of interdependent contribution and at the same time highly cosmopolitan by nature mark the information networks economy. The result is the growth of direct social cooperation in the production of goods and services and also, increasingly, in the very processes of technological innovation. Recombinant innovation and mixture are present in open digital platforms dedicated to solving technical, economic and social problems and in those areas where the boundaries between private economy and direct social collaboration are tenuous.

Crowdsourcing, for example, is a way of solving social, technical, organizational or economic questions by means of an open appeal, a broad invitation to address a given problem based on public mechanisms for expressing criticism. It is a form of design widely used in the industrial world nowadays. As with consumption, in the production and distribution of cultural goods, the borders between the contributions of lay elements and those of experts are becoming blurred. 'Innocentive', for example, is an online network of 300,000 engineers, scientists and entrepreneurs dedicated to finding solutions to big private and public problems in various areas and, outstandingly, in the field of health. The whole process is fantastically accelerated by the multiplication and lowered cost of the means that allow access to these participative forms of cultural production, namely the Smartphone, currently being used by more than a quarter of the Brazilian population (which means around 60 million people).[19] As Pierre Lévy has shown, in 2011 no less than 65% of internauts are neither European nor American and the population around the world with an Internet connection at home has already passed the two billion mark, having grown by 500% since the beginning of the 2000 decade.[20]

A new economy that fosters unity between society and nature, between economics and ethics, questions the most important scientific and political pillar that forms the basis for evaluating social resource use – economic growth. Such questioning is not rooted in any supposedly conservative instinct to paralyse transformations capable of fulfilling human needs and desires. It is essential to pose a question that is notably absent from most of the social sciences: what is the significance and the sense of economic life? The answer offered by the last 150 years is economic growth, an entirely self-referenced and autonomous objective. Economics as a science began to consolidate itself in the last third of the nineteenth century as it gradually removed from its horizon any economic system objectives other than its own expansion. That idea has been at the root of the formation of the macroeconomy from Keynes' time up until today. The emergence of a new economy, on the other hand, presupposes measurements of resource use performance that are centred around its effects on human well-being and the state of the ecosystems.

The most notable recent studies on this theme show that, in spite of the importance of expanding the supply of goods and services to fulfil the basic needs of the billions of people who currently find themselves living in poverty, it is not possible to achieve that objective so widely recommended around the world, in rich countries and in poor, by using economic growth as the general solution. Recent studies conducted by Tim Jackson,[21] Peter Victor and Richard Heinberg[22] – and in Brazil, those of José Eli da Veiga[23] and Ladislau Dowbor[24] – make a convincing defence of the idea that countries attaining a certain level of prosperity and well-being should voluntarily renounce growth as the core objective of their macroeconomic policies. The economic systems of various Organisation for Economic Co-operation and

Development (OECD) member countries are sufficiently mature to allow their response to unemployment not to be an increase in production but rather an increase in their capacity to convert enhanced productivity into more leisure, more community life and a greater contribution to well-being stemming from the local economies.[25] The model Peter Victor has elaborated for Canada, for example, foresees a decade-long decline in the economy, after which it stabilizes. Developing nations, on the other hand, instead of directing their investments to growth in general, should direct it to goods and services that guarantee not employment generically but well-being combined with respect for and regeneration of the ecosystem services. Obviously, in every case, irrespective of the level of material wealth already attained, there will be a need for policies directed at transferring income that are indispensable to combating extreme poverty and reducing inequality. What is important here, however, is that it is not a question of promoting generalized growth and compensating its effects by supporting those that derive no benefit from it; it is a question of fostering the emergence of an economic system in which the innovations lead to a reduction in the need for work, in less consumption of materials and energy, less pollution and improvements in the quality of life.

It must be pointed out, however, that such objectives are far from constituting what could be considered a macroeconomics of sustainability. The different schools of macroeconomic thinking all have one common unified parameter for measuring economic system performance – prices. All the measurements concerning salaries, investments and incomes can be translated in terms of them. A macroeconomy of sustainability has to face the tremendous difficulties involved in handling measurement parameters that are not susceptible to being lumped together in a single form. Those parameters are associated with people's well-being, community cohesion and the various components of ecosystem preservation and regeneration.

In any event it is essential to bear in mind that the current dissociation of economic growth and social well-being is backed by immense scientific and political authority, as can be readily detected in the discussions conducted in institutions like the OECD and the World Bank. In scientific terms, the participations of two Nobel Prize winners and other renowned economists of the international scientific community in the Stiglitz report also reveal an important sign of the times in regard to the current relationship between economic growth and social well-being.[26]

The most important feature of the new economy, in that sense, is the effort made to increasingly enhance the visibility of the foundations and consequences of the different ways of producing wealth and of measuring it. Part of the wealth is handled by markets and is submitted to an exposure of its life cycle and accountability for the material and energy flows involved. Part of it stems from non-market forms of production, some of them direct (like cooperatives and volunteer groups), others indirect (in the way that increasingly occurs in the information networks society). What is even more interesting is that the markets and the non-market forms of production become increasingly mixed and are under decentralized forms of social control. In that way they confront that which, since capitalism began, has always been viewed as a kind of contradiction of terms, namely stimulating innovation in the sphere of a decentralized economy while at the same time transforming economic life into the means of achieving ends democratically determined by society.

This book is structured in four chapters in addition to this introduction. The first attempts to show that the material abundance of contemporary societies is a long way from producing the well-being that would be expected of it. Thus the chapter discusses what human beings' basic needs really are and how far off the workings of economic life are from meeting them.

The second chapter shows that in spite of the gains associated with the expansion of eco-efficiency in production processes, the pressures that threaten the continued existence of the ecosystem services that human life depends on continue to increase. In addition to its limited ability to produce well-being, the world economic system is founded on forms of use and, above all, forms of social distribution entirely incompatible with fighting poverty or satisfying the basic needs of the many.

The third chapter addresses what many do not hesitate to qualify as the equivalent of squaring the circle, namely the possibility that in the sphere of the decentralized economy where the markets play a decisive role, private corporations will respond to socioenvironmental objectives established by direct social pressure and participation and not in a diffuse manner, only influenced by the price system.

The fourth chapter displays one of the most important factors, introducing an element of hope associated with the transition process towards a new economy: the impressive progress registered by cooperation, a decisive feature of the information networks society.

Notes

1 This expression is used by Nobel Prize winner Amartya Sen (2000) and his colleague, Harvard University professor Martha Nussbaum (2011), and it has a double outreach. In the first place, increasing people's liberties is the main objective of the development process. But in second place, liberties are deliberately referred to here in the plural precisely because they are substantive; it is not just a question of the absence of restrictions but rather of the presence of conditions that make it possible for people to choose what they prefer for a life worth living. Anyone who is politically persecuted or oppressed or who is excessively poor is not in a position to make such choices. The theme is taken up again a little further on in the first chapter.

2 One of the single most important documents produced by the international scientific community at the beginning of the new millennium shows that social life depends on a whole set of ecosystem services such as climate equilibrium, photosynthesis, availability of soils, clean water supply and geochemical cycles, as well as other services associated with leisure and contemplation. The main reference here is the 2005 Millennium Ecosystem Assessment, which presents a very worrying portrayal of the current state of such services.

3 In 1988 the United Nations set up a body composed of scientists from various countries which from then to now has prepared five periodic reports on the relations between human society and the climate system. One of the main conclusions drawn by the Intergovernmental Panel on Climate Change (IPCC, 2011) is that if global warming increases the mean global temperature by more than two degrees, the existence of social life itself will be in jeopardy. A study published in a prestigious British scientific review

that takes into consideration what various governments around the world have committed to do to avoid surpassing that two-degree limit shows that there is a good chance that by 2100 the global temperature will actually have gone up by four degrees (New *et al.*, 2011).

4 Peter Victor's book, published in 2008, is perhaps the most important attempt made so far to show that in a developed country (the study was actually made of Canada) it is quite possible to expand employment and people's well-being without needing incessant growth of the economy. The quotation of Peter Victor is taken from an interview on page 22 of a document first published on 9 December 2011 (http://pagina22.com.br/index.php/2011/12/amadurecendo-economias, consulted on 19 March 2012).

5 This conclusion is confirmed by two important books (Bardi, 2014 and Smil, 2014) that analyse the use of materials in contemporary society and its energetic bases.

6 In November 2011, the McKinsey Global Institute published a study showing not only the recent increases in the prices of the most important agricultural and mineral commodities but the volatility of those prices. Their tendency to consistent decline that marked the twentieth century has given way to a tendency to increase, but to do so in response to speculative movements, and they are now subject to great variability, making planning on the part of companies that depend on such products extremely difficult. One of the factors redirecting innovation aims increasingly at constantly improving the yields of materials and energy used in producing the goods and services supply. At the end of 2011, Global Consultants PwC (2011b) published the results of an opinion poll conducted among executives around the world whereby the virtual scarcity of metals for contemporary manufacturing processes was seen as a kind of 'time-bomb' barring the path to further advancement of industrial production. In 2014, at the World Economic Forum, the Ellen MacArthur Foundation and McKinsey launched a report on the Circular Economy (as opposed to the dominant linear economy), which synthesizes this new tendency of sustainability-driven innovation.

7 Some of the best work in synthesizing the challenges involved in attempting to reduce global greenhouse gas emissions has been done by the German Advisory Council on Global Change, and the results were published in 2009.

8 The difference between the greenhouse gas emissions of the United States and Bangladesh refers to the use of fossil fuels only. It is interesting to note that US GNP is 21 times greater than that of Bangladesh but its emissions are 155 times greater and its per capita emissions 74 times those of Bangladesh. That huge disproportion in overall and per capita emissions is far greater than the difference in their levels of wealth. That is just one of many examples of how putting emphasis on reducing differences in wealth levels is not sufficient on its own. It is equally important to determine what patterns of wealth production are going to prevail. The information set out above has been taken from a paper of the World Bank's Environment Department (2007).

9 The document in question is titled *The Great Green Technological Transformation* (UN DESA, 2011), perhaps the most complete, profoundly thought-out and well-documented study of the green economy of all those published on the eve of the Rio+20 conference.

10 "Primary energy is an energy form found in nature that has not been subjected to any conversion or transformation process. Oil and coal are among the forms of non-renewable primary energy while solar, wind and sea energy are among the renewable forms" (http://en.wikipedia.org/wiki/Primary_energy, consulted on 18 March 2012). Physicist Robert Ayres and journalist Edward Ayres published a highly instructive and profound paper on the relationship between economics and energy in 2011.

11 The information is based on a UNEP document published in 2011. Marina Fischer-Kowalski, who runs the Social Ecology Institute in Vienna, was responsible for the report and she structured it around the idea of the existence of a 'social metabolism', as set out in detail in Chapter 2. The reference is UNEP (2011a).

12 The source for this information is an organization that represents US mining corporations (http://www.nma.org/statistics/fast_facts.asp, consulted on 7 December 2011).

13 In their book published in 1993, authors Robert Ayres and Udo Ernst Simonis (1994) define industrial metabolism as being the physical processes that convert raw materials, energy and human work into finished goods and residues.

14 Benefit Corporation is a "new class of corporation required to create a positive material impact on society and the environmen: and to meet higher standards of accountability and transparency" (http://benefitcorpage net, consulted on 31 November 2014). At the end of 2014 there were 1,128 companies operating as Benefit Corporations in 35 countries and 121 industries (http://www.bcorporation.net, consulted on 31 November 2014). Patagonia and Natura are the most well-known Benefit Corporations in the world.

15 Jeremy Rifkin used the term 'lateral power' in a book published in 2011 to represent the opposite of a concentrated, hierarchic power. What is interesting is that the term 'power' is not used merely to express political domination but, in Rifkin's work, to mean the way in which contemporary societies use the resources that are needed for their reproduction. In his latest book, Rifkin (2014) shows that lateral power opens the way to strengthening social collaboration and even to the end of capitalism.

16 Michel Bauwens is the creator of the P2P Foundation, one of the most influential ventures in the cooperative diffusion of culture that the information networks society has made feasible. The idea that the civic should be the foundation for the commons, markets and governments is set out at http://blog.p2pfoundation.net/essay-of-the-day-the-civic-as-the-foundation-for-the-commons-markets-and-governments/2012/03/19 (consulted on 19 March 2012).

17 See http://www.teslamotors.com/blog/all-our-patent-are-belong-you (consulted on 31 November 2014).

18 See http://www.thehandandeye.com/blog/7-31-2014-patagonia-is-going-to-share-their-weed (consulted on 31 November 2014).

19 See Bortolozi (2014).

20 Pierre Lévy is one of the most outstanding scholars of the information networks society.

21 Tim Jackson's *Prosperity without Growth* (2009) is a key reference work for any debate on sustainable development. His conference at the TED is well worth watching: http://www.ted.com/talks/tim_jackson_s_economic_reality_check.html, consulted on 19 March 2012.

22 Richard Heinberg is the author of one of those rare works (Heinberg, 2011) that attempts to relate the crisis that broke out in 2007/2008 not to a supposedly urgent need to reinstate economic growth but, instead, to the idea, central to his book, that growth is actually coming to an end. He is a member of the Post Carbon Institute, and fundamental information on the challenges of sustainable development in the contemporary world can be found on the Institute's website (http://www.postcarbon.org, consulted on 19 March 2012).

23 José Eli da Veiga is a professor at the University of São Paulo and is most certainly the Brazilian in whose works the question of sustainable development and the meaning of the term itself have been most profoundly discussed. His column in the *Valor Econômico* newspaper is one of the most important sources for any discussion regarding the relations between economic growth and ecosystems (see Veiga, 2010).

24 Ladislau Dowbor is an economist and professor at the Pontifical Catholic University of São Paulo. His Internet page is rich in material on the information society and on contemporary dilemmas associated with economic growth (http://dowbor.org, consulted on 25 June 2015).

25 The OECD was founded in 1961. It has 34 member countries, all of which are part of the developed world, with the exception of Mexico. It publishes studies and makes recommendations, almost always embracing the idea that a free market is the best way of addressing contemporary problems.

26 In 2008, the French government created a commission of economists to report on the way in which contemporary societies measure the performance of their economies and the social progress that results from them. One of the most important conclusions that the commission's work produced was that the way that measurement was being done ever since the end of World War II based solely on GNP was completely inadequate for revealing whether or not an economy meets the needs of the respective society. The report Stiglitz *et al.* is available at http://www.stiglitz-sen-fitoussi.fr/documents/rapport_anglais.pdf (consulted on 19 March 2012).

1

POOR IN WHAT WAY?

Introduction

Currently the world economy is five times the size it was just half a century ago.[1] That growth, above all in the last 30 years, has been correlated to an impressive decline in the proportion of poor people in the world population.[2] The fact could tempt one to conclude that the shortest route to demolishing the remaining poverty (which in the last 10 years has started to grow again) would be to accelerate economic growth. The problem is that, increasingly, severe environmental limitations bar the way. Thus it would seem that a *green economy* (and more specifically *green growth*) directed at drastically reducing the material and energy involved in the production of goods and services would be capable of achieving the socioenvironmental objectives expected of the economic system.

However, that conclusion – present with varying degrees of explicitness in several international documents, starting with the one published by the United Nations at the beginning of 2011, known as the Green Economy – is actually untenable.[3] Despite all the increases in material and energy efficiency in the contemporary economy, the pressure on ecosystems continues to intensify. Even if efficiency gains increase further, it is still impossible to conciliate the general and, indeed, universal orientation to economic growth with the ecosystems' limitations. According to Rockström and Klum (2012), there are nine planetary boundaries which, if they are overstepped, will threaten social life itself and in a possibly irreversible manner. Of those nine boundaries, three have already been transgressed beyond acceptable limits: climate change, the erosion of biodiversity and the nitrogen cycle.

The economic consequences of that fact are not necessarily negative, and many companies and social cooperation initiatives have already perceived that. On the one hand, it makes innovation – that is, the opportunity to obtain economic gains by making more efficient use of materials, energy and biodiversity itself – even more urgent and pressing. Furthermore, it could potentially induce a convergent reflection, on the part of companies, civil society and governments, as to the meaning and utility of what they produce for the development process.

Initiatives like that of the already mentioned global movement Benefit Corporation, even though they are a minority, make their mark, not because of any generic principles of social responsibility or by making indiscriminate promises of gains for their shareholders, but rather by committing themselves to creating "a positive material impact on society and the environment, redefining fiduciary obligations to include nonfinancial considerations in their decision making processes, and reporting on their overall social and environmental performance using standards recognized and attested by independent third party protagonists" (http://www.bcorporation.net, consulted on 25 June 2015).[4]

It is interesting to observe that the initiative is actually engendered within the business world itself, albeit it obviously has strong relations with various government spheres as well as the social movements. The reasoning behind it is quite different, for example, from the argument whereby economic growth in general could be very positive if we knew how to deal with its side effects, especially those involving the environment. The real challenge of a new economy (directed at reconstructing the relations between society and nature and between economics and ethics) is different; it means embedding in each step of the production and distribution processes the capacity to create goods and services that are relevant and useful for those individuals, communities and territories with whom the company responsible for producing them maintains relations; and exposing in a clear manner the accounting associated with material and energy flows that the production is based on. In other words, nothing short of a new economic culture altogether, that is, a change of references and values on which business opportunities offered to companies are based.

However, it means that the goods and services emerging from the economic system will no longer be judged only by their indirect effects, their ability to meet a generic demand, the creation of employment positions implicit in their production, or for being based on technical knowledge that might never have existed were it not for the products they are associated with. The judgement will have to take into account the direct effects of whatever is going on in the economy on the lives of people and the state of the ecosystems. It is on the basis of those premises that any discussion of the real capacity of the economic system to reduce poverty and enhance people's well-being must be constructed.

If the ecosystems were an infinite source of support for economic growth, then these ethical and value-related questions would not be so important. However, the fact that boundaries do exist means that an answer is urgently required for the following: *produce for what reason and for whom?* In a world of unlimited resources those questions would be largely irrelevant.[5]

The current discussion on climate change is highly illustrative of this linkage between poverty, material production and the limitations of the ecosystems. To ensure that the average temperature of the planet does not rise beyond a certain threshold (beyond which the consequences in terms of climate unbalance will be catastrophic, with the occurrence of floods, landslides, droughts, melting glaciers and so on), total greenhouse gas emissions need to be curbed. The German Sustainable Development Council (a deliberative entity) has calculated that greenhouse gas emissions for the period 2009 to 2050 must be kept below 750 gigatons in order to ensure a 67% probability of keeping the rise in global temperature to less than two degrees up until the end of this century.[6] If the option for a greater safety margin is taken, with a 75% probability of not exceeding two degrees, then total emissions will have to be kept down to less than 600 gigatons.

It is not so much the numbers that are important here, albeit they obviously represent an extraordinary challenge. The important question to pose is: if there is a carbon space with defined limits and a carbon budget that cannot be exceeded and if we do indeed wish to keep within certain well-understood limits of global temperature increase, then *who has the right to occupy the residual carbon space and with what kind of production should it be occupied?* It matters not whether the object of production is a jet ski or a house; they are both imbued with the virtues of creating employment, involving knowledge, unleashing multiplying effects on economic life and meeting a social demand. But considering the limitation imposed by the carbon space, is it legitimate to fail to examine the merits of the respective purposes of each product and pass judgement on the efforts involved in satisfying the demands for them? If there were technologies available that made it possible to meet both demands and yet not infringe on the limitations of the ecosystems, then such analyses and judgements could be avoided, but the fact is that however great the technical progress towards decarbonizing economic life may be, any such expectation is entirely unrealistic.

This means that the supply of goods and services cannot be evaluated on the basis of formal parameters (employment posts created or tax revenue levied, albeit society obviously needs jobs just as much as it needs tax revenues), but rather, it should involve *substantive criteria* associated with its ability to produce well-being.[7] Actually the reasoning used here is not restricted to the question of greenhouse gas emissions but refers to the entire range of material production. That brings in the decisive question raised in Peter Victor's aforementioned fundamental book: "Is it not the case that the rich countries have to give way to the poor countries by deliberately opting for a slower rate for their own economic growth?"

Clearly this is a risky discussion in at least two senses. The first risk lies in the fact that the fundamental judgement of the real utility of goods for human societies could very well be the antechamber of a conservative authoritarianism that would bar innovations (and accordingly even the construction of a green economy) and pose a threat to the most basic human liberties. At the same time, individuals' freedom of choice is based on certain objective conditions that make it a fiction and a formality that actually disguises the immense inequality that exists in effectively exercising it. Only a radically conservative vision would use the argument of preserving liberties to oppose the urgent need to rethink the question of rights in the occupation of the remaining carbon space and the rights to the use of biosphere resources. In the vast majority of cases, what we see is the conservative vision supporting itself on the argument that the scarcity of resources and even pollution itself will be reversed by technological innovation, provided that the real liberty exists that enables such innovations to advance.

Tim Jackson has identified the second risk present in this discussion: economic growth is not only the basis for the goods and services supply, but, above all, it is the means of creating employment, which, in turn, guarantees social cohesion itself. In contemporary societies, no way has been found to guarantee such cohesion that does not involve improvement in employment levels, and that fact induces the idea that economic growth is an objective that is self-justifying. In that perspective, in order to perpetuate it, measures must be taken to correct any eventual negative effects on the social sphere (such as income concentration) or the environment. In other words, economic growth presents society with a crucial dilemma between having the services and goods on offer to explicitly address and meet social needs with due respect for the limitations of the ecosystems (which is hardly compatible with the idea of generalized growth), while at the same time contributing by improving employment levels and enhancing tax revenues, which can hardly be achieved without economic growth.

Nobody can deny, as will be shown below, that there has been a reduction in poverty practically everywhere in the world. Nevertheless, as the coming items in this chapter will show, the limits of that success are so very clear that they actually underscore the urgency of meeting the challenge of launching the parameters for a new economy in which ethical questions are not treated as marginal or additional aspects but, instead, lie at its very heart.

Converging towards a flat world

There is undoubtedly a streak of irony in the expression used by Thomas Friedman in his two most important books.[8] It is true that the world is converging towards consumer patterns that are increasingly homogeneous, which he expresses in his use of 'flat'. At the same time, however, he admits the existence of the most profound inequality in the use of resources that form the base on which this convergence is actually constructed. In any event, what he, Jeffrey Sachs and innumerable international documents have identified is that, since the last two decades of the twentieth century, there have been clear signs of a reduction of poverty in various dimensions.[9] However, the reduction in question is admittedly a partial one in at least three aspects: it has not involved an important portion of the world's population, whose precarious living conditions make a shocking contrast with the abundance that exists on the planet; income poverty has been reduced much more than other decisive forms of poverty; and the reduction of poverty is correlated with an almost generalized concentration of income (except in some Latin American countries, among them Brazil). Even so, the reduction has been impressive. Nutrition is an emblematic case.

"We consider areas of hunger to be those where at least half the population presents visible signs of nutritional insufficiency," stated Josué de Castro (1980: 59) in his classic *The Geography of Hunger*.[10] If that criterion is used, then hunger is no longer the most widespread form of poverty in the contemporary world. The first edition of *The Geography of Hunger*, published in 1946, denounced the fact that two-thirds to three-quarters of the Latin American population did not ingest enough food to meet their basic bodily needs. In 2010, that total in Brazil was less than 5% and lower than 6% and 7% in Peru and Venezuela, respectively, according to the Global Hunger Index.[11] In Brazil, even in historically problematic regions like the semi-arid and 'Zona da Mata' regions of the Brazilian northeast, malnutrition is no longer part of the daily life of the poorest part of the population. In 1970 hunger was recorded as affecting 37% of the world population: today the one billion hungry in the world represent one-seventh of the total population; even so the figure is, of course, unacceptable, and all the more so is the fact that the formerly declining curve in the quantity of undernourished people has reversed.[12]

"Hunger and underdevelopment are the same thing," wrote Josué de Castro in his usual blunt style; nowadays that close association can be strongly questioned. Hunger has indeed been significantly reduced even in places where other forms of poverty (violence, lack of access to basic services, and the precarious quality of education, basic sanitation and the exercise of human rights) persist and in some cases have even expanded. Furthermore, the number of overweight and obese people is already greater than the number of hungry individuals, which is a clear sign that the workings of the world's food system are in urgent need of profound changes and transformation.[13] What is even more important, the technological optimism of those who believe that increased returns from the land and increases in the productivity of agricultural work are sufficient to guarantee the food abundance that formerly marked the world scenario, particularly in the last three decades of the twentieth century, is now being called into question by the stagnation of the rhythm of growth of those technological gains so typical of the Green Revolution.[14]

In any event, the reduction in hunger is clearly observable and correlated to the notable expansion of a kind of new global middle class. The proportion of individuals living on the equivalent of less than US$ 2.75 a day dropped from 30% to 17% of the world population.[15] By 2030 (i.e. less than two decades from now) half of the world population will have an annual income ranging from US$ 6,000 to US$ 30,000 (values levelled by purchasing power parity), far more than the 29% of the population currently in that income bracket. Since the twenty-first century began, around 70 million people a year have been entering this income bracket for the first time. In 1990 only 1% of the Chinese population was in it; by the end of the first decade of the millennium that figure had risen to no less than 35%. By 2030 no less than three billion people (which means 150 million a year) will be entering a kind of worldwide middle class defined by an average spending rate of US$ 10 to 100 a day *per capita*.[16] The McKinsey report makes use of OECD data to estimate that the middle class will pass from the 1.85 billion registered for 2009 to 4.88 billion in 2030.

What is even more remarkable is the rhythm of this evolution as compared to the historical precedents of transition processes experienced by the developed countries. The United Kingdom, for example, took 150 years to double its GDP after the Industrial Revolution when it had a population of 10 million inhabitants. China and India double their wealth every 12 and 16 years, respectively, and each with a population 100 times larger or 200 times larger if we put them together (McKinsey Global Institute, 2011).

The consequence of that unprecedented drop in poverty levels and the massification of consumption that it led to has been a significant alteration to many corporate strategies that consist of increasing business at the so-called *bottom of the pyramid*.

As an example, in Senegal, Danone launched a liquid yogurt (Dolima) that costs a mere US$ 0.10 a unit. At the close of the twentieth century, only 6% of the company's turnover came from low-income consumers, but by 2009, that figure had jumped up to 42%. In Mexico, the same company sells plastic cups of water for US$ 0.15 a cup.[17] In Bangladesh, Adidas launched a pair of sneakers costing one euro, and the French L'Oreal Corporation sells a shampoo and face cream in India in sample size units costing a few cents each. Quite often the sales system for such products involves direct selling in poor communities. It is also important to mention the union between Nobel Prize winner Muhammad Yunus, creator of the Grameen Bank, and the Danone Corporation, that led to the setting up of Grameen Danone Foods Ltd, which in Bangladesh not only dedicates itself to selling cheaper products but also to opening up new opportunities for creating income among poor populations.

New markets along those lines are not limited to the fields of foodstuffs and clothing alone. While it is true that the Indian company Tata's attempt to market a basic vehicle for the price of US$ 2,200.00, up until the end of 2011, had turned out to be a huge failure,[18] at the same time there are mobile phones on sale in India for US$ 20.00 with call charges of just 2 cents a minute, resulting in five million new clients in 2009 alone.[19] In China tablets are being manufactured (largely based on freely shared knowledge, as Chapter 4 will show) for almost one-tenth the cost of an iPad.

In India this market at the bottom of the pyramid sometimes involves innovations in the products designed to address the population's most elementary necessities (even though it may be in a minor way). That is the case, for example, with the wood stove. At the beginning of 2000, traditional biomass was the energy source for heating and cooking for no less than 2.7 billion people around the world (Victor and Victor, 2003). In India 90% of rural dwellings and 40% of urban ones still depend on those same traditional biomass sources, that is, charcoal, firewood, straw and manure (Shukla, 1997). Respiratory infections are the third most numerous diseases registered in India, killing 400,000 children a year and causing a high incidence of throat cancer, especially among women. In that sense, offering a wood-burning stove that produces more heat and less smoke for just US$ 23.00 has real social significance for the country. Also the discovery of a water-purifying system that costs US$ 43.00 has shown itself to be very efficient and it is already present in more than three million homes. The production of a very simple refrigerator

45 cm high and 60 cm wide, consisting of just 20 parts as opposed to the 200 parts of a conventional one, for a price of US$ 70.00, is also part of this extraordinary expansion of opportunities to gain access to consumption.

This clearly perceptible expansion in the bottom of the pyramid market is not restricted to Asia. The African Development Bank estimates a 60% growth in the contingent constituting the new middle class, which at the beginning of 2011 had reached the figure of 313 million people in the Sub-Saharan countries.[20] Just one decade ago there were only 196 million African people in this group, corresponding to a daily spending bracket of US$ 2.00 to US$ 20.00 a day. While it is true that other estimates, like that of the OECD, are less optimistic in regard to the growth of grassroots incomes in Africa, it cannot be denied that the business opportunities directed at satisfying the demands of markets constituted by people living in poverty are immense.

In Latin America poverty levels have fallen since the 1990s from 44% to 33% of the population, according to the CEPAL.[21] That overall decline is not only due to important income transfer programmes but also to improvements in the occupation and employment situation. Open urban unemployment, which stood at 11.2% in 2002, went down to 7.3% in 2010. An absolutely unprecedented phenomenon in the recent history of the continent is the decline in income inequality that has accompanied the reduction in poverty in some countries. The most emblematic example of that is Brazil. The per capita income of the poorest families, occupying the lowest 10% of the social pyramid, increased by 120% in the period from the end of 1993 to the end of 2008. That corresponds roughly to an average increase of 5.3% a year over the period. From 2005 to 2010, that increase gave economists the impression that, for the poor, Brazil is growing more than China – 10.2% a year. For the richest 10% and for those in the median range of the income brackets, that growth was considerably less.[22] For the first time in decades, the Gini index, measuring inequality in personal income distribution, has fallen from 0.60 to 0.56 in the first decade of the millennium.[23] The contrast with the situation in the developed countries and China is vivid, as will be seen later in this chapter. In urban areas, the Gini index falls significantly in the periods 2000/2002 and 2006/2008 in Brazil (dropping from 0.628 to 0.586), in Argentina (from 0.590 to 0.510), in Chile (from 0.558 to 0.517) and in Paraguay (from 0.511 to 0.486), but remains unaltered in Uruguay and grows in Mexico (from 0.476 to 0.487). In the period 2005 to 2011, no less than 60 million Brazilians moved into a higher income bracket than they occupied before.[24] Over the same period the proportion of poor people fell from 51% to 24% of the overall population and the middle class swelled from 34% to 53% of all Brazilians.

These figures alone are sufficient to demonstrate a positive process on which the emergence of a new economy can be supported. Added to them there is information that reports an almost generalized increase in longevity and in school attendance, greater access to health services and the formation of new opportunities in the labour markets. There is also a particularly important demographic bonus for various Latin American countries insofar as the relative weight of children in the composition of their populations has gone down, with a corresponding increase in the weight of the population of adults of working age who have not yet reached retirement age.[25] In Brazil, for example, between 2015 and 2025 there will be the lowest rate of demographic dependence ever (i.e. the proportion of children 14 or under plus adults over 65 will be lower than the proportion of the population that is economically active).

Before we enter the next chapter and examine the threats represented by the options that have currently been adopted for the reduction of poverty, it is important to underscore how limited that reduction really is and to show the real distance between the material abundance of contemporary societies and the effective satisfaction of the most important social needs, and we will do so below.

Basic needs and capabilities: far beyond mere income

Former Chilean Minister of Agriculture in the Allende government, Jacques Chonchol, used to say that the greatest achievement of the agrarian reform in Chile was not the conquest of the land itself but of the right of a peasant to walk into a bank with his head held high.[26] Just as important as any financing that he might eventually obtain is the fact that he would no longer be excluded as he was before by the feeling of inferiority that he himself associated with his social condition. Entering a bank with his head held high is the exercise of a liberty which in the formal sphere existed even before the agrarian reform, but it could never be put into practice due to a series of social, political and cultural circumstances that made the banks, even if only implicitly, a place where peasants could only enter timidly, shamefacedly and with their eyes cast down, because the banks were not part of their world. Irrespective of what one thinks of the Allende government or its agrarian reform, it was a good example of how one of the most important contemporary thinkers, Amartya Sen, defines development: it is a permanent process that enlarges the substantive freedoms of human beings. The adjective 'substantive' here is very precise; it is not just a question of the formal abstract freedom whereby, in principle, any individual is at liberty to walk into a bank. For that freedom to be effectively exercised, it is essential that the individual should have, and feel that he has, conditions that will ensure that he is not looked on as someone who does not belong there, someone who, in spite of the formal existence of the freedom to enter, is not in fact free to do so. In an article published in 1983, Amartya Sen quotes economist Paul Streeten, for whom "the concept of basic needs helps to remind us that the object of the development effort is to offer all human beings the *opportunity* of a bountiful life".[27]

That is why Amartya Sen and the *capability approach* school he is associated with describe the fight against poverty on the basis of ideas that involve a central ethical and valuing dimension and not just in terms of an increase in people's incomes. Development does not only consist of making goods and services available and the generic possibility for people to access them by obtaining an income. Above all, development involves constructing 'a life worth living' for individuals. Martha

Nussbaum, an important intellectual partner in the work of Amartya Sen, states that the purpose of development is to facilitate a "full and creative" life for individuals in which they can "express their potential and mould a significant existence in keeping with their human dignity". A decisive portion of the conditions that make it feasible to achieve those objectives stems from having access to a set of goods and services such as good-quality education, guarantees of physical integrity (including here socially valued clothing), health, food and a decent dwelling. It is also obvious, however, that life with dignity presupposes elements beyond the basic needs, such as the possibility of not being ashamed in public because of one's appearance, the feeling of being useful to others and of belonging to a community; leisure, spiritual fulfilment and the exercise of creativity; and, above all, the absence of the highly common forms of discrimination associated with race, sex, religion or ethnicity. In India, for example, 75.3% of all men are literate but only 53.7% of women are.[28]

Not everything necessary to live a "life worthy of human dignity" (to use Nussbaum's terms) depends on the market supply of goods and services. In that sense the capabilities for a constructive life cannot be addressed as if they were needs. It is not a question of establishing a hierarchy of goods and services and imagining that once a certain minimum level has been achieved an individual is going to fulfil himself insofar as he manages to acquire more and more. Both the capabilities approach and the basic needs approach are in opposition to the idea that a generic expansion of goods and services provision is always socially beneficial. However, the capabilities approach places emphasis on what individuals are able to do and the conditions in which they are able to elaborate their projects and carry forward a meaningful life. Obviously that presumes that basic needs are met, but it is not restricted to them alone. Being able to appear in public without being embarrassed or ashamed or entering the bank with our heads held high does not depend directly on the goods and services on offer, even supposing the individual happens to be dressed in a socially adequate manner, for example. It is not sufficient that an individual has his basic needs satisfied for him to feel at ease in the foyer of a theatre or participate in a community that handles subjects that may be of interest but are handled on the basis of a digital media network. Basic needs, as Amartya Sen has shown, are normally thought of at around the minimum level. The capabilities, because they involve knowledge, information and sociability dispositions, can be permanently expanded. The fundamental nature of the human freedoms that make up the development process cannot be expressed only in terms of the set of goods with which the individual satisfies his basic needs but, rather, in the capabilities that enable him to be an agent of the construction of his own life. People do not value well-being alone: "The freedoms and capabilities we enjoy can also be highly precious to us and, in the final analysis, it is up to us to decide how to use the freedom we have," declares Amartya Sen.[29]

The core question behind a capabilities approach is '*What can a person do?*' and not '*What should a person receive?*' The approach is based on valuing what Sen refers to as positive freedoms that indicate the real exercise of choice by individuals. That is precisely the reason why, in the transition to a form of economic life in which ethics and respect for the ecosystems' limitations are at the core of all decisions, it does not mean simply overcoming absolute privation while leaving the installed inequality intact. The overriding goal is to promote equality of capabilities and that goes far beyond the mere fulfilment of basic needs.

Thus fighting against poverty and expanding human capabilities is far from being limited to obtaining an income, and income cannot be its only goal or even its most important one. There are two basic reasons why. On the one hand, it is fundamentally important to know what individuals actually do with the income they have. One of Amartya Sen's greatest contributions to economics lies precisely in his deliberate avoidance of viewing the goods and services that fill the individual's consumer basket exclusively in the light of a common abstract measurement expressed in monetary units. It is obviously true that income is one way for people to obtain those goods and services that are important to the achievement of their goals. However, what Sen refers to as 'functionings', that is, those freedoms that acquiring goods and services opens the way to, are far more important. Probably, the Chilean peasant in the example had obtained financing from some local agency before he got to the point of entering the bank. What is important here is not the fact that he would probably have to pay higher interest rates for such financing than he would pay if it were directly done by the bank but, rather, his former exclusion from access to banking services that ought to be truly public and universal.

In a similar way, being in a position to purchase enough food to satisfy their own needs not only avoids undernutrition but also means that individuals can avoid situations of dependence on those who often appear in situations of need to offer loans or donations but in an extortive or humiliating manner. However, if the purchasing power to acquire foodstuffs leads individuals to obesity due to excessive quantities of soft drinks and other industrialized food items, then the person's freedom is being violated by it. The freedoms that Amartya Sen has in mind do not consist of the mere *absence of restrictions* (each one eats what he chooses and it is nobody else's concern). Those freedoms are substantive insofar as they presume the *existence of objective social and material conditions* on which the individual can be the agent of his life projects and broaden the range of choices for a dignified and valuable life. A day cleaning lady who works every day and is a single mother of a family whose children spend the day in the care of their older sister stuck in front of a TV set and bombarded with dubious food product adverts does not have any real choice as to what her children should or should not eat.

Goods and services are not an end in themselves but the means to achieving something far more important – a healthy and meaningful life for individuals and for the community of people with whom they have relations. It is obvious that nobody deliberately chooses to be obese, and so a diet that leads to obesity cannot be classified as a free, well-informed choice made by whoever adopts it. What need to be examined, and judged, are the social conditions of production. That is the core message of the last book of the celebrated North American economist John Kenneth Galbraith, *The Economics of Innocent Fraud* (2004), published when he was 96. The 'culpable' frauds are those procedures like manipulating shares in order to swell executives' gains, whereas the innocent frauds are present in many social scientists' ideas, beginning with the belief in consumer sovereignty, an idea with intellectual roots in the distinction, so dear to neoclassic economic thinking, between choice and preference.[30] In that perspective, individuals' choices are a perfect reflection of their preferences. In the rationale of conventional economics, as Carol Graham's excellent book *The Pursuit of Happiness* (2011) shows, individuals' well-being increases insofar as their possibilities of choice increase. Thus, in that light, economic growth is the necessary condition for any increase in well-being.

To Amartya Sen, John Kenneth Galbraith and Carol Graham, individuals' preferences are to a large extent moulded by social structures, and the poorer the conditions they are living in, the less control they have over them, or – to use Sen's expression – the less they are the agents of the organization of their own lives due to the limited public debate in their sphere. Obese people often opt to consume a certain kind of food product that satiates their immediate desire but at the same time leads to serious health problems in the long term.

Consumption gives place to 'doings and beings' that require the analysis not only of individual income but also of the consequences of whatever use they make of it for their lives. As an example, it is perfectly possible that the income should be destined for the purchase of goods and services that are totally unlikely to facilitate a 'full creative life', to use Martha Nussbaum's expression. Adolescents who get involved in crime obviously have a much higher income than that obtained through licit activities but that does not lead them to having a life worth living. A television set may broaden an individual's access to culture, entertainment and previously unseen experiences and horizons or it may do the opposite and confine the individual's perspective of life to prejudice, cultivating revenge as the means of combating violence and stimulating the most predatory forms of consumption.

The second reason why fighting poverty cannot be restricted to the mere question of income concerns situations in which, in spite of achieving increases in income, individuals face critical situations in regard to their access to basic sanitation, education and health or find themselves living in places where violence is rife and where they are systematically discriminated in their access to the most basic public services. About 2.6 billion people in the world have no basic sanitation provided to them and 884 million have great difficulty in obtaining drinking water on a regular basis.[31] All of those precarious situations are accompanied by diseases that affect children more than any other group, jeopardizing their school attendance and their very learning processes and even causing the death of 1.4 million children a year before they are five years old. One of the Millennium Development Goals is, by 2015, to cut down by half the number of people in the world without access to basic sanitation as compared to the figures for 1990, but it is unlikely to be achieved.[32] In Brazil, the rise in income of the poorest families has meant that colour TV is present in 92% of all households; basic sanitation, however, in 2011, was still limited to 55% of homes. Thus the families have enjoyed an increase in income, but in the vast majority of cases, they continue to face serious health problems stemming from the precarious nature of public investments in basic sanitation.[33] In the greater São Paulo region, for example, in 2010, no less than 10 municipalities (among them Guarulhos and Barueri) had no sewage installations whatsoever.[34] Half of all the raw sewage of the metropolitan area's 28 municipalities is discharged straight into the Tiete River without any treatment.

Comparing income and education situations is also very revealing: in the period from 2000 to 2011, annual per capita gross income in Brazil went up by 32% and reached the figure of US$ 7,689. Over the same period, however, formal schooling expectations actually dropped from 14.5 years of schooling to 13.8 years, according to an article by Flavio Comim, an economist formerly attached to the UNDP in Brazil. Furthermore, he declares, "when we adjust HDI figures to the inequalities that exist in income distribution, education and health in Brazil, we lose 27.7% of the Brazilian HDI. It goes down from 0.718 to 0.519."[35]

Another example of income's intrinsic limitations as an expression of genuine well-being can be found in a project put forward by a city councillor in São Paulo in the second half of 2011 proposing that the lack of vacancies in day care should be compensated for by awarding a day care allowance to the value of 272.50 Brazilian reals. The *Nossa São Paulo* (Our São Paulo) movement, the *Ação Educativa* (Educational Action) organization and the São Paulo Social Forum all oppose the idea because the effective existence of day care is incomparably more important for a child's development than any income that purports to compensate for the absence of that right. Day care develops children's skills in three directions: it stimulates equality between the sexes by creating an environment where the care of children is not an exclusively feminine task; it opens up new fields for the insertion of female labour into the labour market; and finally it accelerates the socialization of children, which of itself boosts their cognitive potential and will have a positive effect on their future schooling performances. In this area also lies one of the most perfidious forms of inequality, and it has not been attenuated in any way by the decline in income concentration registered over the first decade of the millennium in Brazil. A working group set up by the Brazilian Academy of Sciences composed of experts from the fields of neurobiology, economics and cognitive development psychology has shown that, in spite of the expansion of access to day care and schools, there have been no accompaniment or evaluation mechanisms installed to monitor the quality of the educational work. The performance is very poor by comparison with international standards and as indicated by national examination results. Obviously those indicators are not homogeneous and the overall averages do not mirror the situation in most of the schools that accommodate the offspring of inhabitants with the highest incomes.

The work of Chilean economist Manfred Max-Neef, published by the *Dag Hammarskjöld Foundation* in 1991, offers one of the most important contributions to the study of poverty and the various policies directed at overcoming it. First of all, departing entirely from the usual perspective in which the question is addressed by economists, he declares that *human needs are not limitless*. They are susceptible to being enunciated and delineated. Or, in his exact words, "human needs are finite, few and classifiable". That being so, poverty itself needs to be redefined. Poverty should really be referred to in the plural form because it refers fundamentally to being deprived of any one of the fundamental human needs. That idea is central to the formulation of development process objectives. The social and material conditions that allow for a life with dignity do not embrace the infinite expansion of consumption by individuals or by societies. That is perhaps the most important practical consequence of the idea of basic needs. It reflects Gandhi's thought whereby the world has enough for everyone's need but not for everyone's greed, which is, by definition, infinite.

In second place, and precisely because they are not infinite, human needs can be organized in the form of a matrix that involves a set of rights and duties that are inherent to a dignified and constructive life. That matrix consists of nine axiological categories (i.e. basic values), each of which relates to four existential categories, meaning the conditions that enable axiologically defined values to be put into practice, as shown by Table 1.1.

One of those values (axiological categories) is subsistence. The *being* associated with subsistence is physical and mental health, a good sense of humour and adaptability; the *having* is food, a home and work; the *doing* associated with it is feeding and nutrition, rest and procreation; and the *interacting* is the living environment and social localization. As the table organized by Max-Neef clearly shows, in addition to subsistence, the axiological values include protection, affection, understanding, participation, leisure, creation, identity and freedom.

At the same time, they are obviously not fixed values and evolve over time to accompany technical progress. Today we may consider rapid, cheap access to the Internet as a fundamental human right, one of the basic needs of any individual. Similarly, the capabilities that underpin the individual's construction of a decent life need to be consistent with one another. Receiving a high-quality education but being denied the political freedom to express one's opinion and knowledge (as is the case even today in some totalitarian states) means that addressing this particular basic need for education does not actually lead to a decent life for the individual. At the other end of the scale, there are societies with a glaring contrast between political freedom and a degree of human misery that in practice curbs any possibility of exercising the right to participate in public life.

It is obviously inadequate to classify everything beyond basic needs as being superfluous. In that sense it is worth underscoring the differences between Max-Neef's and Amartya Sen's approaches. Unlike Max-Neef, Sen endeavours to make a clear distinction between needs and values. It is on the basis of that distinction, for example, that he makes his criticism of the most consecrated definition

TABLE 1.1 The diversified and limited nature of human needs: matrix of needs and satisfiers

| | | NEEDS ACCORDING TO EXISTENTIAL CATEGORIES | | |
		Being	*Having*	*Doing*	*Interacting*
NEEDS ACCORDING TO VALUE CATEGORIES	**Subsistence**	1. Physical health, mental health, equilibrium, sense of humour, adaptability	2. Food, shelter, work	3. Feed, procreate, rest, work	4. Living environment, social setting
	Protection	5. Care, adaptability, autonomy, equilibrium, solidarity	6. Insurance systems, savings, social security, health systems, rights, family, work	7. Cooperate, prevent, plan, take care of, cure, help	8. Living space, social environment, dwelling
	Affection	9. Self-esteem, solidarity, respect, tolerance, generosity, receptiveness, passion, determination, sensuality, sense of humour	10. Friendships, family, partnerships, relationships with nature	11. Make love, caress, express emotions, share, take care of, cultivate, appreciate	12. Privacy, intimacy, home, space of togetherness
	Understanding	13. Critical conscience, receptiveness, curiosity, astonishment, discipline, intuition, rationality	14. Literature, teachers, method, educational policies, communication policies	15. Investigate, study, experiment, educate, analyse, meditate	16. Settings of formative interaction, schools, universities, academies, groups, communities, family
	Participation	17. Adaptability, receptiveness, solidarity, willingness, determination, dedication, respect, passion, sense of humour	18. Rights, responsibilities, privileges, duties, work	19. Become affiliated, cooperate, propose, share, dissent, obey, interact, agree on, express opinions	20. Settings of participative interaction, parties, associations, churches, communities, neighbourhoods, family

Leisure	21. Curiosity, receptiveness, imagination, recklessness, sense of humour, tranquillity, sensuality	22. Games, spectacles, clubs, parties, peace of mind	23. Daydream, brood, dream, recall old times, give way to fantasies, remember, relax, have fun, play	24. Privacy, intimacy, spaces of closeness, free time, surroundings, landscapes
Creation	25. Passion, determination, intuition, imagination, boldness, rationality, autonomy	26. Abilities, skills, method, work	27. Work, invent, build, design, compose, interpret	28. Productive and feedback settings, workshops, cultural groups, audiences, spaces for expression, temporal freedom
Identity	29. Sense of belonging, consistency, differentiation, self-esteem, assertiveness	30. Symbols, language, religion, habits, customs, reference groups, sexuality, values, norms, historical memory, work	31. Commit oneself, integrate oneself, confront, decide on, get to know oneself, recognize oneself, actualize oneself, grow	32. Social rhythms, everyday settings, settings one belongs to, maturation stages
Freedom	33. Autonomy, self-esteem, determination, passion, assertiveness, open-mindedness, boldness, rebelliousness, tolerance	34. Equal rights	35. Dissent, choose, be different from, run risks, develop awareness, commit oneself, disobey	36. Temporal/spatial plasticity

The **being** column registers personal or collective attributes that are expressed as nouns. The **having** column registers *institutions, mechanisms, norms, tools* (not in the material sense), *laws*, etc. that can be expressed in one or more words. The **doing** column registers *personal or collective actions* that can be expressed as verbs. The **interacting** column registers *locations and milieus* as times and spaces. The word interacting was chosen for lack of a better substitute to the (space and time) idea of the German BEFINDEN or the Spanish ESTAR.

of sustainable development whereby it is seen as satisfying the needs of present generations without jeopardizing those of future generations. Sen's objection is ontological:[36] a human being cannot be reduced to the dimension of the satisfaction of his needs. Development is a process of capability acquisition and empowerment and its objectives go far beyond mere human needs, basic or otherwise. In his remarks on the Brundtland report where the phrase appeared, Sen considers that "while it is true that people have needs, they also have values and place a particularly high value on their skills to reason, appreciate, choose, participate and act.[37] Considering people in the light of their needs alone offers us a very narrow vision of humanity."

Max-Neef's matrix attempts to overcome that limitation by expanding the definition of human needs and including the values that Sen refers to among them. At the same time Max-Neef integrates the needs identified with the capabilities that are required to effectively meet them, which he calls 'satisfiers'.

Nevertheless, however complex the delimitation of what is luxury and what is necessary may be, and even though doing so carries the risk of authoritarianism in putting it into practice, it cannot be avoided or got around in view of the limits that the ecosystems impose on the expansion of goods and services. It is for that very reason that Herman Daly reproduces Max-Neef's matrix in his treatise on ecological economics.[38] The example of climate change shows how important it is to define basic needs with clarity and precision. Based on empirical studies conducted in China, the group headed by Jiahua Pan (of the Chinese Academy of Social Sciences) shows that it would be feasible to keep the limits of greenhouse gas emissions down to a level compatible with maintaining the equilibrium of the climate system if the economy were to be redirected to achieving two basic objectives: first, to provide the material basis for meeting the basic needs of those who are still living in a state of deprivation; and second, to drive that objective forward in the light of technological innovations that make it possible to reduce the consumption of those materials and forms of energy that are behind the greenhouse gas emissions and the assaults on biodiversity. That is why Pan (in the same way and based on the same conceptual structure that inspires the German report mentioned in the introduction to this work) underscores the carbon budget notion: "The concept of a carbon budget is based on two axioms: human needs are limited to an individual's biological aspect, but luxury and waste stemming from emissions are unlimited; although there is actually a geo-physical limit due to the finite nature of our Planet Earth."[39]

The greatest challenge associated with the emergence of a new economy consists of updating the formulation of Gandhi's fundamental question: how much is enough? In principle the formulation of such a question would seem to be incompatible with the workings of a decentralized economy where the greater part of the goods and services supply comes from the markets.

While it is true that the path trodden so far has permitted undeniable victories over poverty, nevertheless we should question whether the best possibilities for making the functioning of the economic system compatible with meeting human needs and respecting the ecosystems that human life itself depends on lie in deepening and improving those very same ways. However much importance we can attribute to the recent progress made against poverty (and not just income poverty), the answer to that question can only be no, and that fact underscores the urgent need for a sweeping revision of the direction being taken by contemporary economic organizations.

Does inequality really matter?

Is it possible, in a modern society, to define the desirable and acceptable level of inequality among its members? Prior to the Renaissance and the emergence of the idea that is at the root of the philosophy of natural right in Hobbes, Locke and Rousseau that all individuals are fundamentally equal, inequalities were to some extent considered natural and it was thought that only some kind of magic event could lead to any kind of social mobility. In contrast, the modern era is marked by individuals occupying positions in the social hierarchy according to attributes that are not allocated by tradition, status or lineage but depend on other elements susceptible to being possessed by 'others', such as money and professional qualifications. Obviously there are innumerable mechanisms for perpetuating current social inequalities, but the essential rule governing the workings of present-day societies is not supported by the existence of traditional perpetuation mechanisms (such as castes or noble titles, for example), even though such mechanisms can still be found in many places (as, for example, the rigorously stratified delineation of what an individual may or may not do in consequence of the caste he or she belongs to). One of the twentieth century's most important political philosophers, John Rawls, dedicated his work to defining the meaning, utility and limits of inequality in modern, democratic society.[40] To that end he established two basic parameters. First, that freedom must be respected in all circumstances: a reduction in inequality must not be used to restrict anyone's freedom; that is merely in keeping with the kind of political and economic liberalism Rawls defended and in a certain sense may be considered trivial. The second parameter is more interesting and deserves to be quoted literally. Obeying 'fair principles' requires that "social and economic inequalities satisfy two conditions. First they need to be linked to functions and positions that are open to all in equal conditions of opportunity and second, they need to benefit the least well-off members of society." The core idea is that no society can advance materially without there being some degree of inequality. What should be the dimension of an inequality that makes it possible to stimulate material progress but, at the same time, to avoid producing iniquitous situations of deprivation and extreme poverty? To ensure that the response should not be a mere reflection of the interests of the protagonists in the discussions, they should be conducted under a 'veil of ignorance', whereby the participants decide what the useful level of inequality would be without having prior knowledge of who will be the eventual occupants of the social positions that the inequality will give rise to. That opens the way for the (impersonal) conception based on reason and debate of a social order that satisfies the universal criterion of justice. To Rawls, that involves the presupposition that the inequalities will result in benefits for the poor and not just gains for the rich.

The next chapter will show that the nature of this discussion undergoes radical alterations in the light of climate change and the material and energy-related impossibility of reconciling the proposal to meet the basic needs with the immense inequalities in the use of ecosystem resources. It must be underscored that the degree of income concentration accompanying current economic growth can hardly be considered useful for the poorer strata of society and, furthermore, it affects the feeling of well-being of all, even those who do not find themselves at the bottom of the social pyramid. Let us take a closer look at this issue.

In the year 2000, the World Bank did not believe that inequalities were a problem provided the increase in global wealth reached the poorest segments, albeit in a lesser proportion.[41] However, during the first decade of the new millennium, studies conducted by economists at the World Bank demonstrated that, contrary to that initial view, inequalities bring with them damage to social cohesion and even jeopardize economic growth itself given that they block the economic initiatives of the poor. Furthermore, the main conclusion of the annual report of 2006 addressing the relations between equity and development directly is that in order for *the power of economic growth to have any significant effect in reducing poverty, it should be directly related to a prior distribution of income*. In the terms of the *World Development Report*: "the growth elasticity of poverty reduction falls with greater income inequality. In other words, the impact of (the same amount of) growth on poverty reduction is significantly greater when initial income inequality is lower."

From 1990 to 2001, for every US$ 100 of world economic growth per capita, a mere 60 cents contributed to reducing the poverty of those who were living on an income of less than a dollar a day.[42] The greater the concentration of income, the less economic growth benefits poor people. Obviously that concentration is liable to be reversed by the increased opportunities that poor people have to benefit in some way from that growth by means of having a better education, better contacts with the labour market and access to health services that enable them to present themselves in better conditions to seek a worthwhile job. Nevertheless, the recent trajectory of the developed countries, where, until recently, there has been ready access to health and education (and above all the tremendous difficulty they have in reducing unemployment and underemployment), casts doubt on the supposition that economic growth has the power of promoting the integrating effects that are expected of it.

One of the most important characteristics of the economy over the last 30 years is that it has led to a shocking increase in inequality precisely in the world's most democratic countries, and to an equal extent in countries distinguished by the great impetus of their economic growth (India and China). The current situation in the developed countries is one of reversing social conquests accumulated over the years since the end of the great crisis in 1929 that marked social life in the United States and Western Europe up until the middle of the 1970s. The synthesis organized by Jean-Pierre Lehman contains impressive information.[43] Although inequality among countries is on the decrease (the world is becoming flat, to use Thomas Friedman's expression, or as Jeffrey Sachs has it, there is a movement of convergence in the world economy), in the interior of the countries the disparities of income and opportunities are becoming more accentuated. Inequality in Britain is at its worst level since 1920, which nullifies a significant part of the social conquests around which the very capitalism of the second half of the twentieth century accommodated itself. The incomes of the 90% least rich Britons remained stable from 1973 to halfway through the first decade of the new millennium, but over the same period, the richest 1% saw their income triple. According to *Financial Times* columnist Martin Wolf, for each dollar generated by the British economic system from 1976 to 2008, 58 cents went to the richest 1%. Economist N. Kristof did not hesitate to use the term 'Banana Republic' in his analysis of the fact that from 1980 to 2005 no less than 80% of the increase in Americans' incomes went to a tiny group of 1% of the population.[44]

In the 15 years from the mid-1990s to the beginning of the 2008 crisis, family income in the 29 OECD member countries rose an average 1.7% a year, but among the poorest 10% it only rose by 1.4%, while for the richest 10% it increased by 2% a year.[45] Those differences may seem small, but when they accumulate over a 15-year period, they are immense. In the United States, the social abyss has become even more profound and the equivalent figures are 0.5% for the poorest 10% and 1.9% for the richest 10%. In Mexico the figures are 0.8% and 1.7%, respectively. This income gap between the richest 10% and the poorest 10% is in the ratio of 14 to 1 in the United States, Turkey and Israel and no less than 27 to 1 in Chile and Mexico. Seventeen of the 22 OECD countries registered increases in their Gini indexes in the category 'income distribution'. What is most striking is that the increase in inequality takes place in spite of the actions of the direct transfer of income and taxes, which have, on average, reduced by a quarter the level of inequality that would have been established had such tax and redistribution policies not been implemented. In 2004, in the United States, there were no less than 37 million people living below the North American poverty line.[46] By 2011, poverty in the United States had already engulfed 50 million people, and the increase in poverty in the United States is not only in absolute numbers but also in the proportion of the poor in the country's total population.

Inequalities in the United States are far greater than the population itself imagines.[47] A recent research survey presented the interviewees with three scenarios (in regard to income inequalities). In the first, income was distributed among people in a fair manner. In another, the patterns of income distribution were equivalent to those of Sweden (but presented in the form of a hypothetical country), and in the third, the richest 20% received 84% of the income and the 20% immediately below them received 11%, also presented as a hypothetical country, with care taken not to reveal that this last was actually the situation in the United States at the end of the first decade of the twenty-first century. There was no observable distinction between men or women or between Democrats and Republicans in their overwhelming rejection (92%) of the last option (the real situation of the United States) or their preferred option equivalent to the situation in Sweden. What is interesting here is that when questioned as to the real extent of income concentration in the United States, people showed a perception of society as much less uneven than it actually is. In the estimation of the majority of those interviewed, the richest 20% own 60% of the income when in fact they detain 84%, and furthermore, the interviewees revealed that they wished that the concentration of income was much lower than what they imagined it to be: ideally the top 20% should not own more than 32% of the income for the distribution to be considered fair.

The speed at which American incomes became concentrated from the mid-1970s on is highly impressive.[48] In 1976 the top of the pyramid, occupied by 1% of the population, received 9% of all income. By 2010 this control was equal to 24%. The CEOs of the biggest North American corporations earned 42 times the salary of an average worker in 1980. In 2010 they were earning 531 times the amount. In the period from 1980 to 2005, no less than 80% of the overall increase in income went into the pockets of the richest 1% of the population.

That difference, between the real inequality and the public's perception of it, is not restricted to the United States. In October 2009, Michel Forsé and Olivier Galland asked a representative sample of French people how much they thought a corporative CEO earns in their country. The answer offered was 859,000 euros, three times lower than the real amount. *Les Rémunérations obscènes* (Obscene Earnings) is the title of the book that sociologist Philippe Steiner has dedicated to this issue.[49] In a European survey conducted in 1999 to identify the vision of the distance between the wages of an unqualified worker and the president of the company they worked for, the answers were 3.8 for Sweden, 5 for Spain, 8 for Germany, 12.5 for the United States, 12.5 for Great Britain and 16 for France. The survey referred to by Steiner used a slightly different methodology than the one applied by Norton and Ariely and went on to ask people what they felt would be a fair ratio for the difference between salaries at the bottom and top of the company's salary hierarchy. The answers were consistently lower than those that the same individuals had considered to exist in reality. At that time (1999) there was already a tremendous gap between the real inequality and the perceived inequality that in the United States it had reached, on average, a ratio of 300 to 1, and in France 177 to 1. In fact, as Philippe Steiner remarked, "The estimated gap responses actually corresponded to the ratio between the wages of an unqualified worker and those of the upper middle class, as if the interviewee were unable to visualize anything beyond that."

The survey was repeated in France in 2010, when it was found that the perception of inequality had multiplied fourfold: in 1999 the French imagined that the president of a company earned 16 times more than a simple worker, but in 2010 this perception had jumped up to 63 times more. Also, the disparity considered to be fair had increased threefold. However, ignorance persists though to a slightly lesser extent: errors in the responses regarding the average salary of an unqualified worker were only 10% to 14%. The responses were totally accurate in the estimates of teachers' salaries in the government school network, and ministers' salaries were overestimated by 23%. However, the degree of error in guessing the salaries of top corporate executives ranged from 300% to 500%.

Inequalities do not just harm those who are in the lower levels of the social pyramid: they destroy the foundations of social life, as shown by an important book launched in 2009 by two British infectious disease specialists, who propose: "The scale of income differences has a powerful effect on how we relate to each other" (Wilkinson and Pickett, 2009). That proposition justifies the subtitle of their book: *Why Equality is Better for Everyone.*

That observation is important insofar as increasing inequality is not restricted to developed countries alone. China is experiencing a process of accelerated income concentration. Its per capita GDP is growing faster than per capita income. If the distribution of income gets no worse, growth will have a positive effect on the poorest segment of the population, but there is a process of increasing concentration of income in course that will limit the effects that the increased GDP can have in reducing poverty. The average income of urban households in China in 1978 was 2.57 times that of rural households, but that disparity had fallen somewhat by 1985, to 1.85, only to soar up again to 2.9 by the year 2001. The study this information was taken from comes to the unequivocal conclusion that "even though China has been successful in reducing poverty, economic growth since the mid-1980s has not led to a corresponding reduction in poverty. The rate of poverty reduction slowed down and some new forms of poverty appeared." Also, it should not be forgotten that when we talk about poverty reduction in China the poverty line adopted there for making such calculations is much lower than the one recommended by the World Bank, for example.[50]

Obviously, all that does not mean that economic growth is not necessary to the developing countries. What is fundamentally important, however, is that growth should be explicitly orientated towards obtaining well-being and at the same time embody respect for the preservation and regeneration of ecosystem services. Peter Victor is very clear on that point and uses arguments similar to those of one of the researchers of the Chinese Academy of Social Sciences, Jiahua Pan (Pan and Chen, 2010), in regard to the question of carbon space and carbon budgeting – namely, "Few would dispute the tremendous contribution that two centuries or more of economic growth have made to raising the standard of living of people in countries fortunate enough to have experienced it."[51] One of the arguments set out in Peter Victor's book is that the biophysical limits of the planet will prevent the kind of economic growth enjoyed by rich countries from being extended to all peoples of the world over the long term. Rich countries should make room for economic expansion in those countries where the need is greatest. What is at stake here is the idea that growth, even in those countries that have already achieved a high level of material wealth, should continue to be the overall goal of macroeconomic policy.

Such questioning becomes even more consistent whenever an examination is made, in the light of well-being economics, of the real utility of goods and services in the lives of people that growth has been capable of offering, as we will see in the next section.

Is more always worth more?

One of the most frequently used arguments in favour of the universally constructive nature of economic growth is that regardless of what is actually produced or offered (within the limits of the law, obviously), it has the triple potential virtue of creating employment, stimulating innovation and allowing tax collection. It is impossible to align a new economy, having the biosphere's limitations at its heart and ethics embedded in the decision-making processes on the use of (public, private and associative) resources, with that postulate. The creation of work posts is absolutely decisive for maintaining contemporary social cohesion, and innovation is indispensable from whatever angle it is considered, and all the more so in view of the need to improve the energy and material efficiency of the economic system. Taxes are necessary for the provision of public goods.

However, not everything the economic system offers to social life is effectively useful. In spite of the smoker's pleasure every time he or she lights a cigarette, it can hardly be considered that their real well-being is expanded by the satisfaction of their vice. But, as everyone knows, cigarette manufacture generates employment, increases tax revenues and even introduces a kind of innovation. The case of cigarettes is just an extreme example of a more generalized problem regarding the effects of consumption on the ecosystems. The fact is, however, that the expansion of consumption is one of the foundations of economic growth, as shown by the work of Tim Jackson and the 2010 Worldwatch Institute report. It is particularly clear in countries with low levels of savings and where consumption (fuelled by credit) grows at a faster rate than income increase, as has notably been the case in the United States and in several European countries as well. In 1980 North Americans saved 11% of their incomes.[52] By 1990 the average figure had dropped to 8%, and when the 2008 crisis burst on the scene, it stood at less than 1%.

An important step towards reversing human societies' severe pressure on ecosystems would be to make significant changes to contemporary consumption patterns, above all those associated with the way of life of the richest segments, not only in the world's most developed countries but in the better-off developing countries as well, and even in those where extreme poverty prevails.

The contemporary discussion on the usefulness of what is produced for individuals, communities and territories calls for an effort to classify goods and their capability to satisfy the needs of individuals. Psychologist Daniel Kahneman, winner of the Nobel Prize for Economics, has shown that the satisfaction that can be obtained by acquiring goods and services is frequently subject to a kind of treadmill logic whereby one keeps walking all the time but without ever leaving the same spot.[53] When an individual acquires a certain item, he experiences a feeling of satisfaction. When his income goes up, he buys what is considered to be a superior version of that object, which gives him greater satisfaction. But that is only for a limited time, after which his level of satisfaction drops to what it was when he acquired the first item. Thus the real power of goods to satisfy people's fantasies and desires is limited and that induces them to indulge in an ever-increasing consumption. Using a very similar line of reasoning is the idea of positional goods put forward by North American economist Thorstein Veblen.[54] The satisfaction of individuals with the income they earn depends on a comparison they make with that obtained by other individuals and not on the absolute level of the income as such or the rise in income they achieve.

There is a considerable volume of literature in psychology and experimental economics examining the reasons behind people's strong propensity for expanding their consumer aspirations, but a more profound analysis of the issue lies beyond the scope of this book. It is important to mention, however, two fundamental and contradictory dimensions that are involved in this tendency to increased consumption.

Easterlin's paradox

The first dimension lies in the so-called happiness–income paradox. Its formulator, North American economist and demographer Richard Easterlin, expresses it succinctly in a paper written together with other collaborators and published in 2011: "at a certain point in time, within a nation or among nations, happiness is directly correlated to rising income, but, as time goes by, increased income does not correlate with increased happiness" (Easterling *et al.*, 2011). Work undertaken to substantiate that idea began in the United States in 1973. Later a team led by Easterlin carried out studies in Japan and European countries and more recently in 17 Latin American countries, 17 developed countries, 11 Eastern European countries and 9 of the world's poorest countries in Africa, Asia and Latin America – some with very high economic growth rates and others with the very lowest levels of expansion of their GDPs. The findings for Latin America showed that the individuals' level of economic satisfaction is not influenced by the general growth of economic activity in their countries. The same result was obtained for 37 of the countries analysed to measure their levels of life satisfaction over periods varying from 12 to 34 years.

The conclusion of Easterlin and his collaborators' work is both singular and important: "If economic growth is not the main route to greater happiness, what is? A simple, but unhelpful answer is that more research is needed. Possibly more useful are studies that point to the need to focus policy more directly on urgent personal concerns relating to such things as health and family life and to the formation of material preferences, rather than to the mere escalation of material goods."

Since the days of Easterlin's early work, the literature on the relations between income and happiness has burgeoned impressively and there has been a notably profound exploration of the various dimensions embraced by the word 'happiness', ranging from immediate fruition, that is, the pleasure that marks the thinking of Jeremy Bentham, the very first exponent of utilitarianism, to the idea that happiness involves living a full and meaningful life – a central idea in Aristotelian thinking and also one of the pillars of the previously mentioned 'capabilities' approach. The economics of happiness stands apart from conventional economic science insofar as it does not deduce well-being directly from access to goods and services and even less from an undefined range of products whose total (translated into the income of the individual) would supposedly denote his or her real wealth. The economics of happiness endeavours to unite the real sentiments of individuals (by means of opinion polls) with information respecting the consequences of the use they make of all that is at their disposal during their lifetimes.

At the same time, it is important to remember, with Amartya Sen, that happiness cannot be considered an absolute value, a means of measurement capable of defining, in its own right, objectives on which the goods and services supply should be organized.[55] On the one hand, happiness is only one of the innumerable conditions for a life worth living. Honour, self-esteem, solidarity and the feeling of belonging to a group and of being appreciated by it are all aspects that contribute to a decent life, and happiness can never be taken as a proxy value that synthesizes all the others.

The following dimension is not supported by opinion polls but offers information on two of the most important economic sectors in contemporary social life and discusses their effects on well-being: the production of foodstuffs and the production of individually owned automobiles. Here, too, it is easy to detect the limitations of the 'theory of revealed preferences' whereby individuals' real preferences are revealed, not by opinion polls but by what they actually spend their money on.[56] The theory of revealed preferences sees the choices made by smokers or obese individuals as an expression of their real preferences and accordingly as contributing to the expansion of their sense of well-being. In fact, as Carol Graham's book, cited earlier in this chapter, clearly shows, obese people are less happy than non-obese people and smokers experience the paradoxical situation of feeling happy when the price of cigarettes goes up because it helps them in their efforts to give up smoking.

The reason for dedicating attention here to food and transport is not just due to the immediate impact they have on individuals' lives, communities and territories but also because of their tremendous weight in regard to employment, tax revenues and innovation systems in contemporary societies. In other words, they are decisive sectors from the point of view of the risks embedded in conducting 'business as usual' represent for the emergence of an economic life in which ethics and respect for the limitations of the ecosystems are at the centre of decisions.

Obesity and traffic jams

There is an almost unanimous feeling in regard to the urgent need to expand global food production. The income of populations that until recently were living in poverty is increasing and a contingent of an additional two to three billion can be expected to incorporate itself into the existing seven billion inhabitants in the course of the next 40 years. In a book published in 2008, Jeffrey Sachs denounces the George W. Bush government for having paralysed its support for family planning programmes in the world's poorest countries on the pretext that it might foster tolerance regarding abortion. As a result, in his opinion, the world population which could have stabilized at eight billion inhabitants will now only interrupt that growth process around the year 2050 with a population of over 10 billion according to estimates made by the UN Population Fund.

The Human Development Report for 2011 states the case very clearly: population growth generates an undeniable pressure on natural resources.[57] Family planning, women's sovereignty over their own bodies, broad access to the health system and the supply of the means to safe contraception would make it possible for no less than 53 million women to avoid unwanted pregnancies to which they are subjected. In countries like Mali, Mauritania and Sierra Leone, less than 10% of women have access to modern means of contraception. In low-income countries, less than 30% of the women use modern contraception methods against 88% in Norway and 84% in the United Kingdom.

However, the needs of an increasingly populous world cannot be met merely by increasing the supply of goods and services. It is also necessary to take into account with two circumstances directly associated with what Amartya Sen calls the *functioning* of contemporary food production.

First, no less than 40% of the United States' total food production is lost every year.[58] In the developing countries, that percentage is a little lower, around 30%. In any event, they are impressive figures and they mean that there is a similar level of waste of fertilizers, land, pesticides, seeds, water and labour. Those losses should be compared to the fact that agriculture is responsible for 13% of all greenhouse gas emissions (excluding those associated with deforestation) and 47% of total methane emissions. It is not hard to imagine the positive effects on the environment and agricultural supply if those losses were cut down.

Furthermore, the impressive victories obtained in combating hunger in recent decades have been accompanied by an equally impressive increase in obesity around the world. The beginning of the twenty-first century marks the beginning of a period when, for the first time ever, the number of obese individuals in the world surpasses the number of hungry people. The average daily food intake of a North American individual is around 3,830 calories, far beyond the recommended level. North American obesity is epidemic. The US Centers for Disease Control and Prevention define an obese individual as one whose body mass to height ratio is 30% above what is considered the normal standard.[59] In 1990, not one North American state had an obesity prevalence above 15% of the population, but by 1999 there were already 18 states in which prevalence was in the range of 20% to 24%, but, even so, not one had passed the 25% mark. In 2008, however, 32 states were found to have obesity prevalence figures among their citizens of over 25%, and in six of them the level was above 30%. According to the National Health and Nutrition Examination Survey (NHANES), the problem is equally serious among children and adolescents. In the period between 1976/1980 and 2007/2008, obesity in children aged two to five jumped from 5% to 10.4%, and in the age group six to eleven, from 6.5% to 19.6%. To make matters worse, obese children are highly likely to become obese adults. In 2010 obesity affected 35.7% of American adults and 17% of their children.

The problem of obesity is not exclusive to North Americans, however. The chronic disease surveillance system developed by the Epidemiological Studies in Health and Nutrition Group at the São Paulo University, headed by Professor Carlos Augusto Monteiro, revealed that in Brazil more than 42.7% of the population was overweight (a serious condition but not so serious as obesity) in 2006, and by 2009, the percentage was up to 46.6%.[60] Globally, the UN Food and Agriculture Organization (FAO) estimates that 1.6 billion people are overweight, a figure higher than the numbers directly affected by hunger.[61]

The World Health Organization (WHO, 2009) has calculated the number of years of potential life lost due to various kinds of diseases. The years lost directly as a result of hunger (that particularly affects new-born and young children) amounts to 200 million years of life a year. Second place in this macabre ranking goes to diseases associated with obesity and excessively sedentary lifestyles, which carry off 150 million years of potential human life. That is almost double the figure attributed to sexually transmitted diseases. In the United States, only tobacco kills more than the combination of obesity and the sedentary habits that accompany it.

Thus, however important it may be to expand global agricultural production, it is absolutely fundamental to find out what ends the global agro-nutritional system serves. Obesity is primarily related to the generalized introduction of ultra-processed foods into human nutrition and to the powerful advertising pressure applied by the industries associated with that sector which drive the formation of predatory habits in daily food routines, as for example transforming soft drinks and similar products into regular components of the daily diet.

A second example, of a similar nature, is the production of individually owned automobiles. In 2011, according to information displayed on the website of the World Business Council of Sustainable Development, the president of Shell recommended that the world should urgently prepare itself to accommodate more than one billion vehicles in the coming years; 40% of them are liable to be electrically propelled. Even when the source of electricity continues to be carbon-based, electric vehicles have lower emissions than those propelled by gasoline. Furthermore, there is an important set of innovations associated with electric cars that involve the use of new materials for batteries and various other vehicle components as well. Electrically powered vehicles are important vectors of innovation systems directed at sustainability, and Brazil's backwardness in research and investment in that direction is a reason for concern. The automobile industry is highly internationalized and there is a serious risk of Brazil, the world's sixth largest producer, becoming isolated and failing to keep up with innovations in the area of electric cars.[62] What is at stake in the dispute between the electric motor and the internal combustion engine is much more than the sources of energy involved. The internal combustion engine has over 4,000 forged or cast-moulded parts in addition to the suspension and transmission equipment installed in a vehicle. Furthermore there is an entire maintenance and workshop sector associated with it, whereas in the case of electric vehicles, maintenance is liable to be far less complex. Special linings for hoods and bonnets will no longer be necessary. That means that the entire circuit of the industry's workings will come into question with this change, one which, in fact, is already taking place in the global sphere.

Nevertheless, however great the technical innovations may be and however successfully they improve the vehicles' material and energy efficiency performances, it is hard to imagine a more unsuitable way of enhancing mobility in metropolitan regions than the individual car. Amory Lovins of the Rocky Mountain Institute has pointed out that in spite of all it stood for throughout the twentieth century, the individual automobile has a cost that is readily perceivable in the form of some basic information.[63] In the United States it called for the paving of arable areas that add up to the size of the states Ohio, Indiana and Pennsylvania put together and with a daily maintenance cost of US$ 200 million. Every year 1.2 million die in traffic accidents and another 50 million are injured. Of that total, 90% occur in developing countries. The World Health Organization estimated that this real massacre eliminated 2.4 million people in 2010 (WHO, 2004). Annual economic losses stemming from traffic accidents are in the range of US$ 65 to 100 billion, more than all the money invested in development aid.

The World Health Organization, however, is not the only UN agency to proffer a critical vision of the automobile as a means of guaranteeing mobility. The UN Department of Economic and Social Affairs (DESA) is unremitting in its diagnosis of the place of the individual automobile in the economic growth process: "there is not enough physical space for the planned increase in the number of vehicles; the result will be serious problems of traffic jams and pollution. To promote sustainable development, an alternative vision of the transport sector is needed that abandons excessive reliance on private motorization." In spite of all the promises associated with new forms of energy for their engines, the transport sector is currently where the greatest increases in CO_2 emissions are taking place. The enhanced vehicle efficiency achieved in the period from 1970 to 2006 failed to avoid an increase in greenhouse gas emissions of no less than 130% worldwide. The data on pollution of the atmosphere and its effects on human health are equally alarming.

What is important in regard to the emergence of a new economy is embedded in the final conclusion of Amory Lovins' work: "the automobile industry of the late twentieth century is arguably the highest expression of the Iron Age". Furthermore, its energy inefficiency is great: "Of the energy in the fuel it consumes, at least 80 percent is lost, mainly in the engine's heat and exhaust, so that at most only 20 percent is actually used to turn the wheels. Of the resulting force, 95 percent moves the car, while only 5 percent moves the driver, in proportion to their respective weights. Five percent of 20 percent is one percent – not a gratifying result from American cars that burn their own weight in gasoline every year."

That energy inefficiency multiplies exponentially when the alarming level of traffic congestion that is now so typical of the majority of the world's metropolitan regions is taken into account. Reports on average vehicle speeds in traffic in the city of São Paulo show that it is often faster to walk than to go by car. Thirty-two per cent of people in Brazilian cities with over 100,000 inhabitants take over an hour every day getting to work.[64]

Currently world automobile production stands at 70 million units a year.[65] That means that the one billion mark Shell's president has predicted will be reached (if the current rate does not intensify further) in 2025. From the point of view of the relationship between wealth and well-being that is the focus of this chapter, the consequence will be to intensify pressure to ensure that "roadwork design predominates in the design and organization of major cities", to borrow a phrase from architect Valter Caldana.[66]

Owning an automobile continues to be one of people's most cherished aspirations, especially in developing countries. There is an accentuated price reduction associated with single-owner cars being exported by China, and owning a car has begun to replace the desire to own a motorcycle in the consumer dreams of those currently emerging from the situation of poverty they lived in up until a few years ago. However, the chances of harmonizing the expansion of the vehicle fleet with a sensation of well-being derived from using this means of transport are highly remote, given the limitations of urban and metropolitan spaces.

It is not only architects and urban planning specialists who have realized that fact; the automobile industry itself is becoming increasingly aware of it. The image of the car as an expression of individual freedom and autonomy is being cultivated less and less, especially among young people. Phil Patton, commenting on the Audi Urban Future Award, demonstrates that the automobile industry is facing a problem with its reputation, which bears increasing resemblance to that of the tobacco companies.[67]

Conclusions

Economic growth is not a panacea for achieving well-being. It is of fundamental importance to evaluate what it means not only in terms of its general social effects (expansion of goods and services supply, creating employment, boosting tax revenues and stimulating innovation) but, above all, in terms of its direct impacts on people's lives, on communities and on territories. In that sense it is a means and not an end in itself, and the definition of the objectives it means to achieve must embrace ethics and values. It is no longer good enough to merely evoke material wealth, tax revenues, jobs and innovation. The supposedly automatic link envisaged in the economic thinking that currently prevails, that would connect those fourfold expansions to an enhancement of greater social well-being, is irreparably flawed and that fact alone is sufficient to justify and underscore the urgent need for the emergence of a new economy essentially centred on meeting basic needs. Placing the economy at the disposal of the development process means orientating its individual units and even private interests towards opportunities to make gains and create values based on the measure of well-being obtained and not on any abstract parameters of wealth that supposedly result in well-being. The experience of the last few years has shown that this supposed mechanical link between wealth and well-being is increasingly problematical. Moreover, when it is examined from the angle of the preservation and the regeneration of ecosystem services that human societies depend on, then arguments favouring radical changes in the way we organize contemporary economic life become stronger than ever, and that is what we will go on to examine next.

Notes

1 This information can be found in the aforementioned work of Tim Jackson.
2 The number of poor is currently shamefully high in view of the wealth of contemporary societies. However, the percentage of the total population that is poor has gone down to an extraordinary extent. The numbers of people hit by hunger went down steadily in the period from 1970 until the mid-1990s. From then on, however, it has been increasing incessantly. A good explanation with graphs illustrating the evolution of hunger in the world can be found at http://www.worldhunger.org/articles/Learn/world%20hunger%20facts%202002.htm (consulted on 21 March 2012).
3 Green Economy, *Pathways to Sustainable Development and Poverty Eradication*. See UNEP (2011b).
4 See https://www.bcorporation.net/sites/all/themes/adaptivetheme/bcorp/pdfs/B%20Corp_2011-Annual-Report.pdf (consulted on 21 June 2015).
5 Skidelski and Skidelski (2012) reject the idea of this association between ethical limits to the expansion of production and the degradation of the services provided to human societies by the ecosystems. The arguments they put forward to show that degradation can be overcome by science and technology are not very convincing especially if they are read in the light of the already mentioned book by Rockström and Klum (2012).
6 This important report, with a preface by Angela Merkel and former Indian Prime Minister Manmohan Singh, was launched at the 2009 Copenhagen Climate Change Conference and is highly instructive and informative in regard to the relations between climate change and inequalities. Its repercussions, however, were undeservedly slight. See German Advisory Council on Global Change (2009).
7 The reference here is to the work of the great German sociologist Max Weber (1864–1920). The economic calculation in money and capital is formal insofar as it does not take into account any criterion other than the values involved in the operations. On the other hand, substantive rationality involves the purposes or ends that motivate the resource use. Modern societies are typically notable for the growing prevalence of formal rationality associated with the economic calculation in money and capital. In spite of the obscure style of the work in which this distinction is made, it is, nevertheless, worth consulting. The distinction in question is set out in paragraph 9 of the second volume of *Economy and Society* (Weber, 1990).
8 Thomas Friedman is a *New York Times* columnist and his two books (2005 and 2010) are important reference works for the contemporary discussion around the question of sustainable development.
9 Jeffrey Sachs was a special adviser to Kofi Annan and had an important role in designing the millennium goals, a set of goals adopted by the United Nations to fight

poverty. While it is true that in the 1990s the young economist was party to the unconditional stability policies preached by the International Monetary Fund (he was an adviser to the governments of Bolivia and Poland on their application), today he is one of the global exponents of the fight to reduce inequalities and in favour of sustainable development.

10 This is one of the most important Brazilian social science works and can be viewed as being the first essay on social ecology. The analysis of the indissoluble union between natural conditions and social life in the Brazilian northeast and the Amazon in the late 1940s is as exemplary today as it was then (Castro, 1980).

11 The Global Hunger Index has been published since 2007 by three prestigious organizations – the International Food Policy Research Institute (IFPRI), Concern Worldwide and Welthungerhilfe. The index is a tool that unites three indicators: the percentage of undernourished individuals in the population, the prevalence of underweight children and the infant mortality rate (IFPRI, Concern Worldwide, and Welthungerhilfe, 2010).

12 This information has been taken from the entry 'Hunger' on Wikipedia (http://en.wikipedia.org/wiki/Hunger, consulted on 22 March 2012) and is supported by UN FAO documents.

13 The information is supplied by the World Health Organization (http://www.who.int/topics/obesity/en, consulted on 22 March 2012).

14 During the 1960s, gains in yields of cereal crops in world agriculture rose by 3.2% a year. In 2000 that rate went down to 1.5% a year, as shown by another important study published by the FAO (2009).

15 The information is set out in a paper published by the global consultants Goldman Sachs (2008).

16 This information can be found in McKinsey Global Institute (2011).

17 Information that was published in the *Wall Street Journal* (Passariallo, 2010).

18 Information taken from the *Economist* (http://www.economist.com/node/21526374, consulted on 22 March 2012).

19 See Bellman (2009).

20 See Wonacott (2011). The optimism of Wonacott's report is not shared by the OECD report on that continent which shows a reduction in poverty in course but at a much slower rate than expected; see OECD (2011a).

21 There are various sources of information on this issue. The most complete one is the CEPAL collection of reports, *Panorama Social da América Latina* (Social Panorama of Latin America), which can be downloaded from http://www.eclac.cl/cgi-bin/getProd.asp?xml=/publicaciones/xml/9/41799/P41799.xml&xsl=/dds/tpl/p9f.xsl&base=/dds/tpl/top-bottom.xsl (consulted 25 June 2015). There is also an excellent synthesis in the UNEP document and that of the Red Mercosur, published in 2011.

22 The median is the value that separates the set of lower half values for a given variable from the set of upper half values.

23 The Gini index is a coefficient used to measure the inequality among values in the distribution of a given frequency. Its commonest use is in regard to income distribution. A Gini index of zero indicates that there is a perfect distribution, among members, of the values in question: in the case of income it would mean that its distribution was entirely fair, whereas a Gini index of one means that inequality is maximal and a single individual receives all the income.

24 Information taken from the *Observador Brasil 2012*, a survey conducted by Cetelem BGN of the BNP Paribas group (http://www.cetelem.com.br/portal/Sobre_Cetelem/Observador.shtml, consulted on 24 March 2012).

25 Information provided in the work of Alves (undated).

26 I was privileged to hear this statement made as part of Chonchol's account of his government experience.

27 This reference to the article of 1983 appears in Sen (1984).

28 Information set out on page 6 of Nussbaum's (2011) book.

29 This phrase has been taken from one of the fundamental books written by Sen and published in 2009 (page 9).

30 Neoclassic economic thinking is what has dominated teaching and research in economics from the end of the nineteenth century up to the present moment. Its basic hypothesis is that process, products, income and its distribution are determined in a competitive manner in the markets, and that from that process results the best possible allocation of productive factors and consequently the best state of well-being. Its two most important premises in regard to human behaviour are rational decision making and the inherent self-interest of individuals. There is a good presentation of the subject on Wikipedia (http://en.wikipedia.org/wiki/Neoclassical_economics, consulted on 22 March 2012).

31 Information displayed on page 8 of global consultants KPMG's important 2012 report.

32 A commitment made by 193 countries, in the sphere of the UN Millennium Development Goals, to achieve certain fundamental objectives by the year 2015, namely: reduce extreme poverty, universalize primary education, promote gender equality, reduce infant mortality, improve maternal health, combat epidemic diseases and others (http://www.un.org/millenniumgoals, consulted on 22 March 2012).

33 IBGE data summarized at http://www1.folha.uol.com.br/cotidiano/908789-brasil-ainda-sofre-com-falta-de-saneamento-basico-aponta-ibge.shtml (consulted on 22 March 2012).

34 This is from data of the *Instituto Trata Brasil* in the report of Reina (2010).

35 The Flavio Comim article quoted here can be read at http://www.ihu.unisinos.br/noticias/502580-idh-como-uma-onda-no-mar (consulted on 22 March 2012).

36 In philosophy, ontology is the doctrine concerning the nature of being.

37 Sen discusses the consecrated idea of sustainable development in what is possibly his most important text addressing an environmental theme, published in the *London Review of Books*.

38 Herman Daly is the most emblematic figure of contemporary ecological economics. It is a subject that explicitly sets out to consider the economic system as merely part of a much larger system that it is dependent on, namely the ecosystem. In 2004, Daly and Joshua Farley published their manual *Ecological Economics*.

39 Jiahua Pan is a renowned scientist in the field of climate change. His 2010 article written together with Ying Chen is strongly influenced and inspired by Amartya Sen's ideas.

40 John Rawls' most important work, *A Theory of Justice*, was published in 1971 and is considered to be one of the most important classics of twentieth-century political philosophy. The quotation below can be found on page 291 of the 1993 edition.

41 The World Bank produces an annual report on development, the *World Development Report*. The 2006 edition discusses the relations between equality and development (http://siteresources.worldbank.org/INTWDR2006/Resources/477383-1127230817535/082136412X.pdf, consulted on 25 June 2015). Elasticity, in the sense used by economists, is a measure of the sensitivity of a given phenomenon to the causes that are capable of making it vary. When income is very highly concentrated, then economic growth benefits the poor even less than when the inequalities are less marked (thus poverty reduction is not very elastic in regard to economic growth); inequalities remove the poor even further from opportunities that economic growth might offer in terms of employment and new productive occupations.

42 The calculation is set out in the work of Woodward and Simms (2006), published by the UN DESA.

43 See Lehman (2010).

44 'Banana Republic' was the expression used by Kristof to refer to the United States of the second decade of the twenty-first century (Kristof, 2010).

45 The issue of inequality (which is often only addressed in the aspect of income inequality and consequently in the singular instead of 'inequalities') has also come to occupy an increasingly important place on the OECD agenda, as a work published on which the information is based clearly shows (OECD, 2011b; http://www.oecd.org/dataoecd/32/20/47723414.pdf, consulted on 23 March 2012).

46 This information is presented in a book written by Philip Bartlett Smith and Manfred Max-Neef (2011). Bruni and Zamagni (2010) announce the increase both in the

absolute numbers of poor people in the United States and as a proportion of the overall population.

47 This is the outstanding finding of a research survey conducted by two professors, one belonging to the Harvard Business School and the other to Duke University (Norton and Ariely, 2011), who applied the philosophical principles of John Rawls to their research work.

48 The information is set out in the above-mentioned work of Kristof (2010).

49 See Steiner (2011). The quotation at the end of the paragraph is taken from pages 14 and 15 of Steiner's book.

50 The information is based on the work of Angang *et al.* (undated) and Deng and Gustafsson (2011).

51 The quote is taken from pages 154 and 155 of Victor's book (2008).

52 This important piece of information is set out in Masterson's book (2011).

53 The fundamental importance of Kahneman's work resides in his attempt to go beyond the common presuppositions of various economic schools of thought in regard to what goods best represent well-being. He shows (Kahneman and Krueger, 2006) that the determinants of a sense of well-being go far beyond the question of possessing material goods and often refer much more to momentary circumstances and individual characteristics. In any event, his work of 2006 corroborates the validity of several opinion polls regarding the question of well-being which have shown that there is no close linear relation between increases in wealth and greater happiness. In the conclusion of their work, Kahneman and Krueger praise the initiative undertaken by the Kingdom of Bhutan in creating a national well-being indicator (alongside the traditional indicators of production and income) and pointed out that the United Kingdom and Australia are making efforts in the same direction. The contrast between the apparent amply ambitious scope of their work and the narrowness of the conventional approach to the question of well-being is clearly expressed in the last phrase of the text: "In the final analysis we suspect that many politicians feel themselves to be much more comfortable with the idea of minimizing a certain concept of extreme poverty than with that of maximizing a nebulous concept of happiness."

54 The US economist and sociologist Thorstein Veblen (1857–1929) drew attention to the aspect of the quest for status and the conspicuous and ostentatious nature of the consumption of certain high-income segments of modern societies.

55 This is an issue discussed by Sen in his aforementioned 2009 book.

56 The theory of revealed preferences' starting point is that people's preferences cannot be observed directly and that in reality they reveal themselves in what they do with their resources. It is in this aspect that the theory identifies preference and choice and does not in any way enter into questions of foundations, origins or conditioning factors or anything else influencing the formation of preferences that will eventually give rise to choices. Little (1949) explains that "if then it should be possible to explain that an individual's behavior is consistent it should be possible to explain it without any reference to anything other than the behavior itself".

57 Every year since 1990, the UN Development Programme has launched a report in which it displays the Human Development Index (HDI) ratings, a parameter that seeks to synthesize (albeit in very imperfect form) the social situations of various different countries.

58 This information is provided by the UN FAO and is formally set out in the report on the Green Economy (UNEP, 2011b). Roberto Smeraldi recalls in a personal communication the importance of distinguishing loss from waste. In the field of nutrition, they tend to be inversely proportional to one another; when losses are relatively high, waste is relatively low, and vice versa. Losses are mainly related to the pre-consumption phase and they are most abundant where there are deficiencies in technology, logistics, storage and infrastructure. Waste, on the other hand, is associated with consumption itself, when there is an abundant supply and higher income levels. Curiously enough, Brazil has both these phenomena.

59 Information supplied by the US Centers for Disease Control and Prevention can be found in the document 'U.S. Obesity Trends. Trends by State. 1985–2008' (http://www.cdc.gov/obesity/data/trends.html, consulted on 23 March 2012). The technical definition for obesity is taken from the work of Ogden *et al.* (2012). It makes it clear that obesity does not mean being a little overweight. An adult with a height of 1.75 metres is considered obese if he or she weighs more than 92 kilos!

60 See Monteiro (2010).

61 Monitoring of the causes associated with mortality can be found in various reports like the one published in 2009 by WHO.

62 The sources of information here are two articles published in the newspaper *Valor Econômico*: Santos and Medeiros (2009) and Olmos (2009). Santos and Medeiros demonstrate Brazil's dependence in relation to "the anachronistic metal-mechanical chain". Olmos' article is particularly important insofar as it highlights the Brazilian tendency to accommodate itself to the inefficient internal combustion engine in view of the importance of ethanol.

63 The information is drawn from Chapter 2 of *Natural Capitalism*, written by Paul Hawken and colleagues. The second chapter ('Reinventing the Wheel') can be downloaded from http://www.natcapage org/images/other/NCchapter2.pdf (consulted on 23 March 2012).

64 http://www.estadao.com.br/noticias/cidades,um-terco-dos-brasileiros-leva-mais-de-uma-hora-para-chegar-ao-trabalho,759794,0.htm (consulted on 23 March 2012).

65 The information is given in a text of Marli Olmos (2009).

66 The urban designer was interviewed by the *Estado de São Paulo* newspaper on 2 August 2009 (http://brasil.estadao.com.br/noticias/geral,um-terco-dos-brasileiros-leva-mais-de-uma-hora-para-chegar-ao-trabalho,759794, consulted on 21 June 2015).

67 There are those who do not hesitate to refer to the automobile industry as a 'tobacco-like problem' (http://designobserver.com/feature/audi-urban-future-summit-2011/31388, consulted on 27 December 2011).

2

THE MYTH OF THE IMMATERIAL

Green economy is not the same as green growth

Introduction

The idea of goods and services growth as the universal pathway to well-being is being increasingly discarded, even by economists. What most of the recent work regarding it has contested is not just the way wealth is expressed but the very outreach and meaning of goods and services production as the basis for obtaining a good quality of life in contemporary societies. In his account of a UN meeting on the issue, Jeffrey Sachs (2011) goes so far as to speak of "the importance of seeking happiness rather than national revenue". In that regard it is important to avoid two common misunderstandings.

First, economic growth is a condition that enables the construction of infrastructure and the provision of services (education, health, culture, mobility, connection) capable of meeting the needs of billions of people, above all in developing countries. Thus there cannot be any question of a general suppression of it. However, even in developing countries, it is imperative to significantly modify the forms in which economic growth materializes itself. It is not feasible, for example, that producing individually owned cars should continue to be one of the essential vectors of economic expansion despite all the harm and impairment this means of transport causes to the designing of sustainable cities, to the health of individuals and to the vigour of territorial communities. The progress made in terms of new materials and energy sources for automobiles will only acquire any real meaning if their use is shared, if the number of vehicles in circulation is drastically reduced, if there is effective support provided for the provision of mobility through collective forms of transport and, above all, if urban layouts and designs are constructed with people in mind and not cars. Therein lies much more than a simple factor of restraint. It constitutes an extraordinary opportunity to do business, as the American company Zipcar shows. It is explicitly directed at clients who want all the comfort implicit in having their own individual vehicle but are prepared to share its use by means of hire arrangements. All the site's advertising stimulates the shared use of goods and consequently represents considerable savings for individuals and for society as a whole.

Another practice that cannot be recommended as the basis for economic development is stimulating the consumption of highly energy-intensive processed food whose ingestion has a direct connection with the global obesity epidemic. As can be seen from the above-mentioned documents, there is growing concern in the World Health Organization with diseases related to people's lifestyles and their ingestion of industrialized foods: diabetes and hypertension are the two most important. The principal consequence pointed out in the preceding chapter is that the capability of economic life to produce well-being will be increasingly subjected to public judgement and in ways that go far beyond anything that prices alone could achieve.

This is where the second misunderstanding comes in; limiting is not the same thing as paralysing. The space that exists for generating prosperity by means of goods, services and innovations directed at boosting social well-being is immense. Business opportunities in that direction will improve as the real costs of the predominantly predatory forms that have been the hallmark of our economic development become fully revealed.

There are two decisive areas (strongly inter-related) in which such opportunities for simultaneously doing business and producing well-being exist: the *green economy* and the *information networks economy*. In both cases innovation is at the heart of all the new opportunities. There is nothing worse, however, for the emergence of a new economy that has respect for the ecosystems at its centre and in which ethics commands the decision-making processes, than the image so recurrently projected, that the information networks and the green economy are a kind of dematerialized (and consequently inoffensive) option, a kind of shortcut to perpetuate growth as the driver and finality of the economic organization. What is really at stake is not conquering new techniques in order to maintain current patterns of doing public and private business where the order of the day is 'growth', even if they manage to clean up their undesirable externalities. If that were the case, the opportunities for creating value in the information society would be integrally subjected to the prices system, and that simply does not happen. A growing portion of innovation, production of well-being and the prosperity of contemporary societies responds to forms of social relations in which the markets play an irrelevant role. Up until now, expanding knowledge, strengthening social networks, making discoveries and facilitating invention have all been almost immediately linked to increases in market exchanges and, accordingly, are conditioned to economic growth.

One of the central features of a new economy in which ethical considerations are at the heart of decision making (and that is starting to take place in the information networks society) is that the achievements stemming from the collective intelligence of the social groups is no longer exclusively conditioned by the private property system and consequently are not expressed in the form of prices or in the aggregation that composed the GDP. That means that the creation of value is no longer restricted (and in fact has never been restricted) to what is bought and sold, even though the markets and the companies obviously continue to play a decisive role in social life. To use an expression coined by one of the co-founders of the think tank *Esfera*, located in São Paulo's *Casa da Cultura Digital* (Digital Culture House), the creation of value lies "in the ability to *join the dots together that were formerly separated*, to make things exist that did not exist before, and to be useful to people".[1]

The *green economy* and the *information networks society* open the way for unprecedented innovations. The wish to obtain well-being and respect for the ecosystems in the sphere of a decentralized economy where the markets play a decisive role must be met outside of the currently prevailing parameters in which the contents and the metrics of social capability to produce utilities can only find expression in economic growth. One of the most important aspects of the previously mentioned Stiglitz report is its recognition of the immense magnitude of goods and services delivered outside the regular market sphere of social life. Domestic work, looking after children and caring for old people are among the most obvious examples of the immense importance of social activities that are not mediated by the markets. An information networks society will stimulate a desirable smudging of the sharp boundaries – that have marked recent history, at least since the Industrial Revolution – that separate activities involving free, voluntary cooperation from those carried out for private gain. The frontiers between business and civil society are becoming fluid. Information, knowledge and science are public goods increasingly important to the contemporary economy. That reduces the distance separating what the great classics of social science have always treated as mutually hostile worlds.[2]

The core idea of this chapter (focused on the *green economy*) is that the rhythm of *decoupling* of goods and services production from their material and energy bases could be speeded up considerably and enable the achievement of extraordinarily positive social and environmental results. From the public, private and associative angles, doing that poses some crucial challenges to the advancement of contemporary knowledge and technological innovation. It involves new energy sources and, more than that, new ways of using energy, materials and what, up until now, has been considered to be waste. Even so, however crucially important this *decoupling* may be, it is incapable of compensating for the destructive effects that the increase in goods and services supply has on the maintenance and regeneration of the basic ecosystem services. It cannot overcome social reproduction's inherent entropy even if eco-efficiency is enhanced far beyond present levels. The decoupling of what is being produced from the energy and material base that its production rests on is merely *relative* and is accompanied by an increase, in absolute terms, in resource consumption.

Furthermore, in some sectors like agriculture, where not even this relative decoupling is occurring, growth's destructive effects on the ecosystems are not so much the result of the ingress in the markets of those who until recently were living in poverty (although obviously their pressure cannot be ignored) but, above all, from the concentration of resource use in the hands of the rich. No less than half of all global greenhouse gas emissions stem from the planet's 500 million richest inhabitants, as shown by Figure 2.1.[3]

In addition to this social concentration of emissions, there is a similar concentration of energy materials use, as has already been pointed out in the Introduction. The prospect of a global population increase of three billion people in the coming years represents such an intense pressure on the ecosystems that – at the present rate of development – technological innovations directed at economizing material and energy and reducing greenhouse gas emissions will be incapable of counterbalancing its effects. At the same time, as the preceding chapter explained and we will examine in greater depth here, inequality burgeons to such an extent that it will reduce even further the chances of new discoveries and inventions managing to harmonize economic life with the maintenance of ecosystem services that the human species actually depends on.

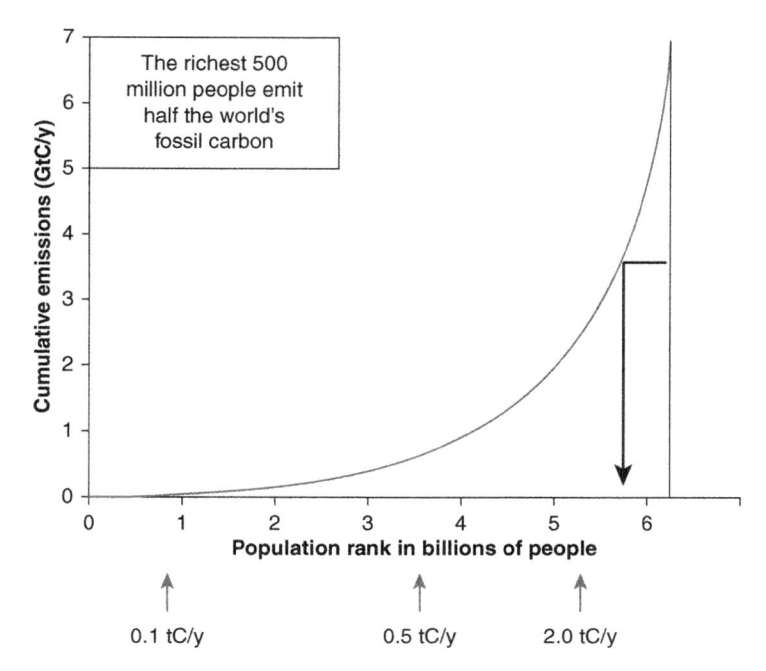

FIGURE 2.1 Who emits?

Source: Pacala (2007).

The economy of the knowledge of nature

Increasingly, multilateral organizations, the corporate world and civil society itself have been making use of the term 'green economy'. It involves three fundamental aspects.

The first is certainly the best known and corresponds to the transition from the large-scale use of fossil fuels to the use of renewable sources of energy. In that regard, Brazil is in a privileged position insofar as its energy matrix can lean heavily on hydroelectric power and ethanol and, since the beginning of the second decade of the twenty-first century, on wind energy. While in the world at large the average participation of renewable energies in the economy is around 13%, in Brazil it is over 45%; in the richest countries, it stands at around 7%.

Figure 2.2 illustrates the world economy's great dependence on fossil fuel sources of energy. It must be pointed out that it separates the renewable forms of energy (the dark band at the top) from biomass (the pale band at the bottom). It so happens that by far the greater part of the energy produced on the basis of biomass comes from burning firewood, charcoal and dry manure for heating purposes and above all for cooking. It is a source of energy for 1.4 billion people who have no access to electricity, and it should not be confused with modern biomass such as that which fuels vehicles in Brazil (and in parts of the United States).[4] Since the 1950s there has been a great increase in the world economy's dependence on

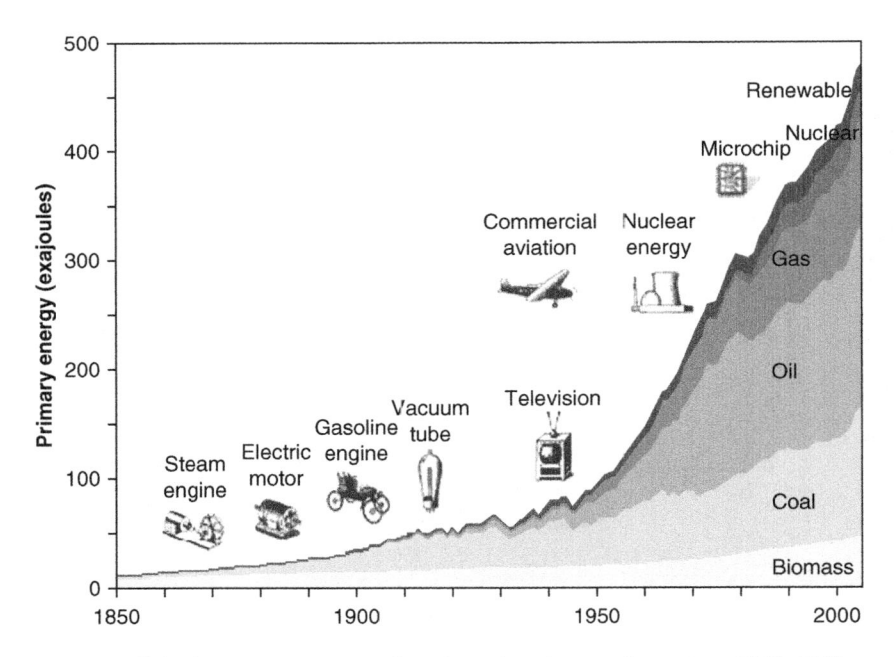

FIGURE 2.2 Rise in energy consumption since the nineteenth century, 1850–2000

Source: *World Economic and Social Survey* (UN DESA, 2009, p. 48; http://www.un.org/en/development/desa/policy/wess/wess_archive/2009wess.pdf, consulted on 24 March 2012).

fossil fuels as its source of energy, and as will be shown later on, that dependency is not decreasing.

The second fundamental dimension of the green economy lies in promoting and taking advantage of products offered by biodiversity, based on what Brazilian geographer Bertha Becker refers to as the *economy of the knowledge of nature* economy in contrast to the current *economy of the destruction of nature* economy.[5] The idea is to create value chains associated with (wood or non-wood) forest products and ecosystem services and to ensure that business based on those chains benefits population groups that live in areas rich in biodiversity. A document that was produced as part of the International Year of Biodiversity (2010) was prolific in regard to the innumerable economic opportunities it identified that could derive from that kind of exploitation.[6] The private sector has also publicized important initiatives in that direction.[7]

However, doing business involving the economic use of products and services associated with the world's most important, and at the same time most fragile, biomes has so far fallen short of what might have been expected from reading the literature produced during the International Year of Biodiversity. The effective construction of value chains based on forest products for medicinal, cosmetic and industrial purposes has been extremely modest. Up to now, biomimicry, considered by some studies to be the most advanced of all contemporary industrialization processes, is still a long way off from materializing all its great potential.[8] It is true that the predatory occupation of the Brazilian Amazon has been largely curbed, not only as a result of public policies directed at combating deforestation but equally as a result of social coalitions that have managed to transform the profiles of municipalities formerly included in forest destruction blacklists, and which are now coming off them, like Paragominas in Pará and Alta Floresta in Mato Grosso.

Those small signs of progress, however, fail to compensate for the timidity with which this fundamental dimension of the green economy has been addressed so far. The precarious nature of investments in science and technology in the region is one factor that explains the contrast between the wealth embedded in its biodiversity and the effective economic use that is being made of it. This is clearly revealed in an important document produced in 2008 by the Brazilian Academy of Sciences dedicated to the question.[9] Even today it is impossible to discern whether economic use of the standing forest does not take place because it offers a corporate prospect that is not very realistic or if what is behind it is the precarious nature of public and private investment in that direction. In any event, what can readily be detected is that this second dimension of the green economy falls far short of expectations. Today, the Amazon is the scene of gigantic projects for energy production, oil exploration and mining whose results bring no benefits to local populations, threaten traditional communities and contribute nothing towards the sustainable use of biodiversity.[10]

The third aspect of the green economy is not directly or immediately associable with the exploitation of biodiversity, although it does have short- and long-term consequences for the ecosystems. This third dimension refers to offering goods and services on the basis of techniques capable of reducing pollution (beginning with greenhouse gases), reusing an increasing proportion of its rejects and, above all, cutting down on the materials and energy around which the production processes are organized.

Successes achieved in that direction are impressive whether viewed as a whole or examined in the form of localized examples. The problem is, though, that such progress is still very far from being sufficient to allow economic growth to continue without jeopardizing climate equilibrium, biodiversity, and material and energy supplies themselves.

The approach to this issue will be expressed in the form of two closely linked basic propositions, addressed in the items that follow.

1   Conciliating development process requirements with the preservation and regeneration of the major ecosystem services that human societies depend on will only become possible by *changing the management of materials and energy* that current forms of production are based on. The possibility of accruing economic gains with strategies that envisage a more intelligent use of materials and energy is immense and their effects on societies and ecosystems are potentially highly positive. That increased efficiency is already taking place in part, and public policies are being designed to intensify it, particularly by creating sustainability-orientated innovation systems. These will be examined below.

2   Despite the benefits already obtained and the immense potential yet to be exploited, eco-efficiency still does not constitute a shortcut that could lead to *the perpetuation of growth* as the mainstay of the relations between society and the economy. Reductions in energy and materials consumption stemming from technological innovation have not been and cannot be sufficient to allow the economy to overcome the limitations imposed by the ecosystems which society depends on. To use Leonardo Boff's (2011) observation, "the Green part represents a mere stage in a larger process. Production is never entirely eco-friendly." What is in fact at stake are the consumer patterns of contemporary societies and, above all, their impressive and ever-increasing inequality. The reduction of that inequality is one of the most important challenges, and if it is not faced the green economy will be bereft of much of its effective outreach, as will be seen later in this chapter.

Less and less material, less energy, less emissions . . .

In 2011, the UN Environment Programme's (UNEP) International Resource Panel published an important report on the processes by means of which the use of natural sources and its impacts on the environment could be uncoupled from economic growth. The main author of the report, Marina Fischer-Kowalski, runs the Social Ecology Institute in Vienna, Austria. Her research programme is structured around the concept of *social metabolism* and more particularly *industrial metabolism*. It is an approach that analyses the reproduction of human societies by studying the ways in which they make use of the materials and energy they depend on and, at the same time, the way they manage the refuse resulting from their productive processes. The metabolism concept in the case of society is not limited to biochemical aspects alone but embraces the material and energy flows that human society depends on. From a strictly biochemical angle, birds' nests are not part of birds' metabolisms, but they are fundamental to any study of their reproductive processes.

The same line of reasoning applies to human societies in regard to the material and energy that their reproduction is based on.

It must be remembered that for the vast majority of social sciences such an approach is entirely strange. In the interior of classical thinking, the works of Marx and Engels are among the few exceptions to that rule. The metabolism between society and nature is at the heart of their thinking right from their early writings up to Marx's *Capital*. They never mistook value (the work necessary to produce goods and services) for wealth, or forgot that one of the essential components of the latter stems from nature and not from human work. In a text he wrote towards the end of his life, the *Critique of the Gotha Programme*, Marx underscored that work itself is an expression of a natural force, a capacity human beings have to transform nature and obtain from it the utilities they need. However, that is an exception in the interior of classical thinking, and to it could be added a part of cultural anthropology and its studies of traditional societies with an emphasis on their material foundations. The most emblematic example is the treatise *Argonauts of the Western Pacific* by the founder of modern ethnology, Bronislaw Malinowski.

In neoclassical economics, value is given a definition that makes no reference to the materials or energy contained in the goods and services supply or to the waste stemming from their production, all treated alike as 'externalities'. In the same way, ever since its creation by Keynes right up to the present, macroeconomics has always conceived social life as a self-sufficient closed cycle in which income and product circulate between households and companies (or, at the most, including governments and philanthropic entities), without attributing to materials, energy, pollution or biodiversity any function other than that which expresses itself in the markets.

However, it is not only economics that turns the metabolism of social life into an abstraction. In the sociology of Durkheim, in his own words, "the social explains the social", with no reference to the relations between society and nature. In Max Weber's work, with the notable exception of a passage in the final part of *The Protestant Ethic and the Spirit of Capitalism* (where he evokes the exhaustion of oil and coal deposits), society is analysed from the angle of what occurs in the relations between individuals and social groups.[11]

Romanian economist Nicholas Georgescu-Roegen played a decisive intellectual role in formulating what can be called, without fear of rhetorical exaggeration, a *new paradigm for reflecting on economic life* constructed around the idea that it is not enough to do as traditional economic science does and reduce materials, energy and pollution to the language of prices and evoke the idea of externalities whenever that reduction proves to be impossible.[12] At the root of belief in the continuity of incessant economic growth lies the idea that when sources of material and energy that social reproduction depends eventually become scarce they will be replaced by other, more efficient ones provided that the process is conducted in a way that is appropriate for the free functioning of the markets. In that light human intelligence is seen as constructing a world of infinite resources totally at variance with the notion of entropy. The idea is that capital and work are capable of uninterruptedly substituting whatever is offered by Nature (material, energy, water, biodiversity, climate . . .), while at the same time, through the achievement of eco-efficiency, the pressure on those resources will increasingly diminish. It is exactly that vision that makes it possible to contemplate economic life as being reduced to terms of capital and work without considering that material, energy or pollution have any conceptually relevant role at all.

The translation of all the components of the economic system into one common unit of expression (prices), thereby abstracting their material, energetic and biological bases, is one of the decisive bases for the conviction that the future will be a replica of the past and that accordingly there are no limits to economic growth. That conviction seriously underestimates the importance of materials and above all of energy in the economic system. One of the most outstanding researchers in this field, Robert Ayres, sums the question up in a book published jointly with Edward Ayres in 2011: "Physical energy plays a far more important role in productivity and growth than most economists, business advisers and government experts have ever imagined. Energy services are not just a part of the economic system; they are, to a great extent, what drives economic systems."

In spite of Georgescu-Roegen's work having been vehemently rejected by the most important economists of the day, when it was published in the 1970s it actually led the way to one of the most fecund present-day social science research programmes, and the UN 2011 report on decoupling is a manifestation of that.[13] In the last 20 years, this programme has also led to attempts to alter the paradigms used to measure the performance of economies.

The concept of 'aggregated national material flows accounting' is just one example, now widely used in the European Union.[14] Germany, Japan and Switzerland have commissioned public governmental reports on it, estimating the materials needed for their goods and services productions. Since 2001 the British National Statistics Office has been publishing accounts of material flows; Japan has set the establishment of a 'sound material-cycle society' as a national goal – a society based on a healthy life cycle in respect to the materials use it is founded on.[15] Their environmental reports begin with the observation that "rapid economic growth has been associated with generating vast accumulations of waste and increasing scarcity of resources".

The same kind of calculation can be applied to energy use and the various forms of pollution, especially greenhouse gas emissions. The core question is: *has the technical progress of contemporary societies managed to make economic growth base itself on the decreasing use of materials and energy and an ever-diminishing level of pollution?*

The response to that question embodied in the UNEP report for 2011 is that the more efficient use of material resources *per unit of wealth produced* is a process fully underway. In the OECD member countries, from 1975 to 2000, the use of physical resources per product unit (the so-called material intensity of economic life) fell almost by half, which is an impressive achievement. Generally speaking, in 2002 each unit of global GDP was produced using an average 20% less material resources than in 1980. The energy use intensity of the US and British economies fell by 40% in the period from 1980 to 2009, and the same phenomenon was observed in global GDP, where intensity of energy use has been going steadily down.[16] Since 1980 carbon intensity in the global economy has gone down from 1 kilogram for every dollar's worth produced to 770 grams. Vaclav Smil's important work shows that during the twenty-first century global GDP increased 22-fold, fossil fuel consumption 14-fold and emissions 13-fold, which indicates a steady gain in energy efficiency, reflected in the production and reduction of emissions per unit produced over the course of that period.

There has also been notable progress in eco-efficiency in certain sectors and local instances; the quantity of water used in soft drink manufacturing has fallen, and so has water use in sugarcane washing for the ethanol production process. Even in the US coal production sector there has been important progress: the units implanted in the twenty-first century emit 40% less CO_2 than those that predominated in the twentieth century (Boyce, 2013). Big retail chains have reduced the amount of water used by their individual outlets. Containers made from other organic materials are replacing plastic recipients. Brazil has especially good rates of recycling, as high as 56.7% in the case of PET bottles. Tetra Pak intends to recover 40% of its packaging to serve as industrial raw material by 2014 (Adeodato, 2010). The recovery of recyclable paper, which represented 38.3% of total consumption in 2000, was over 43.7% by 2008 (Fontes, 2010). Aluminium recycling has also registered remarkable progress. In 2010, Brazil recycled no less than 97.6% of aluminium cans for beverages, totalling 239,000 tons of scrap aluminium, the equivalent of 17 billion individual cans. Although the United States produces much more than Brazil, they recycle much less – just 58.1% of what they consume. The transformation of slag formed during steel production into natural aggregates and ingredients for the manufacture of cement is part of a process of energy co-generation that mirrors this collective effort to improve energy and materials use and reduce the volumes of waste materials stemming from production processes. Whirlpool in Brazil has reduced the energy consumption of its products (especially freezers and air conditioners) by half.[17] Equipment specifically designed to reduce water consumption is increasingly present in all the markets. The Decca company launched a shower heater in 2011 that mixes water and air and consumes a mere 6 litres of water a minute, saving up to 480 litres a day in a household where four people bathe for 10 minutes each, once a day. A hotel in Campinas (São Paulo) has substituted soap and water with an enzyme-based product that dispenses with the use of water altogether and it has managed to save a huge 30,000 litres a month in keeping its kitchens clean (Silva, 2011).

In the United States there was a noticeable improvement in the ratio between fuel consumption and the distance travelled, especially in the period between 1970, when it stood at 13.5 miles per gallon, and 1991, when it was 21.1 miles per gallon.[18] In the light trucks category, the fuel performance per mile is also positive, with distance per gallon increasing from 10 miles in 1970 to 18 miles in 2009. In Holland, an increase of 50% in GDP in the period 1990 to 2008 did not prevent the use of fertilizers (an important source of water contamination) from declining from a mark of 100 in 1990 to less than 40 in 2008, and in the same period there was a drop of 85% in the use of sulphur dioxide by the economy as a whole.[19] Success was far smaller in reducing greenhouse gas emissions, however; biodiversity losses were not reversed to any meaningful extent, nor were the problems with the nitrogen cycle.

One of the major obstacles to the progress of eco-efficiency is the opportunity for economic gains offered by practices based on predatory methods. It cannot be stated too often that, at the beginning of the second decade of the twenty-first century, three of the world's largest companies are oil companies: Shell, Exxon and BP. As Jeremy Rifkin aptly points out, there are another 500 companies circling those giants and together they are responsible for about one-third of the total global GNP.

That largely explains frequent cases where an innovation capable of economizing materials and energy but that requires an immediate increase in costs is not developed any further because of an inability to construct a consensus among producers in regard to the elimination of conventional methods and in view of the difficulty to obtain the necessary state regulations for materials that are often highly specific and that call for a lengthy discussion in the legislative sphere. At the end of 2011 a federal judge impeded the implementation, in the state of California, of regulations governing greenhouse gas emissions originating from motorized vehicles by using the argument that it would be a transgression of American commercial legislation.[20] The law foresees an analysis of the production life cycle of all fuels and favours locally produced fuels because of their lower transportation costs. That was considered to be illegal. In Brazil the case of ecological asphalt is also emblematic (Pupo, 2011).

The mixture in question contains 15% to 20% of rubber derived from used tyres and is around 30% more expensive than traditional asphalt. On the other hand, it lasts longer and that effectively reduces the real difference between production costs. The technique also improves road surface adherence and accelerates water absorption on rainy days. In spite of these last advantages there is not the slightest chance of this technology ever being used on a large scale.

The most advanced country in the world in regard to decoupling economic growth from material and energy use is Japan. Under the aegis of its Top Runner Program, manufacturers or importers of a significant range of industrial products commit themselves to a public display of the energy performance of each item of goods and establish clear energy consumption goals.[21] The Program started off with nine products in 1998 and by 2009 the number had gone up to 21. Since it began, energy efficiency has improved by 68% for air conditioners, 55% for refrigerators, 78% for fluorescent lamps and 23% for automobiles. Here we have all the most important ingredients of a new economy directed at improving the metabolic performance of human societies, namely limitations on energy consumption, innovation in the form of stimulating reduction in the use of materials and energy, and public display of the material and energy bases that the production processes employ. Even Japan, with an energy consumption equivalent to half that of the United States, showed it was capable of reducing energy consumption during working hours in Tokyo by 15% after the Tsunami struck in 2010.

In the European Union, an increase of 1% in GDP was accompanied by a mere 0.4% increase in materials and energy consumption – a clear demonstration of the decoupling of the wealth generated from its material and energy bases. During the twentieth century the use of material resources for production purposes increased eightfold, but global GDP was multiplied by no less than 23. The 2011 UNEP report on this decoupling phenomenon notes that this progress was not the result of any international policy designed to achieve it. It actually took place against the background of a generalized decline in raw materials and energy prices. In other words, the world economy gave out no signs of any scarcity of those resources to the economic agents making use of them, and furthermore, examples of policies specifically designed to improve the quality of resource use are rare and very recent.

In a book published jointly with Edward Ayres in 2011, Robert Ayres shows the huge extent of the opportunities that exist for improving materials and energy management. The construction of a bridge leading to a low carbon economy depends on such improvements. Co-generating energy, for example, currently being practised by over 1,000 US industries, could readily be multiplied 10-fold. That would mean guaranteeing 10% of the United States' electricity-generating capacity without burning a single barrel of oil or a gram of coal and doing so at a far lower cost than those involved in building thermoelectric plants. Even in Brazil, where there is immense potential for co-generating electricity, only 15% of power actually comes from that source, as opposed to 50% in Denmark and 38% in Holland.

The inefficiency of the United States' huge coal-fired generating plants is absolutely shocking, and over the last 40 years the technology employed in them has remained practically unaltered. Robert and Edward Ayres calculate that for every seven units of potentially useful energy contained in coal entering coal-fired generating plants, only one actually ends up performing anything useful for society. There is a glaring contrast between the tremendous technological progress represented by an iPad, for example, and the technological backwardness of the energy base on which its production actually rests.

One of the most important objects of concern for industrial ecology is evaluating the efficiency with which primary energy (like that contained in a barrel of oil, for example) is converted into what physicists refer to as 'useful' mechanical, chemical or electrical 'work'. The green economy has a strong focus on intensifying efficiency and reducing losses in that conversion process. However advanced the technology employed may be, losses in conversion are always inevitable; they are inherent in the entropy of any physical transformation. However, there are immense possibilities for improvement. The aggregate efficiency figure for the conversion of primary energy into useful 'work' in the United States is 13%, higher than in Russia, China or India, but trailing behind Japan, the United Kingdom and Austria, where the figure is 20%.[22] Even that higher figure of 20% actually means that *four-fifths of all the high-quality energy extracted from the earth are simply wasted.* Immense gains could be obtained by making full use of all that wasted energy.

In spite of the increased recycling rates of paper, aluminium and PET bottles referred to above, there is still an immense untapped potential for economizing on materials through reuse, as shown in the 2011 UNEP report *Towards a Green Economy.* The industrial practice of remanufacturing electric motor components, aircraft parts, compressors, photocopiers and others could represent annual energy savings equivalent to 10.7 million barrels of oil, the equivalent in terms of the energy production of five nuclear power stations. The Caterpillar Corporation is the leading industrial user of reused materials and has three plants expressly dedicated to that end. No less than 70% of the weight of a typical modern machine could eventually be reused in its actual condition and a further 16% could be recycled. Xerox and Canon have been using such practices since 1992.[23]

Patterns of domestic consumption, however, will also have to change significantly: German households consume on average 210 kilowatt-hours per square metre. In newly constructed buildings, that goes down to 95 kilowatt-hours, and in those buildings where energy and materials savings are a specific objective (passive house projects), the figure can be as low as 20 kilowatt-hours. This type of housing construction has been progressing in Europe ever since the 1990s, but in the United States, up until 2009, the first of its kind had yet to be completed.

There are, however, extraordinary obstacles in the way of those immense potential savings and they are found as much in the conventional processes of factor use as in the existing infrastructure, which is not designed to consider reuse of material and energy. They also exist in the pricing system itself, which fails to indicate the social costs of pollution, the use of water and especially greenhouse gas emissions.

The Trucost consultancy estimated the environmental costs of the world's 3,000 largest global corporations and compared them to the profits of the same companies.[24] Only three criteria were adopted: greenhouse gas emissions, use of water and waste production. The result is highly impressive. If they had to pay for their use (and destruction) of ecosystem resources, their gains would fall by no less than 40%. Eventual payment of those costs presupposes changes in the functional infrastructure of present-day societies, and implanting such changes then would be no mean task.

Some of those obstacles are being overcome and there has been some expansion of the economic system's efficiency in energy, water and materials use and a reduction in the volumes of greenhouse gas emissions, water-borne pollutants and solid waste per unit of wealth produced. Nevertheless, Vaclav Smil (2011) has estimated that the current transition calls for a far greater effort to transform the energy base of social reproduction than has ever been made at any other historical period of transformation. The sheer physical dimensions of the fossil fuel-based energy system are immense, embracing coal mines and coal-fired thermoelectric plants, 50,000 oil fields, 300,000 kilometres of oil pipelines and 500,000 kilometres of gas pipelines. Somewhere from 15 to 20 trillion dollars is the amount necessary to alter the infrastructure of the energy supply of the world economy.[25]

Even if such investments were feasible and the interests associated with fossil fuels were to lose some of their enormous power, and even if the innovation systems directed at sustainability were to be greatly accelerated, expanding the decoupling process now in course, all of that would still not make it possible to neutralize the environmental impacts of a supposed 'green growth' process. The very construction of a new metabolism whereby the reproduction of human societies stops destroying ecosystem services and starts to regenerate those that have been degraded will only be possible if there is first a drastic reduction in inequalities and economic growth ceases to be the objective and the yardstick of relations between the economy and society.

. . . nevertheless, now more than ever

The Philosopher's Stone is a legendary alchemical substance supposed to be capable of transforming base metals into gold or silver and also credited by some as being an elixir of eternal youth. The overwhelming majority of economic science adopts a stance on energy issues not very far removed from the faith of the alchemists in the possibilities of obtaining gold and eternal youth. The baseline for constructing a new relationship between society and nature in which innovation, ethics and limits guide resource management is that there is no miraculous Holy Grail for energy problems. Furthermore the transition to a new economy will probably have to continue supporting itself throughout the twenty-first century on the large-scale use of fossil fuel sources of energy. That fact has two consequences: on the one hand, as we saw in the preceding item, it is of fundamental importance to improve energy use and management, and the progress achieved in that direction can be boosted significantly by means of sustainability-oriented *innovation systems*. On the other hand, it is equally important not to succumb to the illusion that present-day societies are capable of freeing themselves from fossil fuel energy in the coming three or four decades and at the same time perpetuating the incessant production of goods and services by means of a supposed 'green growth' process. It is true that, since the beginning of the twenty-first century, the power coming from solar and wind energy has increased at an exponential rate (see Abramovay, 2014). Nevertheless, nowadays investments in fossil fuels are bigger than ever.

Furthermore, even if eco-efficiency is greatly boosted, researchers in this area have shown that the absolute increase in production and consumption is a powerful counterweight to any gains obtained from the advancement of technology. It is true that the same level of economic activity can be obtained based on different materials and having different impacts. That is what makes technical innovation and eco-efficiency so important. At the same time, however much innovation progresses, economic life that is universally growth-oriented clashes irremediably with the maintenance and regeneration of the services ecosystems provide to human societies, beginning with the climate system. Let us examine the energy aspects first.

There is a common saying that the Stone Age did not end because stone became scarce, suggesting that the same could be said about oil and the civilization it has supported.[26] There is a flaw in that expression, however, because it tends to ignore the finite nature of fossil energy. Saying that there is still enough stone to go around even though the Stone Age is over and so oil will still be welling up even after the Fossil Energy Era is over is a perilously misguided perception. It reminds one of the promises of the US nuclear energy industry of energy so cheap that its price couldn't even be measured.[27]

Since the early 1980s up until today, more oil has been consumed than is immediately available on the earth's surface. In the period from 1970 to 2010, world oil production expanded at the rate of 0.9% a year, whereas consumption went up at the rate of 1.5%.[28] It must be borne in mind that this apparently small difference becomes gigantic when it is projected in time.

More than half the potential of the great wells in the Persian Gulf region has already been extracted, and from now on there will be an irreversible decline in their yield. Figure 2.3 illustrates the phenomenon very well. The barrels represent the production potential contained in recently discovered wells, by years. It can be seen that

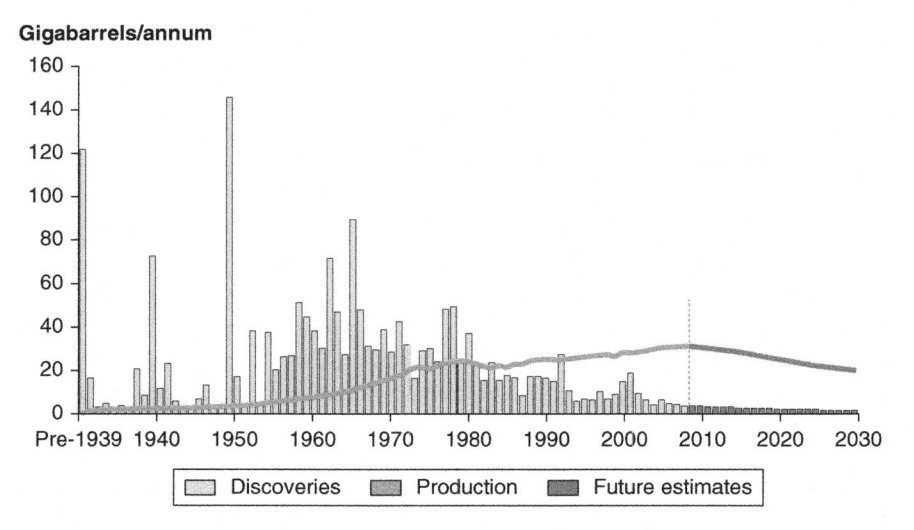

FIGURE 2.3 Conventional oil production is below consumption. World conventional oil discoveries and production, 1939–2010, and projection until 2030

Source: UNEP (2011a).

the maximum was achieved in 1950, with other peaks between 1960 and 1970, but after that the wells show a steady decline in yields although production as a whole continues to grow (horizontal line). Exxon's document *The Outlook for Energy* (2012) shows that more than 95% of the oil being offered today was actually discovered prior to the year 2000, and more than 75% prior to 1980.[29] In recent decades, for every three barrels consumed, only one has been discovered in new deposits (Rifkin, 2011).

That takes place against the background of constantly increasing global oil consumption. By 2011 it had hit the mark of 88 million barrels a day, 2.3 million more than in 2010 (Casselman, 2011). US geological research has estimated that the planet has deposits of three trillion barrels of viscous (heavy) oil, which would nominally be sufficient for the next 100 years. On the face of it, that seems like good news; it would give us time to move forward with innovations to accelerate the transition to a low carbon economy based on renewable energy sources.

The optimism induced by that information, however, is plagued by two problems. The first refers to the possibilities and costs of using existing oil reserves. The second involves the real chances of alternative forms of energy. Let us take a closer look.

Of the 1.6 trillion barrels of conventional oil that geologists estimate to exist, only 400 million barrels are recoverable using present-day technology, and that cuts the 100 years down to a little over 15! The gloomy prognosis is brightened by the prospect of technological innovations such as the injection of steam into the deposits to make the oil less viscous and enable it to rise to the surface, something that is already being done and is known as a non-conventional form of oil exploitation. Brazilian pre-salt deposits and the explorations in the Arctic are the new frontiers for these non-conventional oil sources. The problem here is that the steam injected into the subsoil needs to be heated up to 300°C so that both water and energy will be needed. We cannot ignore the fact that very frequently the oil reserves in question are located in deserts, so that the companies involved will have to use sea water, and decontamination and desalinization of the sea water will be essential to the success of the venture. All of that means spending a lot more energy to obtain the energy contained in the oil itself.

That is just one example of a generalized tendency that can be examined under the heading of 'energy return on energy invested', the energy expended per unit of useable energy obtained.[30] From 1930 to 1940, when the wells were abundant and highly productive, for every unit of energy expended in extraction, 110 units were obtained embedded in the crude oil. It is important to realize just how much energy oil contains; three spoonfuls of it contain energy equivalent to that expended by a human being in 8 hours of labour. So this cheap slave, found in very high-yielding wells, is at the root of the quadrupling of the global population in the twentieth century and the spectacular increase in agricultural production over the same period.

Oil continues to be the energy-rich substance it always has been, but the costs of extracting it are going steadily up. In 1970 its energy yield was 23 units of energy for every unit spent in extracting it. In the new wells being exploited today, that ratio is down to 1 to 8, and in the offshore explorations like the Brazilian pre-salt deposits, it is around 1 to 10. In the areas of tar sand deposits in Canada, the ratio is 1 to 3, so that while it is true that oil exploitation is not over, the process of winning it is using up more and more energy. Geopolitical factors have an important influence on the costs of exploiting and exploring for oil. While 44% of global consumption takes place in the United States and Western Europe, the reserves, at the beginning of the twenty-first century, were largely found scattered among politically unstable countries, and that puts additional pressure on the exploration of areas that are environmentally fragile and where costs of extraction are very high, like the deposits in Alaska, Canada and Brazil. In spite of the environmental problems involved and the energy inefficiency of extracting oil from tar sands in Canada, that country has the second largest volume of oil reserves in the world, surpassed only by Saudi Arabia, and it is the United States' biggest oil supplier, contributing 21% of all US importations of that energy source (Rifkin, 2011: 59). This desperate search for fossil energy obviously has a growing cost; in 2010 the costs of oil imports by the OECD countries went from US$ 200 billion at the beginning of the year to US$ 790 billion by its end.

Table 2.1 shows the major consumer countries and the location of the major reserves. Sixty per cent of the currently available oil lies in politically problematic countries.

What stands out extraordinarily in this context is that the global transport systems, instead of adapting themselves to these restrictions, are doing just the opposite and heading in the direction of increased consumption of materials and fossil fuels, and consequently increased emissions, as can be seen from the information displayed in Box 2.1. Against the background of rising costs associated with the use of oil, the gains obtained by automobile industries in the performance of engines are counterweighted by the increasing use of fossil fuels in the American transport systems, with global consequences that can only be disastrous.

TABLE 2.1 Who owns and who consumes oil?

Global reserves		Global consumption	
Country	Part. %	Country	Part. %
Saudi Arabia	19.9	United States	25.1
Canada	13.6	Western Europe	18.9
Iran	10.3	China	8.3
Iraq	8.7	Japan	6.5
Kuwait	7.7	Russia	3.7
Emirates	7.4	India	3.0
Venezuela	6.1	Canada	2.6
Russia	4.6	Brazil	2.5
Libya	3.2	Saudi Arabia	2.4
Nigeria	2.7	Mexico	2.4

Source: Sperling and Gordon (2009). Sperling and Gordon gathered the data from the US Energy Information Administration's publication *International Energy Outlook*.

BOX 2.1 AUTOMOBILES: THE UNBRIDLED GROWTH OF AN INEFFICIENT INDUSTRY

In the United States, fuel consumption per distance travelled fell considerably in the period from 1970 (13.5 miles per gallon) to 1991 (21.1 miles per gallon), as was shown in the previous chapter. Since then, however, progress in that direction has been absolutely minimal. From 1990 on, fuel consumption of cars stagnated around the figure of 21 miles to the gallon, and for light trucks, a previous period of gains was interrupted and the figure stuck at 18 miles to the gallon up until 2010. As the fleet of vehicles has continued to grow, the result has been that overall fuel consumption on the part of American cars, pick-ups and sport utility vehicles, which was on the decrease in the period 1975 to 1995, has begun to grow again. In the case of cars it has been relatively slight, in the order of 0.1% a year over the period 1970 to 2009. Light trucks, however, stand out with an increase in the order of 4.2% a year, despite the notable increase in engine efficiency. Even over the first 10 years of the new millennium, fuel consumption by the US light truck fleet rose at a rate of 1.5% a year. Once again, that may not seem like much, but over the years it has a gigantic effect.

In 2009, when the United States already had 245 million vehicles in circulation of which 44% were in the 'light truck' category, much heavier and higher on fuel consumption than conventional passenger sedans. What is most remarkable is that in 1975, right after the first 'oil crisis', these overweight private vehicles represented only 24% of the total sold. In 1970 sales of ordinary cars were six times higher than light truck sales in the United States. In spite of the two oil shocks, the participation of the heavier vehicles in the overall sales market went steadily up, and in 2001 more light trucks than cars were being sold. It was only in 2008 that sales of ordinary cars began to exceed those of the heavier-type vehicles (albeit to a very slight extent). However, in 2010, light truck sales took the lead once more among the sales of new vehicles. In other words, the response of the automobile industry to the energy crisis was actually to launch models with higher fuel consumption.

Those figures are totally at variance with the usually projected image of the automobile industry (whose turnover, if it were the GDP of a country, would place it in sixth place among the world's economies), as a sector renowned for high levels of innovation. The individually owned car powered by an internal combustion engine is impressively inefficient, as was seen in Amory Lovins' analysis set out in the preceding chapter; its engine invariably wastes somewhere between 65% and 80% of the energy it consumes. It is the fruit of the union of two eras on the verge of extinction, the Iron Age and the Oil Age. To make matters worse, the supposed innovations consist much more of increasing

(Continued)

(Continued)

the power of the engines and the speed and weight of the vehicles than in any reduction in their fuel consumption. In 1990, an automobile could go from 0 to 100 km/hour in an average of 14.5 seconds. Today that time is down to 9 seconds, and in some cases just 4. Consumption figures have only gone down in places like Japan and Europe where governments have set obligatory targets to that effect. It was only when the crisis of 2008 broke onto the scene that such targets first appeared in the United States. It is one of the least innovative sectors of contemporary industry insofar as it only innovates in aspects that are of no interest (speed, power, weight) and resists innovating in the most needful areas (savings in fuel and materials consumption).

In a world whose economy is already well over the limits of the ecosystems' possibilities, that cannot be viewed as a merely national problem. At the end of the first decade of the millennium the United States was responsible for 20% of all CO_2 emissions, and the transport sector's participation in those emissions has gone up from 31.5% in 1990 to 34.2% in 2009. In the United States, the transport sector, which formerly emitted 6.1 billion metric tons of greenhouse gases a year (not just CO_2), expanded emissions to reach the mark of 7.1 billion metric tons in 2007 and, even though there was a drop in 2009 to 6.5 billion tons, that amount is still three times greater than the entire set of Brazilian emissions.

What is most disturbing is that wherever innovations have occurred they have been directed much more at satisfying individuals' desires to own bigger, faster and more powerful cars than to addressing any real public interests for more economical vehicles or shared use of vehicles. It was only in 2007 that, for the first time in 32 years (the previous occasion was right after the first oil crisis), US law imposed fuel economy targets on the vehicles produced by its automobile manufacturing industry. Prior to that, in 1980, for example, the transport sector consumed 50% of all oil used by the United States, and by 2009 that percentage had gone up to no less than 70%, by which time the overall consumption of oil in the country had also gone up. The space for innovation is so great that the government is pressuring for performance to improve from the current 20 miles to the gallon to reach 54.5 miles to the gallon by 2025, after two decades of technological stagnation in this area. It is important to underline the literal nature of the expression 'individual vehicle', given that, in a country where there are more cars than driving licences, the percentage of trips made with single-person occupation rose from 80% to 88% of total trips in the period 1980 to 2000.

Even if the pattern of growth in the automobile industries in other parts of the world is one of less waste of energy and materials than in the United States, the current prospect of 100 million vehicles a year entering the market in 2017 is disturbing because of its effects on climate equilibrium and urban organization, especially in the developing countries.

The expansion of the world's car fleet between 1990 and 2009 was at the rate of 2.3% a year. The greater part of that increase can be attributed to Asian countries, and current tendencies show that the trend will probably continue for quite some time. Over the last two decades, the rate of increase in the Chinese automobile fleet has been 14.6% a year; for India, the figure is 8.3%, and for Indonesia, 7.8%. In Brazil the increase has been 3.6% a year, and in Argentina 2.2% a year, over the same period. While in 1960 two-thirds of the world's vehicle fleet was in the United States, today that figure has fallen to 20%, and in 2009 the United States had an average of 828 cars for every thousand inhabitants. In India the ratio was 14.4, in China 46.2 and in Sub-Saharan Africa 24.2. Even if the ratio per individual does not get up to American levels, the forecast that the motorization index for China will be 375 individual vehicles for every thousand inhabitants by 2030 is highly worrying (McKinsey Global Institute, 2011). In Brazil the automobile industry expects to raise the motorization index from 154 to 250 vehicles per thousand inhabitants (Borlina Filho, 2011). The fact that from 2010 to 2011 the percentage of people living in the city of São Paulo who considered the traffic situation to be 'terrible' rose from 37% to 55% has not had the slightest effect on the industry's plans (Ribeiro *et al.*, 2011).

However, the greatest harm associated with this mode of transport becomes apparent when the cars are stationary. The space for parking automobiles is acquiring growing importance in various cities around the world. In São Paulo, of the total area of privately constructed buildings in 2000, almost half was dedicated to parking space for automobiles (Leite Jr *et al.*, 2011). While cities like New York and San Francisco are stipulating a maximum limit for areas to accommodate cars (inducing the use of other means of transport), São Paulo and Los Angeles go the opposite way and stipulate a minimum area that construction companies must provide for private parking, thus stimulating what Sperling and Gordon unhesitatingly refer to as 'car-centrism'.

Sources: *Transportation Energy Data Book* (http://cta.ornl.gov/data/index.shtml, consulted on 24 March 2012) and Sperling and Gordon (2009).

Throughout the twentieth century, a general decline in the price of commodities masked the global costs of this growing use of energy resources and materials.[31] In the Brazilian pre-salt, for instance, exploitation costs rose 250% in the period 2003–2013 (Ramalho, 2015). With the advent of the first decade of the new millennium, there was an unprecedented reversal of that trend, and high and volatile prices of commodities became the rule, as shown by Figure 2.4: all the drops in prices registered in the twentieth century have been wiped out since the beginning of the new millennium.

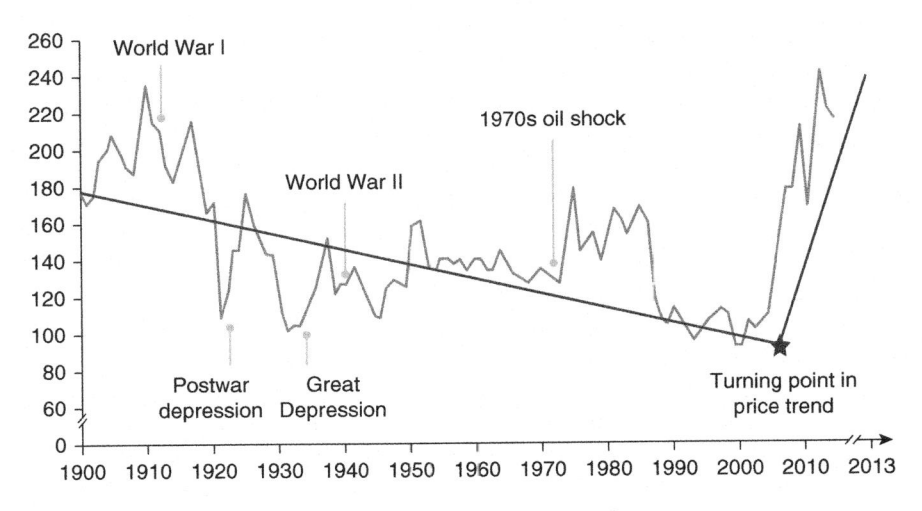

FIGURE 2.4 The volatility of commodity prices in the twenty-first century

Source: McKinsey (2012).

The increases in energy costs associated with exploration and exploitation of materials and energy are not restricted to oil alone.[32] Even if nuclear energy overcomes the vigorous contestation it faces today, the investments in producing reactors are immense and, like oil extraction, the costs are growing. Furthermore the deposits of high-grade uranium ore are rapidly being exhausted, thereby elevating economic and energy costs involved in obtaining it. Coal is no different. It is true that coal production in the United States has risen by 2% a year since 1940, but the sources of high-energy coals have already run out and as a result more and more energy has to be expended to obtain the same amount of available energy in the exploitation of coal. The background to this lower energy yield situation is a forecast made by the International Energy Agency to the effect that from 2008 to 2030 American consumption of coal will increase by 47%.

During the last decade, global coal consumption in the United States, India and China (which has become a massive coal importer) has gone up to an impressive extent. The intensity of oil participation in global GDP continues to fall (albeit at a modest rate), but the intensity of coal participation over the same period has gone right up, and the first decade of the new millennium has been dubbed the 'coal revival' decade, contrasting with the 1990s when gas predominated.[33] In the decade starting 2000, China alone has installed more coal-fired generating plants each year than the total number of such plants existing in the United Kingdom.

In the case of other minerals there is also a scenario of rising costs associated with extraction. In the case of iron, for example, known reserves in 2010 would allow for the present rate of exploitation to continue for another 75 years, with the additional advantage, as compared to oil, that the deposits are not concentrated in high-risk countries and are in fact widely dispersed (McKinsey Global Institute, 2011). However, the rhythm of the discovery of new deposits has slowed down since 1997 and the costs of exploiting deposits have gone up noticeably since 2002. Even though there is no scarcity in absolute terms, it is possible that the most fertile sources are already close to being worked out. Figure 2.5 shows that the sources of material that feed the world economy are becoming scarcer and exploiting them is becoming increasingly costly.

But in addition to those materials that economic life is directly dependent on, the indirect effects of mineral exploitation need to be taken into account. The *ecological rucksack* concept does exactly that. It is fundamental to any contemporary study of social metabolism and it is directed at calculating *how much material needs to be displaced to produce certain mineral goods* (Behrens *et al.*, 2007). To produce one kilogram of aluminium, for example, 85 kilograms of materials need to be moved around. The drop in mining yields has led to an increase in this volume of material displaced (the ecological rucksack). The 2011 UNEP report on decoupling shows that the displacement of materials involved in some branches of mining increased threefold in the course of the twentieth century with accompanying increases in impacts on the land, on water availability and the use of energy. That information correlates with the drop in mine yields (the amount of metal that can be extracted from a given mine) for copper, nickel and gold mining.

But one could ask whether this scenario of scarcity on the availability side and rising costs in the exploitation of fossil fuels (and in the energy costs of those materials that the goods and services supply is based on) will be compensated for by the gains stemming from the use of renewable energy sources. Won't solar, wind, geothermal and biomass energy be capable of creating a context in which increasing energy costs are counterbalanced by this offer of energy from new sources? The

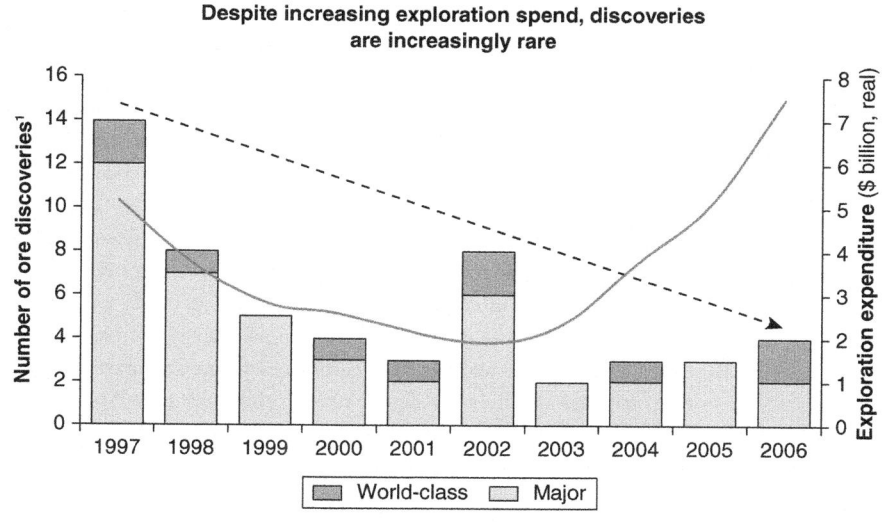

1 All metal and mining materials; latest data available to 2006.

FIGURE 2.5 Minerals: the low-hanging fruits have vanished

Source: McKinsey (2012).

second problem inherent in such optimism with regard to energy availability sufficient to make growth of the global economic system perennial (apart from the growing signs of exhaustion of the supplies of materials and energy it is built upon) is that however much hope we are disposed to place on renewable sources, their baseline is so low that it is going to be a long time before they come to represent anything really significant in the global energy matrix. There is ground for optimism in this field, as shown by Jacobson and Delucchi in an impressive study published in *Scientific American* (2009) showing that a world whose energy matrix is almost entirely based on renewables is technologically possible in 2030. But, once again, the incumbent fossil actors' investments in energy are creating infrastructures that promote oil, coal and gas beyond their technical and economic efficiency.

Admittedly renewables' current growth rate is extraordinary.[34] In 2008 and 2009, modern forms of renewable energy contributed 47% to the increase in global electricity-generating capacity.[35] The developing countries have been responsible for more than half of that elevation. In 2009 wind energy expanded by 32% and solar increased by 53% in comparison with the previous year. Biofuel participation in the global energy matrix of the transport sector went up from 2% to 3%. There has also been a considerable increase in decentralized use of renewable energy sources. The learning curves associated with renewable energies have led to a reduction in their prices: the silicon used in photovoltaic cells dropped in price from US$ 65 a kilogram in 1976 to US$ 1.4 in 2010. The cost of producing wind-sourced energy in the United States went down from US$ 4.3 per watt in 1984 to US$ 1.9 in 2009.

Even so, the overall picture is worrying. That figure of a 13% participation of renewable energies in the world energy matrix largely represents biomass used for cooking and to a lesser extent for heating purposes in very poor countries; in other words, traditional sources of energy harmful to health and hardly sustainable. The more promising energies have global matrix participation baselines so low that they are almost ludicrous: 0.1% for solar energy, 0.1% for geothermal energy, 0.2% for wind energy and 2.3% for hydroelectric energy (and the limited possibilities of expanding hydroenergy plants are well known). In terms of modern forms of bioenergy, so far only ethanol produced from sugarcane can actually offer energetic and economic efficiency despite all the optimism associated with cellulose-derived ethanol, which would theoretically make it possible to broaden the range of raw materials that could be used to produce energy from biomass. Currently a mere 1% of the world's energy matrix consists of modern renewable energy forms.

Although there are some countries that can count on a significant participation of renewable energy sources in their energy matrices, they are few. Apart from Brazil, only four countries in the world (Indonesia, Peru, Angola and Malaysia) have fossil fuel participation in their total emissions lower than 20% (World Bank, 2007). Eighty-nine per cent of Japan's emissions stem from fossil fuels, and the figures are 87.5% for the United States, 81.2% for South Africa, 70.4% for China and 56.8% for India. Even if renewable energies were to advance at a much faster rate than they have done up until now, it is not very realistic to imagine that in the next 40 years fossil fuels will play an insignificant role in the global energy matrix. The conclusion set out in one of the most important recent documents on the subject produced by a UN agency is unequivocal: "nowhere is the rhythm of technological change anywhere near to what is necessary to achieve the goal of full de-carbonization of the global energy system by 2050 or thereabouts" (UN DESA, 2011).

There are two consequences of that fact. The first, highlighted in the chapter on *manufacturing* in the UNEP report on the green economy (elaborated under the direction of Robert Ayres), refers to the urgent need for enhanced efficiency in energy management. The aim of such improvement is that the same quantity of fossil fuel (entailing thereby the same quantity of emissions and the same expenditure of energy in its extraction) can result in greater quantities of goods and services. That is the underlying idea of decoupling, and it is without a doubt a crucial aspect of the green economy.

The second consequence is that however great those gains in efficiency may be, they are always offset by "economic and demographic growth: the total volume of emissions and the use of energy and materials continues to grow in spite of the decline in emissions and amounts of material used per unit product. Unless there is an absolute decoupling, economic growth will carry on implying greater demands for energy and resources to the point of putting the health of our basic natural resources in jeopardy" (UNEP, 2011b: 249).

Although, in 2002, each unit of GDP produced made use of, on average, 26% less material resources than in 1980, the absolute growth of global GDP annulled that gain in efficiency: in spite of the decline in use in relative terms, the absolute amounts of material consumed over the period increased by 36%, as shown by Figure 2.6.

The prospects for the period 2002–2020 are that the increase in productivity per unit produced will be counterbalanced by an *increase in the consumption of materials of*

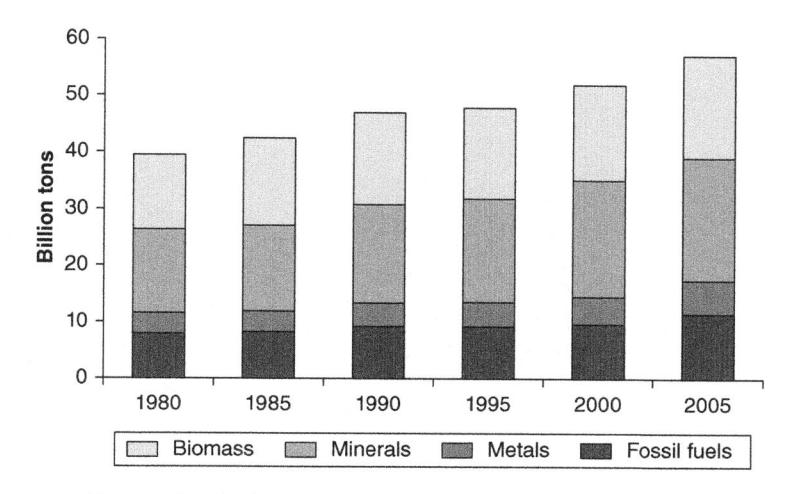

FIGURE 2.6 Rise in the absolute consumption of materials, 1980–2005

Source: European Environment Agency (2010; http://www.eea.europa.eu/soer/synthesis/synthesis/chapter7.xhtml – see Table 7.1: consulted on 25 June 2015).

almost 50%, accompanied by devastating impacts on the climate and the ecosystems. If the present rate of increase in *natural resource* extraction is kept up, by 2030 humanity will have expanded extraction to the level of 100 billion tons a year to meet the needs of material production, as Figure 2.7 clearly shows. However much prospecting technology and improvements in material use may improve, it is obvious that this trajectory can only lead to the eventual exhaustion of exploitation possibilities.

Although in the course of the twentieth century global GDP managed to grow using less and less energy and materials and reducing emissions per unit produced, in the first decade of the new millennium that tendency reversed, as shown above. While it is true that in the first years of the decade greenhouse gas emissions increased at a lesser rate than global GNP, in 2010 and 2011 carbon intensity in the global economy started to grow again. From 2000 to 2007 there was an annual decrease of 0.7% in greenhouse gas emissions per unit of GNP (see PwC, 2011a). That is far below the reduction needed for human societies to have a chance of keeping global warming down to less than two degrees, and furthermore, that figure only represents a relative decline. But as has been mentioned, when crisis broke out once more, even that slight decrease was interrupted, and the increase that was registered was largely due to increased intensity of coal use in world GNP. China was not the only one responsible for that; in the United States the use of coal is also on the increase.

The International Energy Agency has forecast that global GDP will multiply four times over the period 2010 to 2050. In the chapter on *industry* in the UN report on the green economy, Robert Ayres shows that the forecast is based on the supposition that energy prices will remain stable, which is not a very realistic prospect and contradicts the estimates of the most prestigious global consultations

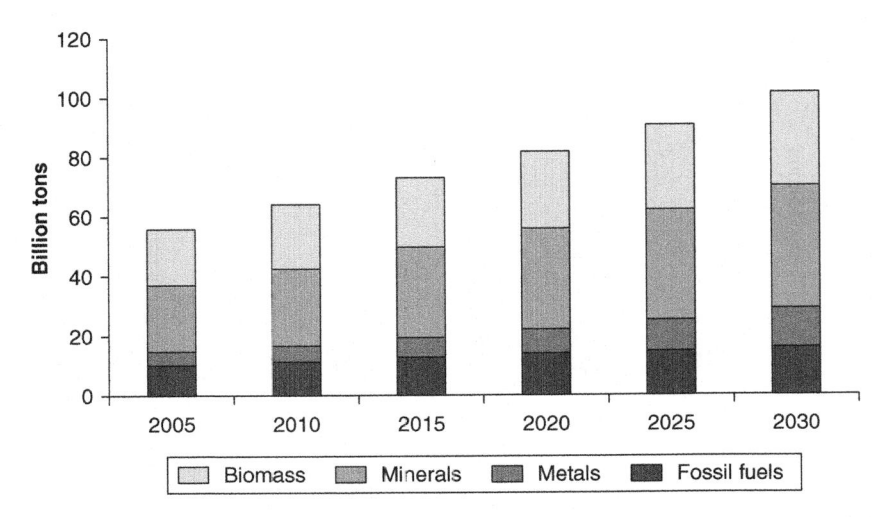

FIGURE 2.7 Business-as-usual scenario for worldwide resource extraction, 2005–2030

Source: KPMG (2012: 22).

concerning this issue and referred to in the course of this chapter. In fact, the growth of that dimension would only be possible if the efficiency of primary energy conversion processes to produce effective work were to undergo a spectacular increase. This scenario was highly unlikely until now, but the prospects relating to solar and wind energy and the progress in energy storage seem to be opening new and promising perspectives for the timing of decarbonization. The Solutions Project, directed by the author of the study already mentioned, published in *Scientific American*, converted his forecast of 100% renewable energy in business by 2030.[36]

Another important point to remember is that the apparently positive eco-performance of OECD member countries in the course of the twentieth century was not based on technological gains alone. Many of their more highly industrialized processes were transferred to emerging countries and above all to China (see Box 2.2). That transfer of industrial activities and production tends to blur the accounts and demonstrations of material and energy flows of the richer countries and shifts from them the responsibility for the associated greenhouse gas emissions. It is well known that China recently became the biggest emitter of greenhouse gases on the planet. If however the emissions associated with its export products are discounted from the total (attributing responsibility for emissions to the consumers), then the Chinese emissions drop by about a third from the present total (see Clark, 2009). Obviously the calculations become even more complex if they are aggregated to the emissions of countries that export the raw materials used by Chinese industries. No less than 70% of Brazilian iron and steel sector exports (one of the country's most carbon-intensive industries) are shipped to China. That means that part of the apparent drop in energy intensity and in carbon intensity of developed economies is actually transferred to industrial processes that are high-energy consumers, big greenhouse gas emitters and utilize raw materials whose extraction has no commitment to significant technological innovations. The same goes for energy production, which in Latin America (especially in the Amazon) is strongly linked to products destined for exportation. Let us examine this aspect in greater detail.

BOX 2.2 THE UNSUSTAINABLE LIGHTNESS OF THE GLOBAL ECONOMY

The world economy is becoming heavier than ever. We saw above that at the beginning of the millennium humanity was extracting no less than 60 billion tons of just four materials from the earth's surface: biomass, metal ores, non-metal ores and fossil fuels. That amounts to 9 tons per capita. We also saw that in the UNEP report in which that information was published in 2011, the programme's executive director, Achim Steiner, recommended that the average figure should be reduced from 9 to 6 tons by 2050, otherwise there could be a collapse of the capacity to provide the goods and services necessary for social reproduction.

(Continued)

(Continued)

So what actually happened in the first decade of the millennium? The weight of the economy increased even further and reached the mark of 70 billion tons. Per capita equivalent went from 9 to 10 tons in just one decade. The main drivers of this explosion, according to a UNEP report published in 2014, are the big developing countries. The Asia and Pacific region (that includes China and India) consumed 10 billion tons of materials in 1980 (less than a third of global consumption at that time). Today it consumes 40 billion tons, more than half the global total (UNEP, 2014).

The metabolism rate/ratio (i.e. the consumption of material, energy and biotic resources compared to the social wealth) of the Asian economy is on the increase. In the 1980s the region's GDP increased 4.2% a year while consumption increased 4.8% a year. That may seem to be a very small difference, but over the years it has huge effects.

In 2012 the *Journal of Industrial Ecology* published a special issue on this topic showing the increasing pressure that the bigger developing countries were putting on global resources (Hashimoto *et al.*, 2012). Today Chinese consumption of materials is almost at the same level as European consumption and stands at 14 tons per capita. According to the same source, Brazil's metabolic rate has doubled in the last 35 years and is drawing closer to that of China.

And what about the developed countries? Both the UNEP report and the *Journal of Industrial Ecology* state that their metabolic rates are relatively stable because the expansion of consumption is supported by increased productivity. That means wealth can be offered using less and less material. Those societies are showing the way forward by decoupling the goods and services on offer from the material, energetic and biotic base that supports them.

If that hypothesis was confirmed, then, in the developed countries at least, the global economy would be passing through a healthy process of dematerialization that would show the way to sustainable development in a strategically decisive manner. In that case, thanks to scientific and technological progress, economic growth could continue without overstepping the boundaries of ecosystem limits and thereby threatening the very existence of social life.

Unfortunately, however, that hypothesis has been refuted in an important paper published by the United States' prestigious *Proceedings of the National Academy of Sciences (PNAS)* (Wiedmann *et al.*, 2013). Previous calculations made by the UNEP and those published in the special issue of the *Journal of Industrial Ecology* were based on the relation between the GDP of each country and national extraction of the materials needed for its reproduction (subtracting exports and including imports of such materials). However, they failed to take into account the weight of materials contained in industrialized products that those countries imported. Nobody can ignore the fact that in almost all of the developed countries there has been a shift of industry, especially in the direction of China. However, the consumption by the inhabitants of the world's richest countries has not diminished.

The *PNAS* article calculated the global economy's *material footprint*. The idea is to find out not only how much of the four materials mentioned above a country extracts from its own surface but also how much of them is contained in the products which the country imports. In this approach, the iron that Brazil exports to China and that is present in an iPad being sold in Great Britain is included in the calculation of the material footprint of British consumption.

From that angle, the apparent lightness of the rich world disappears. Decoupling of the wealth from its material and energy base clearly occurs to a much lesser extent than seemed to be the case. The use of materials extracted domestically by the developed world actually only went down because the materials were extracted and transformed in other countries and not because technical progress had made the economy more frugal in its use of materials.

The overall result is that when the *material footprint* of consumption is calculated, the world appears to be far less homogeneous and flat, to use Thomas Friedman's phrase, than anyone could have imagined. It is true that total Chinese consumption of materials (16.3 billion tons) is almost double that of the United States and four times that of Japan. The Chinese per capita consumption of material, however, is less than half that of America. The parsimony of the Japanese in their use of material is only apparent: their material footprint is almost equal to that of America and Britain. Of the 16.3 billion tons of materials that the Chinese use every year, no less than 7.3 billion correspond to their exports, that is, to the consumption by people living in other countries.

Thus when international trade is included in the calculation of the social metabolism of the world's richest economies, the weight of their material footprint is immense. This unprecedented revelation shows that, however essential it is to enhance the efficiency of contemporary production systems, it does not remove the urgent need to rethink consumption patterns and the meaning of all that the economic system offers to social life.

Resource use in Latin America[37]

Latin America and Sub-Saharan Africa are two regions in the world where material, energy and biotic resources are still superior to the amounts of land and water needed to produce what they consume and to reabsorb the residues generated by their goods and services supply side. To use the specialist term, their biocapacity is bigger than their ecological footprints. That triumph has been a decisive driver in their recent economic growth. Nevertheless, the pressure on ecosystems is so great that if no change in direction is made, the relation between ecological footprint and biocapacity will inevitably invert.

How efficient has Latin America been in making use of those natural resources on which its component countries depend?[38] From the Rio 92 event up to the present day, there has been important progress in the field of renewable energy especially in Brazil and Paraguay (in virtue of Itaipu hydroelectricity and ethanol production), in socioenvironmental planning in various spheres, in the reduction of organic waste in water and, since the middle of the last decade, in the declining rates of deforestation. In the last two decades of the twentieth century, the intensity of the presence of organic contaminants in water expressed as a proportion of GDP fell significantly in Uruguay, Brazil, Chile and Argentina, although in Mexico it increased. Even so, and indeed in spite of those examples of progress, the overall picture reveals an international division in the use of resources that is in no way favourable to Latin America (or Africa).

In recent years, Latin America has experienced a process of primarization of its economy. With the knowledge society in full swing, primary goods, which stood at 42% of Latin American exports in 1998, had expanded their participation to 53% of the total by 2008. In Brazil the proportional increase was even greater: iron ore, oil, soy, meat, sugar and coffee, which made up 28.4% of all exports in 2006, had by the end of 2011 come to represent 47.1% of total exports (see Gerbelli, 2012). An important consequence of that process is that currency surpluses stemming from exports have contributed to enhancing the value of local currencies, lowering the costs of imports and, consequently, having a negative effect on the progress of local industries, in that way acting as an impairment to the progress of industry. Primarization and deindustrialization walk hand in hand.

The process of primarization, however, does not jeopardize the whole of industry, but affects mostly those industries with the greatest content of innovation and intelligence. In Latin America the proportion of products with a high contaminating potential – an international parameter applied to Brazil by a team led by Carlos Eduardo Young, from the Institute for Applied Economic Research, one of the authors of the UNEP and Mercosur Network reports – is on the increase. During the 1990s the participation of this kind of industry in the Latin American economy was on the decrease. In the last decade, however, almost 40% of Brazil and Argentina's industries were in the category of high contaminating potential. From 1998 to 2007 those sectors grew by no less than 230% in Latin America, while at the same time industry as a whole was experiencing a generalized decline, with the possible exception of the Mexican 'maquiladoras'.

Another startling aspect of the global insertion of the Latin American economy becomes apparent when a comparison is made with the net changes in the world's forested areas. While in Europe, North America and Asia (in this last, only in the last decade) forested areas are expanding (albeit often as a result of homogeneous tree plantations that actually reduce biodiversity), in Africa and Latin America they continue to diminish. In spite of the reduction of the rate of deforestation over the last decade, Africa and Latin America have the largest reserves of forests where an economy of the destruction of nature, not an economy of the knowledge of nature, is overwhelmingly prevalent.

It is not just in the nature of its international insertion alone that Latin America is drawing away from sustainability; the same is true of its domestic consumption patterns. In Mexico, for example, the flow of materials that its economic life depends on is constantly on the increase. If we consider just the case of fossil fuels, minerals, building materials and biomass (that is to say, a calculation in the moulds of the one made by the UNEP report on decoupling), the average annual per capita consumption by the Mexicans ranged from 7.4 to 11.2 tons in the period 1970 to 2003. In that total the importance of biomass participation remains constant, while that of the non-biotic materials is on the increase, thereby intensifying the impacts of the economy on the ecosystems.

The fundamental conclusion arrived at by the UNEP and Mercosur Network reports is that Latin America is further than ever from the longed-for dematerialization of economic life that is the major feature of the information and knowledge era. Any transition to a green economy presupposes a new international division, not of labour but of the very use of the ecosystems. At present, there is no macroeconomy of sustainable development. When it does eventually emerge, one of its main pillars will consist of making clear to global society that the abundance of some resources that are concentrated in certain regions is merely apparent. At this moment, the social meaning of the use of these resources should receive more attention than the eventual income that they are able to generate.

A revolution hardly green at all

Malthusianism became a widely condemned concept as far back as the second half of the nineteenth century, and today the term evokes not only a reactionary political posture but grossly misguided forecasts. The fact is that the English vicar Thomas Robert Malthus defended the interests of the big British landowners of his day and elaborated a scientific law pointing to apocalyptic results that fortunately turned out to be mistaken. His law proposed that while population growth was a geometric function, the rhythm of increases in agricultural production was merely an arithmetical progression. The brutal but inevitable results foreseen were that only great nutritional crises and the deaths of starving people could make the satisfaction of human needs compatible with the production possibilities of agriculture and livestock farming.

The achievements of the Green Revolution are often cited as typical examples of how far Malthus was wrong in insisting on the limits that nature imposes on the growth of material production. In that example agriculture would figure as a resounding example of the decoupling of the goods and services on offer from the material base on which it rests. It is true that world grain production went up from 824 million tons in 1960 to almost 2.2 billion tons in 2010. Furthermore the surface area reaped per capita dropped by more than 50% over a period of 60 years, and that took place against a background in which the world population multiplied 2.3 times over, going from 2.5 to almost 7 billion people. That remarkable performance was only possible because of the use of seeds, whose high productive potential was fully exploited by the massive application of chemical fertilizers and the widespread use of pesticides. In many countries (more in the developed countries and Latin America than in Asia) those changes were accompanied by large-scale mechanization, and that all led to a tremendous increase in the productivity of agricultural work.

Decoupling actually took place with land and labour (less labour for the same amount of land) and production, which requires less labour and less land over time. It was not identifiable in other aspects that were decisive in agricultural and livestock production growth processes. Pollution, erosion of biodiversity and consumption of nitrogenated fertilizers all increased far more than production. In that sense, unlike the phenomenon observed in most of the industry, *decoupling of agriculture* cannot even be classified as relative. While it is true that grain production tripled from 1960 to 2010, over the same period *global consumption of nitrogenated fertilizers multiplied almost ninefold*. Figure 2.8 displays the increase in production as a function of the available land surfaces. But for that to happen, the consumption of nitrogenated fertilizers has had to increase even more.

As a result, the prospects for continuing to increase the yield from the land using the prevailing production techniques are highly doubtful. That is reinforced by evidence of a kind of ceiling for agricultural yields which in tropical areas in particular show a tendency to lower with the onset of climate change phenomena. The global implications of that situation are shocking. The UN FAO forecasts that the world's calories offer per capita by 2050 will be less than 2,000 (see the FAO's 2009 report).

It is true to say that, in recent years, progress in Latin American agricultural production has resulted less from the expansion of the areas under agriculture than from the intensification of their use. That intensity, however, strongly relies on the

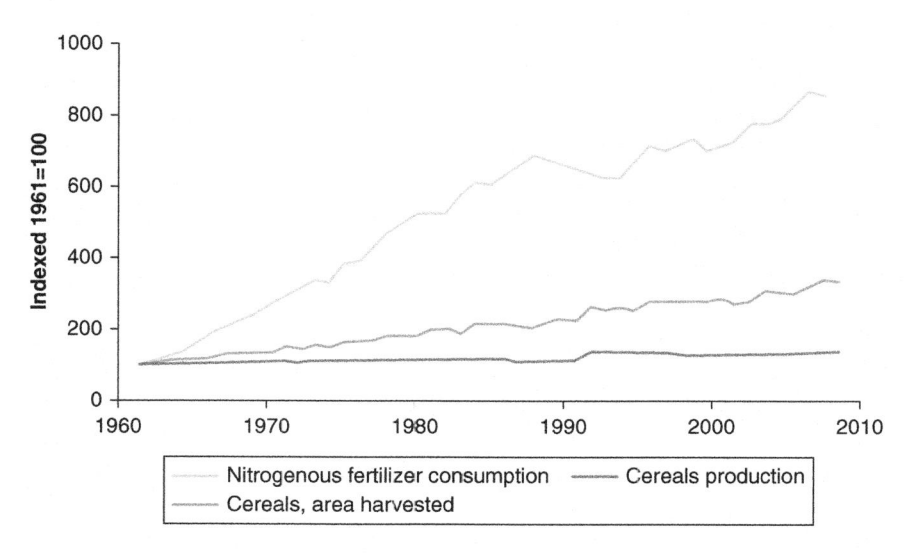

FIGURE 2.8 In agriculture, there is not even relative decoupling. Global growth of cereals production and fertilizer consumption, 1960–2010

Source: UNEP (2011a: 21).

large-scale application of nitrogenated fertilizers and the use of pesticides. In 1961, for every thousand hectares under cultivation, Chile applied 4 tons of fertilizer, as the PNUMA/Red Mercosur's 2011 report demonstrates. By 2007, almost 35 tons were being applied to that same thousand-hectare area under cultivation. In Brazil the figures range from 2 to almost 45, as the UNEP and Mercosur Network reports show. It must also be remembered that Latin America is a great importer of nitrogenated fertilizers and potassium, and that in view of the continent's role in supplying the world with agricultural products, that fact constitutes a serious risk for global food and nutritional security itself.

Furthermore, that intensification in the use of nitrogenated fertilizers is at the root of one of the three dimensions in which contemporary societies have crossed the ecosystem boundaries beyond which the very existence of social life is endangered.[39] The other two dimensions are climate change and biodiversity. Nitrogenated fertilizers join the increased amounts of phosphorus being dumped into freshwater systems and the oceans (UNEP, 2011b). In the United Sates alone, an estimated US$ 2.2 billion are spent on problems associated with the eutrophication of water.

Even though agriculture and livestock production have increased far more than the expansion of the areas of land dedicated to them, nevertheless, the conversion of natural habits for agricultural production purposes has increased by 0.4% a year over the last 50 years. At first sight that does not seem to be very much, but when it is multiplied by 50, then the cumulative effects it introduces are tremendous. To make matters worse, in the first decade of the new millennium, with the surge in demand largely stemming from populations that were entering into new food consumer markets, that rate went from 0.4% to 0.6% a year. If that pattern is maintained through to 2050, it will be entirely incompatible with the maintenance and preservation of those ecosystem resources that human societies are dependent on.

The growth of contemporary agriculture is based on an intensive energy model. To produce a kilogram of beef with the cattle in feedlots, 9 kilograms of vegetable products are needed (FAO, 2010). A kilogram of pork requires 4 kilograms of vegetable products, and for poultry the ratio is 2 to 1. The last few years have seen a tremendous advancement in productivity, in the genetic improvement of races and in animal husbandry and management. Even so, if Americans' meat-eating habits (120 kilograms a year) or even the average consumption in the other developed countries (over 80 kilograms a year) were to be generalized in the world, it would lead to the consumption of such huge quantities of vegetable products that it would inevitably lead to a collapse of the supply of food. Brazil's case is particularly serious: meat consumption (beef, pork and chicken) was 94 kilograms per capita in 2010.[40] The annual growth rate since the beginning of the twenty-first century has been 1.6%.

Furthermore it is always wise to bear in mind that the 30% of the world's surface currently dedicated to cattle raising was once occupied by an exuberant biodiversity. Obviously human exploitation of such landscapes always involves some degree of alteration to their ecosystems. The problem is that cattle raising is the most important factor with direct responsibility for the degradation of the planet's biodiversity. Of the 35 most important environments in the world, in terms of the richness of their biodiversity, no fewer than 23 are threatened by cattle ranching (FAO, 2010). The problem is not restricted to producing meat from terrestrial animals: for every 10 sharks or tuna fish or other large predatory fish that inhabited the oceans in the first half of the twentieth century, today there is only one (Foer, 2010). The problem is so extreme that researchers at the University of British Columbia's Fisheries Center (Canada) have not hesitated to use the phrase 'war of extermination' to describe contemporary fishing activities.

In addition, livestock raising on its own is responsible for 18% of all the world's greenhouse gas emissions. It actually surpasses the total emissions of the transport sector, and furthermore, in spite of its surprising dimension, the FAO calculation may actually be an underestimate. Two specialists attached to the Worldwatch Institute, Goodland and Ahnang (2009), have tried to show that. They claim that the FAO calculation has not taken into account the effects on the climate of animal respiration, which represents no less than 21% of global emissions, and if it were added to the FAO's 18%, the figure jumps up to a huge 39% of all greenhouse gases released into the atmosphere. This is not the place to go into the technical details of that discussion but rather to remember that the consumption of meat actually represents considerably more than the 18% calculated by the FAO. In Brazil, calculations made in 2009 show that cattle raising alone is responsible for almost half the country's greenhouse gas emissions.[41]

One could ask whether the erosion of biodiversity and the energy resources that support the growth in meat production and consumption are the inevitable companions of the well-being represented by eating meat. Excessive consumption of meat is "the primary source of saturated fats responsible for the high risk of cardiovascular diseases, diabetes and various kinds of cancer". That warning can be found in an editorial of a serious British public health review,[42] and it has been corroborated by material published by an American scientific journal dedicated to cardiovascular diseases which shows the high probability of an association existing between obesity and high levels of meat consumption.[43] The fact is that it is an eating habit that is not only harmful to the individual but is associated with the predatory use of increasingly scarce resources on a planet where the population is liable to increase by a third and still has the challenge to face eliminating the situation of hunger in which many live today.

The workings of the global food and nutrition system – its high rates of energy and materials consumption and its negative impacts on human health – mean that it is far from participating in the most important achievements of the green economy in various areas of economic life. If we are to feed nine billion people then we must "freeze the footprint of food immediately".[44]

Essential research carried out by American oceanographer Sylvia Earle points in the same direction (Earle, 2009). It shows for example that half the shallow-water corals in the world have been on the decline since 1950 and that there are as many as 400 areas where they have died, suffocated by nitrogen-rich pollutants coming from the land, and that the acidification of the oceans stemming from climate change jeopardizes the life of corals even further.[45] The devastation unleashed by open water fishing has already decimated 95% of the stocks of codfish and tuna, and there is no way those losses can be compensated for by raising them in captivity. There is not only the problem of diseases in fish farming (as shown by the incidents with Chilean-farmed salmon) but the far greater problem of the high energy costs involved: tuna and swordfish, for example, need to consume 25 tons of meat to produce 1 ton of their own. Furthermore, those species are not destined to be consumed by the world's hungry but by the higher income groups around the world. Fortunately the prospects for freshwater fish farming raising herbivorous fish species are much more promising and have a good chance of prospering.

Conclusions: the three limits

Materials, energy and greenhouse gas emissions: there is a steady accumulation of information in course showing the total impossibility of reconciling the conservation and regeneration of ecosystem services with the objective of perpetuating growth as the basic universal condition for economic life to function. The new political scenarios presented by the International Energy Agency after the Conference of the Parties (COP)[46] in Cancun at the end of 2010 are highly discouraging: if all the commitments to reducing emissions made by the countries that have set themselves targets are added together, then the prospect that opens up is of a four-degree rise in global temperature (see New *et al.*, 2011). The main consequence of that revelation is the impact it has on the *strategic driver for the emergence of a new economy*, namely the *struggle to reduce inequalities*. In that regard the UNEP's 2011 report delivers an important message when it views the reduction of inequalities as the main axis of sustainable development itself.

The greatest challenges to decreasing the impacts of economic life on the ecosystems are not merely technological, albeit the dimensions of the difficulties impeding the acceleration of the decoupling process should not be underestimated; the greatest difficulty, and one that cannot be addressed under the aegis of a mythical 'green growth', is that any changes in the current form of social metabolism presupposes drastic alterations to the patterns of materials and energy use.

'Green growth' is a mythical concept insofar as it believes that a generalized expansion can persist as the central objective of the economy because, supposedly, new technologies will be capable of constantly reducing the amounts of material and energy it uses and the emissions stemming from its provision of goods and services. The previous section of this chapter clearly shows, in the case of agriculture, how completely unrealistic that tenet is. Two consequences stem from this fact.

The first is that economic growth, that is, the use of materials and energy and the occupation of carbon space by anthropic emissions, must be the object, not only of intense technological innovation but also have limits imposed on it: the right to the use of the materials in question can no longer be defined by market mechanisms alone, nor can their use be planned exclusively in the light of generating the revenues the market needs for its very existence. If the economic system were a closed circuit, then its limits would lie at the frontiers of its production possibilities (to use a category dear to economics manuals) and, accordingly, would be represented by the capital and the labour needed for it to function and provide society with what was expected of it. However, as it is actually an open system depending on materials and energy and producing waste with cumulative and potentially dangerous effects (as, for example, climate change, erosion of biodiversity and soils and contamination of water), so the use of resources cannot be subjected exclusively to the formal logic involved in the workings of the markets but the substantial calculations embracing those materials, energy, emissions and degradation of the soils and of biodiversity.

It is not just a question of improving the methods used to estimate the real costs and returns of economic life (although that in itself would be a considerable gain), calculating the losses embedded in activities that bring no benefits to people or to nature and including other costs that cannot be expressed directly in the form of prices (such as domestic work). What it is really about is transforming the very objectives of economic life in such a way that the fundamental parameter for obtaining goods and services becomes the scarcity of the material and energetic elements that it rests on.

It is in this aspect that the conclusions of this chapter connect with those of the first chapter, namely that satisfying basic needs and placing the economy at the service of increasing human capabilities are objectives in consonance with the conservation and regeneration of the ecosystem services that human societies depend on. The way for that to happen, however, does not lie in generalized economic growth, but in making increasingly better use of resources (by means of innovation systems directed at achieving sustainability) whereby the objective and meaning of material production are oriented towards meeting basic needs and expanding human liberties within the limits of the ecosystems' possibilities. It is not just a question of improving eco-efficiency in providing goods and services, but rather a question of collectively rethinking the consumer patterns and habits of contemporary societies. Furthermore the issue does not affect individuals alone but the corporate strategies themselves. The next chapter will examine a problem that many consider the equivalent of trying to square the circle, namely that retailing companies themselves adopt profit strategies that are no longer based on the ever-increasing consumption by their customers. It is worth quoting here the statement of the President of Unilever UK and Ireland in his preface to a report published in 2011 on the future of consumption in 2020: "corporations will have to change their ways of doing business in order to be able to offer sustainable growth over the long term. The old model of ever increasing consumption, and growth at any cost, is broken."[47]

The second consequence is that it will be impossible to respect those limits if the inequality so typical of contemporary societies persists. In addition to the strictly ethical aspects examined in the preceding chapter, the material expression of inequality (in resource and energy use and in emissions) is an obstacle impeding the emergence of a form of social metabolism compatible with the resources of the ecosystems. The per capita emissions of the inhabitants of Bangladesh in 2007 were 0.27 tons. In the same year, the average American emitted 74 times more – 20.01 tons. There is a similar immense distance separating material and energy consumption levels, as the introduction to this book shows. What is at stake is not just the fact that it is physically unfeasible to maintain present rates of increase in consumption of material (biomass, fossil fuels, building materials and minerals) because, if it were maintained, by 2050 the consumption of materials would go from the current 70 billion tons a year to a huge 140 billion tons a year according to the calculation made in the UNEP report on decoupling. What is at stake is the fact that even the objective of stabilizing the levels of consumption and fostering a reduction in the amounts per capita (currently standing at 9 tons, and which would be down to 6 tons when the world population hits the 10 billion mark) is not feasible if the average American or Canadian continues to consume six times more than the average Indian. Obviously inequalities within the countries themselves are just as important as those among the nations.

Increasing efficiency and reducing inequality in the use of resources are the strategy objectives of a new economy which has ethics at the heart of its decision-making processes and supports itself on a social metabolism capable of guaranteeing the healthy reproduction of human societies.

Notes

1 The *Casa da Cultura Digital* is a set of 40 groups (companies, non-governmental organizations) that have in common not only their use of information network society devices but a culture of sharing knowledge and their results (http://www.casada-culturadigital.com.br). Daniela Silva is the person who speaks of this ability to 'join the dots'.
2 The expression 'mutually hostile worlds' has been taken from one of the most important economic sociology books of our time, written by Zelizer (2004).
3 Figure 2.1 has been taken from the work of Stephen Pacala, director of the Environment Institute at Princeton University. There is an interesting conference of his based on these data given at the International Institute for Applied Systems Analysis (http://www.iiasa.ac.at/iiasa35/docs/speakers/speech/pdf/Pacala_speech.pdf, consulted on 24 March 2012). Another worthwhile conference of his can be found at http://www.youtube.com/watch?v=2X2u7-R3Wrc (consulted on 24 March 2012).
4 Information found in the work of KPMG (2012).
5 Bertha Becker headed the team that conducted the study *Um projeto para a Amazônia no século 21: desafios e contribuições* (A project for the Amazon in the twenty-first century: challenges and contributions) (CGEE, 2009).
6 The most important UN publications marking the International Year of Biodiversity are the set of TEEB papers – *The Economics of Ecosystems and Biodiversity* (http://www.teebweb.org, consulted on 25 June 2015) – and the *Global Biodiversity Outlook*, derived from the Convention on Biological Diversity (http://www.cbd.int/gbo3, consulted on 25 June 2015).
7 Volans' (2010) document on Biosphere Economics and the book *Global Canopy Program* are good examples (GCP, 2010).
8 Biomimicry is an expression popularized by Janine Benyus and means, in her expression, "looking to nature for inspiration for new inventions" (http://biomimicry.net/about, consulted on 25 June 2015).

9 Up until 2012 at least, the practical effects of this document on the organization of research in the Amazon, published in 2008, have been very modest (ABC, 2008).

10 For the non-Brazilian Amazon, Little (2014) has demonstrated these aspects empirically. In regard to Brazil, see the excellent document presented to the candidates in the second round of the presidential elections in 2014: Imazon (2014).

11 In the final paragraphs of his classic work, Max Weber speculates on the overwhelming influence of the "modern economic and technical order associated with production in series using machines, which actually determines, in a violent manner, the lifestyles of all individuals born under the aegis of such systems and not merely those affected directly in their economic acquisitions, and, who knows, may well go on doing so until the last ton of fuel has been spent" (Weber, undated, page 130/131).

12 An excellent and instructive presentation of Georgescu-Roegen's thinking can be found in Cechin and Veiga (2010) and in the book by Andrei Cechin (2011).

13 The most important institutional expression of this research programme is the International Society for Ecological Economics (http://www.ecoeco.org/, consulted on 21 June 2015), better known as 'ecoeco', organized in various countries. On decoupling, see UNEP (2011a).

14 Material flows accounting is a method for quantifying material use on the part of modern societies. Several European countries (Great Britain, Austria and the Netherlands) regularly publish statistics portraying their use of resources. Important studies in this area can be found at the website of the SERI (http://seri.at, consulted on 25 June 2015).

15 The Japanese Ministry of the Environment offers an interesting and instructive explanation (http://www.env.go.jp/recycle/3r/approach/hokusai_en.pdf, consulted on 25 June 2015).

16 Energy use intensity measures the relation between GNP and the energy consumption on which it is based.

17 This information appeared in the special Sustainable Business supplement published by the *Valor Econômico* newspaper on 29 May 2011, in various reports written by Sérgio Adeodato.

18 The *Transportation Energy Data Book* provides the figures given at http://cta.ornl.gov/data/index.shtml (consulted on 24 March 2012).

19 The information is contained in an important PBL report, *Exploration of pathways towards a clean economy by 2050: How to realise a climate-neutral Netherlands* (http://www.pbl.nl/en/publications/2011/exploration-of-pathways-towards-a-clean-economy-by-2050-how-to-realise-a-climate-neutral-netherlands, consulted on 23 June 2015).

20 The case is reported on the Environmental Leader website (http://www.environmentalleader.com/2012/01/03/judge-blocks-low-carbon-fuel-rules, consulted on 3 January 2012).

21 See Nordqvist (2006) and http://www.eccj.or.jp/top_runner/index.html for information on the results obtained (consulted on 25 June 2015).

22 The calculations can be found in the excellent chapter on manufacturing coordinated by Robert Ayres, in the already mentioned *Green Economy Report* (UNEP, 2011b: 55).

23 In 2014 the Ellen MacArthur Foundation and the global consultancy firm McKinsey launched, via the World Economic Forum, a very ambitious report on this issue. The Circular Economy is becoming, more than a proposal, a movement which counts on the participation of some great global corporations (World Economic Forum, 2014).

24 The information gathered by Trucost is available in the already mentioned work of KPMG (2012).

25 This estimate was made in the *World Economic and Social Survey 2011* (UN DESA, 2011).

26 The author of this phrase is the former Oil Minister of Saudi Arabia, interviewed in 2005 by the *New York Times* (http://www.nytimes.com/2005/08/21/magazine/21OIL.html?_r=0, consulted on 25 June 2015).

27 'Too cheap to matter' was the term used by Lewis Strauss who, in 1954, was head of the US Atomic Energy Commission. It became so famous that there is even an entry on

Wikipedia about it (http://en.wikipedia.org/wiki/Too_cheap_to_meter, consulted on 23 June 2015).

28 The *Transportation Energy Data Book* of the US Department of Energy is the source for this piece of information. The publication sets out an impressive amount of information on energy production and consumption in the world at large (http://cta.ornl.gov/data/index.shtml, consulted on 25 June 2015).

29 Information found in the Exxon 2012 publication *The Outlook for Energy: A View to 2040* (http://cdn.exxonmobil.com/~/media/global/Reports/Outlook%20For%20Energy/2015/2015-Outlook-for-Energy_print-resolution, consulted on 23 June 2015).

30 The fundamental book written by Homer-Dixon (2008) explores the concept itself and presents the information set out here.

31 The already-mentioned work by the World Economic Forum, McKinsey and the Ellen MacArthur Foundation publishes the data on this reversal.

32 The book by Chris Martenson (2011) offers impressive information on this subject. Its data are corroborated by Ugo Bardi's book, from the Club of Rome (http://www.clubofrome.org, consulted on 25 June 2015). Bardi shows that the Club of Rome has never sustained the imminence of raw material exhaustion during the twenty-first century. Its central idea, since its pioneer work (Meadows *et al.*, 1972), was that the energy costs associated with this material exploitation would be increasingly high. And this forecast is fundamentally correct, as shown by Bardi's (2014) excellent book.

33 Intensiveness measures the extent to which wealth production depends on the factor being analysed – how factor-intensive it is. Over the last 10 years each unit of GNP has been produced using less oil but more coal: it was thus less oil-intensive and more coal-intensive.

34 My article published in 2014 brings more information about the strength of innovation and cost reduction in wind and solar energy (Abramovay, 2014).

35 The Intergovernmental Panel on Climate Change (IPCC)'s 2011 report is the source for the information here.

36 http://thesolutionsproject.org, consulted on 17 November 2014.

37 The data of this part come from PNUMA/Red Mercosur (2011).

38 This question is posed in the PNUMA/Red Mercosur 2011 report.

39 The team headed by Johan Rockström of the Resilience Center at the University of Stockholm published a study in *Nature* delineating nine ecosystem frontiers that, if crossed, could be dangerous for human existence itself. In addition to the three mentioned (climate change, the phosphorus cycle and biodiversity, for which the limits have already been transgressed), there are another five, namely destruction of the ozone layer, acidification of the oceans, use made of fresh water, concentration of solid particles in the air and chemical pollution; see Rockström *et al.* (2009).

40 The *Correio do Estado* newspaper published this information in its issue of 24 March 2012 (http://www.correiodoestado.com.br/noticias/consumo-de-carne-per-capita-aumenta-17-5_97280, consulted on 24 March 2012).

41 The work undertaken to produce this information was done by Mercedes M. C. Bustamante (UnB), Carlos A. Nobre (INPE) and Roberto Smeraldi (Friends of the Earth – Brazilian Amazon) with the participation of Alexandre de Siqueira Pinto (UnB), Ana Paula Dutra de Aguiar (INPE), Jean Page, H. B. Ometto (INPE), Karla Longo (INPE), Laerte Guimarães Ferreira (UFG), Luís Gustavo Barioni (EMBRAPA) and Peter May (Friends of the Earth – Brazilian Amazon). See http://www.inpe.br/noticias/arquivos/pdf/Resumo_Principais_Conclusoes_emissoes_da_pecuaria_vfinalJean.pdf (consulted on 25 March 2012).

42 *Public Health Nutrition* (2005): 8(4), 341–343.

43 The publication in question is the *International Journal of Obesity* (2009): 33, 621–628.

44 This expression was coined by Jason Clay in a paper published in 2009.

45 The respective information appears in an interview that Earle gave to Claudio Ângelo, published in the 16 October 2011 issue of the *Folha de São Paulo* newspaper (http://www1.folha.uol.com.br/fsp/ilustrissima/il1610201105.htm, consulted on 23 June 2015).

46 One of the UN Framework Convention on Climate Change's decisions was, from the mid-1990s on, to hold annual conferences to evaluate progress made in combating climate change. The seventeenth conference was held in Cancun, Mexico, at the end of 2010.

47 It is the introduction to an important report on consumption tendencies through to 2020 elaborated by the Forum for the Future with the support of Unilever and Sainsburys: Consumer Futures 2020 (http://www.forumforthefuture.org/project/consumer-futures-2020/overview, consulted on 25 March 2012).

3

THE FROG AND THE SCORPION

Could capitalism ever show consideration for the world at large?

Introduction

Convinced that the request was made in good faith, a frog agreed to carry a scorpion on its back to cross the river. After all, if the scorpion were to sting him, the scorpion would also die. In the middle of the crossing, however, the frog felt the scorpion's sting penetrate deep into his back. Before he went under, sad and perplexed, the frog received the following explanation – I am a scorpion and that is the way scorpions are.

Is it possible that the story could be any different in the case of capitalism? After all it is a system in which individual companies do their best to expand their gains, consumers are anxious to expand the set of goods and services they have access to, and governments act largely to ensure that those two objectives are achieved. So, in such conditions, how would it be possible for the economic system to have any objective other than its own perpetual expansion? In a world where corporations are legitimized by their profits, governments by the growth rate of their GDPs and individuals seek the means to buy more and more, the central objective of the economic system can only be growth. If we think differently, won't we be behaving in the same way as the frog in the story, innocently believing in the scorpion?

There are two reasons that allow us to give a negative answer to that question, and they are essential elements of the transition to a new economic life in which ethics and respect for the limitations of the ecosystems are central to the decision-making processes. This chapter is dedicated to the first reason, which concerns corporate socioenvironmental responsibility. Clearly the current use of the term rarely goes beyond an attempt to throw dust in the eyes of the credulous; scorpion smooth talk. Unlike the creatures in the fable, however, capitalism is better comprehended in the light of its history and what its actors actually do, and not as having an inveterate and unchangeable nature. One of the most important historic phenomena in contemporary capitalism is the increasing *exposure of private business to various forms of public judgement* that far transcend the sphere of the market (but which nevertheless often find an expression in the price of products or share values or in the value attributed to company brands). Unlike the frog in the story, society is not merely passive and receptive in regard to the economy.

Corporate socioenvironmental responsibility is not just a unilateral gesture on the part of the private sector, an opportunistic tactic to clean up its image. It is in fact a response to a more or less diffuse set of pressures that broaden corporate risk and oblige the companies to transform the links that they base their business activities on. Image is not synonymous with reputation.[1] It is not something external, a mechanical smile manipulated for the company by ingenious communicators. Reputation is constituted by durable social relations imbued with informative contents, conceptions, ideas and values about what doing business means and what the correct methods are to achieve success; that is to say, it is about a broad set of shared meanings on the basis of which the actors involved identify themselves as belonging to a given social field. Accumulating reputation capital does not solely depend on financing, constructing, producing and selling but also on alliances, relations with various social actors and influencing cultural patterns to legitimize the company's activities. The potential to effect social change embedded in those relations is unforeseeable. What is worse than blindly believing in the scorpion's word is the cynical attitude whereby any change in corporate behaviour is automatically dubbed as being merely cosmetic and that underlying it is the need to ensure that the true nature of the company (increased gain) is not betrayed.

The second reason why there is at least a possibility for growth not to be the universal objective of a decentralized economy is that the frog has decided to propose a different kind of excursion to the scorpion, one in which the latter will have less chance to use its venom. In the information network part of the creation of value, wealth and prosperity is based on non-market forms of social relations. In a decentralized society in which the corporations wield immense power and the markets have a decisive role in the allocation of resources, the spaces by means of which social cooperation (not strict individualism) makes it possible to expand prosperity in both the public and private spheres are on the increase. What is even more interesting, as the next chapter will show, is not just the fact that the world of cooperation among people represents an alternative to the dominating world of the markets; what is just as important as expanding those forms of cooperation and reciprocity is the fact that they do not confine themselves to parallel universes, alternative and eternally in the minority, but vigorously penetrate the very sphere dominated by the logic of prices. It is precisely this mixture of domains (market and direct social cooperation), that up until recently were sealed off from one another – and, indeed, were mutually hostile – that constitutes one of the most promising pathways that might enable social actors to orientate part of their behaviours on the basis of motives in which ethics and respect for the ecosystems have an outstanding status. That is where the key to the transition to a new economy lies.

But first let us examine the reasons that make it possible for us to get away from a relationship between the economy and society that had such a tragic ending when the frog took the scorpion at its word.

The insertion of the economy into social life

The idea that the corporate world might voluntarily become a decisive actor in building socioenvironmentally constructive production models must be seen as a paradox.[2] Nobody actually doubts that it is in the scorpion's nature to make use of its venom. That paradox generally triggers two diametrically opposite reactions. One is extremely salutary and consists of a set of denunciations of a kind of green hypocrisy that is no more than false propaganda. American advertiser John Kenney, responsible for the campaign that transformed the world's second largest oil company from British Petroleum into Beyond Oil, expressed his profound deception: "I think that Beyond Oil is just propaganda," he said.[3] In the same vein, American Auden Schendler gave the following warning as an environmental executive: "the idea that ecological postures are always fun, easy and cheap is a dangerous one. Going green means very hard work. The whole thing is highly complex and not always profitable. Companies need to set the ball rolling and effectively start doing something."[4]

But there is also another kind of criticism directed at companies that involve themselves with socioenvironmental considerations which consist of reiterating that a private company's obligation is to produce profits for its shareholders. According to this view, any digression from that purpose will have two negative consequences – the first for the shareholders, whose returns will be threatened by such a demagogic dispersion of efforts; the second would be for society. When a company dedicates itself to matters other than obtaining profits – within the sphere of legal activities, obviously – it creates a distortion in the market's ability to allocate productive resources in a balanced, rational manner. That belief is present in American corporate administration journals and reviews and also in segments of the judiciary which do not hesitate to condemn companies whose distribution of profits takes any interests into account other than those of the shareholders.[5] According to this point of view the scorpion's venom is important in the evolutionary process and ecosystemically useful!

There is a large intellectual foundation for that view, but its most profound elaboration is contained in the ideas of one of the twentieth century's greatest social thinkers, winner of the Nobel Prize for Economics, Friedrich von Hayek. In a famous text written in 1945, he defends a point of view whereby prices contain all the information that not only enable individuals to make decisions but also guarantee that society as a whole makes the best possible allocation of available resources. It does not matter to an individual or a company why the market requires a certain type of screw or why the consumer prefers paper bags to plastic ones; the only thing it is important to know is what the market wants, how much it needs and at what price. If each company seriously concentrates on finding the answers to those difficult questions and the state guarantees the enforcement of the law and the markets are allowed to operate freely, then it is likely that the economic resources will be used better than they would be if someone tried (for social or environmental reasons, for example) to plan what should be done with those resources. "In a system where knowledge of the relevant facts is dispersed among many people, prices can act to coordinate their separate actions," Hayek (1945) explains. What actually foster coordination, human cooperation, are not the actions specifically aimed at achieving it. It is a system that no one has control over and which transmits the information needed to all decision makers: the market, through the medium of prices.

According to adepts of Hayek's views, the problems delineated in the first two chapters of this book stem from the fact that the price system failed to exercise its informative function completely or properly. The solution then would be to improve its functioning and not to interfere in this way of transmitting economic information, which is the market. An interesting contemporary version of that point of view can be found in a work published by the Australian Institute of Economic Affairs: companies are drivers for innovation and do not have to bother themselves about themes with public interest (see Henderson, 2004). Profit is the measure of the company's contribution to social well-being, and accordingly the idea of corporate social responsibility is liable to do more harm than good.[6] In the same vein, adepts of the agency theory and of guiding companies strictly in accordance with the shareholders' interests are fundamentally opposed to the idea that a company should have multiple objectives, believing that it is an economic organization that can only be evaluated in terms of profits and performance.[7] The term multiple objectives is taken to mean relations with actors that are not directly and immediately involved with the business activities that the company is dedicated to. As long as the company has paid its taxes, its workers and its suppliers have delivered its products to its customers, is not being sued for tax evasion or slave labour conditions and, after all that, has managed to distribute dividends, then it is obviously fulfilling its social function satisfactorily. The dividends paid out to shareholders are a kind of proxy for the company's utility in the social as much as the private sphere. It is not required to explicitly dedicate itself to relevant social actions for it to be considered as having a constructive social role in society. It is in that sense that Hayek makes his distinction between human actions (pulverized in billions of individual gestures) and human design (incapable of arriving at the results it proposes in view of the complexity of social life and the impossibility of any planning organization ever possessing the entire gamut of information contained in the billions of transactions taking place among the economic agents) (Hayek, 1967).

It is not hard to sprinkle those ideas with seasonings taken from the left of the political menu: the capitalist company is looking for profit, and the only way to curb its (scorpion's) lust to exploit and devastate is through the action of the state (or, eventually, no one quite knows when, through revolution). Robert Reich, former Labor secretary in the Clinton administration, denounced the idea of corporate social responsibility as being a kind of smokescreen to obscure the indispensable role of the state in social organization (Reich, 2008).

It does not matter whether the idea is left-wing inspired or liberal, what is important is the notion that the company, the market and, in the end, the economy are expressions of an autonomous sphere of social life that functions all the better when it receives the least possible conscious, deliberate, voluntary interference from society. It is as if the true immutable nature of the capitalist company (the relentless unconditional quest for profit curbed only by the force of law and the state) were known and taken for granted. That being the case, transformation could only be superficial, cosmetic and deceptive. The criticism of any possibility of companies responding to socioenvironmental demands other than those strictly required by law is, in the final analysis, based on the idea that capitalism and the economy actually work because they are in some way separate from society, free from its pressures.

So when society decides to manifest itself in the economic sphere, in the life of the companies and in the workings of the markets, the result can only be demagogy (left-wing version) or the poor allocation of resources (liberal version). Social pressure for justice, equality and sustainability should be expressed through the public sphere, by the state and in the form of laws; it should never be allowed to interfere with corporate life.

Markets far beyond the spheres of supply and demand

Situating ethics and respect for the ecosystems right at the heart of economic decisions demands a complete break with the way markets are viewed by most of economic science. What is at stake is the rigid separation of economy and society, as if the former were exclusively an expression of private interest and the latter expressed itself only in the public sphere. The theoretical basis for that dichotomy is a mistaken vision of what the markets signify in contemporary social life.

In a 1977 paper paying homage to Karl Polanyi[8] – which to a certain extent served to guide a considerable part of the research programmes of contemporary institutional economics – Douglass North declared: "It is strange how little discussion there is in economics literature and economic history on the central institution on which neoclassical economics is founded – the market."[9] In a similar vein, another winner of the Nobel Prize for Economics, Ronald Coase, in a text dating back to 1988, remarked that "although economists claim for themselves the study of the market, in modern theoretical economics the role of the market is more in the shade than that of the company".[10] Contemporary economists are merely interested in the "determination of market prices", but the "discussion on the market place as such has disappeared altogether". It is the market as a historical fact with a geographic location and made up of flesh and blood people and not just the general coordinating mechanism that tends to be permanently obfuscated. In the vast majority of cases, economists do not actually study the markets; they suppose them, which is quite different.

The markets cannot be treated as if they were the scorpion's eggs, magical figures, abstract meeting points of buyers and sellers; as automatic, impersonal mechanisms of coordination between individuals, otherwise independent of one another. They are social structures: recurrent forms of interaction that are endowed with certain permanence and are subject to sanctions. That definition opens the way to understanding what everything points to as being a new and fundamental phenomenon for the construction of a new economy: the incorporation of environmental and ethical values or even social equality into the markets themselves. That does not mean that the markets will take it on themselves to address all the great political challenges facing present-day societies, but quite simply that they are not autonomous and independent as their canonic images in economics manuals would have us believe. Instead they find themselves entirely immersed in social life and entirely subject to its influences. Hence the increasing importance of a number of companies that promote what a research group led by Olivier Godard at the Paris *École Politechnique* refers to as anticipated conflict management; far from merely reacting to possible flaws in their products or negative consequences stemming from their production processes, contemporary companies organize themselves in such a way as to accrue legitimacy and credibility in what they do.[11] It is much more than a question of marketing or image. There are systems of legitimacy that make it possible to justify company actions, and the absence of them considerably increases uncertainty regarding the company's future horizons. What is at stake goes beyond the moral disposition of each individual businessman. What is important here is that there are social phenomena that interfere in industrial organization itself, and all the more so when its field of activity is closely bound to the production of collective goods.

Many surprising examples can be given. At the end of July 2006, the Brazilian Vegetable Oils Association (ABIOVE) and the National Association of Cereals Exporters decided that starting from October of that year they would no longer purchase soybean coming from recently deforested areas of the Amazon, and that is now rigidly controlled through the use of satellite images and aerial photography. In the very few instances where the determination was disregarded, the industries kept their word and did not purchase the product from the offending producers. Various NGOs formed part of that initiative, including Greenpeace, Conservation International, The Nature Conservancy and WWF. The Ministry of the Environment also takes part in monitoring the moratorium. In 2010, the Brazilian space research institute INPE began using "a tool specially designed to detect the presence of agricultural crops in deforested areas based on a satellite image classification system". It should be noted that the use of this new technology has made it possible to increase the total area and the number of polygons being monitored. An ABIOVE communiqué informs that "all polygons with more than 25 hectares of deforested land have now been included".[12] Up until 2010 the available technology only detected areas greater than 100 hectares. Another important fact is that in the 2007/2008 harvest 48,809 hectares were monitored, but by the time of the 2009/2010 harvest the area monitored had jumped to 302,000 hectares, within which there were 63,000 hectares of soybean.

Obviously, the soybean moratorium alone will not be enough to put a halt to the absurd deforestation of the Amazon, and there is some evidence that one effect of the new version of the Brazilian Forest Law under discussion in the House of Representatives since 2011 and approved in 2013 has been to stimulate new outbreaks of deforestation. It is also possible that, in many recently deforested areas, soybean has simply been substituted by other crops that are not detected by the technology used for soybean monitoring. Furthermore, the moratorium is restricted to areas deforested after 2006, and those cleared previously are considered acceptable. More importantly, however, while soybean has stopped expanding into the Amazon, it continues to be the vector of destruction in the Brazilian savannah (Cerrado), a biome that is home to one-third of all Brazil's rich biodiversity – over 10,000 plant species, 800 bird species and 160 mammal species – and where "14% of all the waters that flow in three major river basins have their origins – the Amazon, the São Francisco and the Parana-Paraguay".[13]

In spite of all those drawbacks, the moratorium expresses at least three new and important aspects of the workings of contemporary markets:

1   The moratorium is voluntary and its scope goes beyond the minimum requirement of the law. To farmers with land in the Amazon biome, the Forest Law currently in force concedes the right to clear the natural vegetation from 20% of their areas, but in the terms of the moratorium, not even that 20% is acceptable. The fact that the initiative is private and voluntary in no way detracts from its outreach in the public sphere. One of the most interesting features of these agreements among private and associative actors is that they eventually serve as a source of learning and inspiration for public policies. In other words, a voluntary agreement does not mean that the state is absent nor does it belittle government policies in any way.

2   The soybean moratorium has its origins in a set of denunciations in the international sphere made by NGOs specifically linking deforestation in the Amazon with the global food system. In 2006 Greenpeace published its report in English and Portuguese titled *Eating Up the Amazon*.[14] The document not only underscored the connection between soybean and Amazon destruction but specifically named three international giants in the sector (Archer Daniels Midland [ADM], Bunge and Cargill). The NGO also named animal feed processors, supermarket chains and fast-food chains, particularly McDonald's. It proposed a soybean system that would be capable of inhibiting new waves of deforestation associated with the sector. On the down side the same document proposed that Brazil should desist from producing genetically modified soybean altogether, but in that Greenpeace was unsuccessful. In any event, the role of the NGOs was crucial in achieving the moratorium.

3   The third important feature of the moratorium is the idea of traceability: it is no small matter in a country with a strong tradition of 'patrimonialism' and semi-feudal landholding patterns that landowners should publicly reveal how they are making use of private resources. Soybean is just one example; increasingly

companies are revealing the material and energetic bases of their production. That is a decisive characteristic of the functioning of the new markets in the transition to a new economy where ethics and respect for the ecosystems are preponderant in the decision-making processes.

Soybean is not an isolated case; the moratorium is an expression of new forms of organization among the social actors and, in turn, of Amazonian economic life itself. The Sustainable Amazon Forum, for example, brings together NGOs like the Socio-Environmental Institute, the *Saude e Alegria* (Health and Happiness) Project, Imazon and Friends of the Earth – Brazilian Amazon, important social movements like the National Rubber Tappers Council and, at the same time, on the corporate side, Vale do Rio Doce, Petrobras, Alcoa, Philips, ABN, Banco Itaú, Banco da Amazônia and others.[15] Bringing together such a varied group of actors is unprecedented and a sign of civil society's intention to interfere in the way the corporate world decides to allocate its resources. Obviously, the success of these early steps is not guaranteed, but they could not even be attempted if private companies were to be considered as being unconquerable strongholds of an economic rationale to which social life had no access, like a scorpion that any prudent frog would be careful to avoid having any dealings with.

Similarly, as Chapter 2 pointed out, various municipalities in the Amazon region have managed to come off the deforestation blacklist precisely because their businessmen have been willing to give public visibility to the consequences of what they do in the sphere of their private businesses. That change in attitude has been in response to a considerable range of pressures: cuts in credit access determined by the federal government, intensification of surveillance and inspection, loss of economic opportunities due to an external perception of their predatory use of resources (which predominated up until recently) and the great damage done to the reputations of municipalities and companies doing business with them. What is important here is that the turnaround that has enabled many of those municipalities to come off the blacklist, starting with Paragominas, has been the result of a social coalition that involved NGOs, companies, rural workers' unions, cattle and crop farmers' unions and government bodies from various spheres of government, and furthermore, this agglomeration has managed to change significantly the social meaning of business being done there. The goals of zero deforestation, environmental registration (with the technical support of NGOs) and legalization of the municipalities' entire cattle herd have all made it possible to produce certified beef that can be commercialized through big retail outlet chains. Paragominas has also established a carbon accounting scheme aimed at neutralizing all its greenhouse gas emissions.[16] That improved legal environment has attracted a 52 million dollar investment in the form of a Medium Density Fiberboard factory that will be using local raw materials drawn from formerly degraded areas. The charcoal-burning installations have been totally eradicated because they were a stimulus to the illegal use of wood and child labour. Forty-five municipalities have joined the programme, which is supported by a fund created on the basis of a donation made by the Vale do Rio Doce corporation.

Replanting areas of gallery forest with the specific aim of guaranteeing water supplies to São José do Xingu, in Mato Grosso, involves 340 cattle ranchers and is being supported by the Socioenvironmental Institute. A campaign launched in 2004 titled 'Y Ikatu Xingu' (Kamiura language; 'Save the good waters of Xingu') stimulated the formation of a forest species seed collectors network, and the seeds are being planted on the farms and ranches using agronomic techniques that the Socioenvironmental Institute has put at the rancher's disposal.[17] This is one of the noblest uses of the standing forest, namely using it to regenerate degraded areas, and it is being done by partners who up until recently were applying the very practices that produced all that degradation.

All these examples are expressions of one of the most interesting and promising features of market formation in the contemporary world: price mechanisms are beginning to lose their traditional monopoly as the information device that determines the allocation of social resources. Other ways of organizing competitive processes are now joining price mechanisms and they involve public exhibition of syntheses of indicators demonstrating the effects of production and product use on social life and on the natural heritage that the production is based on. It is not merely a question of acknowledging the economy's 'externalities' and addressing them under duress from the enforcement of state legislation and interventions. It now goes beyond that and consists of identifying and measuring how each economic sector makes use of resources whose private nature is coming under increasingly demanding socioenvironmental scrutiny. Another interesting example in the same vein comes from the pharmaceutical industry.

In 2007, Oxfam International published a report containing astonishing information on the production and consumption of medicines. Just 15% of the world's inhabitants consume no less than 90% of all the medicines the sector makes available on the market. The industries concentrate their research on products that have nothing to do with the most frequently occurring diseases. Of the 163 new products launched in the period 1999 to 2004, only three were of any relevance to the diseases that predominate in poor countries. The sector dedicates its efforts excessively to protecting intellectual property rights to the detriment of the access of the very poor to what they have most need of. The compensation of those practices by acts of philanthropy does not solve the problem and effectively places needy populations and their governments in situations of acute insecurity because they never know for sure whether they will be able to count on the provision of the medicines they lack.

The fact of Oxfam launching such a document is not so surprising as the appearance of another document, in 2008, that was actually elaborated with strong support from the pharmaceutical industry itself, in which new parameters for sector evaluation were presented. The surprising parameter is the 'access to medicine index', which classifies the industries according to their social behaviour and not their profitability, as has traditionally been the case.[18] That index strongly questions the traditional model whereby the big laboratories make their gains by patenting the rights of access to the innovations they produce. Indeed, that model is being frankly contested by the systematic breaking of patent rights being authorized by the courts in various countries. In that context, Oxfam's statement that the industry needs to find ways of doing its business whereby responsibility for access to medicines actually becomes part of its core business becomes much more than mere wishful thinking. The index in question is elaborated by a variety of social actors: industry, universities, consultants, governments, religious organizations and Oxfam itself. It attributes weight to various aspects of sector performance that have never previously been expressed in their accounting. The way laboratories manage the question of access to medicines, the consequences of their research in fighting the so-called neglected diseases, the question of fairness and equality in their price policies, and patents and licensing policies are just some of the items evaluated in composing the index. Some investment funds have already adopted the use of that index as a criterion in their decision making on investments in the sector.

The access to medicines index is just one example of a more widespread tendency to make the insertion of the economy and the companies into the social sphere one of the main sources of its own vitality. Obviously the pharmaceutical industries have an interest in elaborating the index. That is not due to any intrinsic charitable spirit. What is important here is that the interest is not the result of any separation between politics and economics, between the world of causes and the aseptic world of business. Quite the opposite; it stems from a joining process, the permeability of the companies in relation to what is going on in the social world. The idea that – within the sphere of legality – the company does what the market requires, and that when the market fails it is up to the government or the NGOs to step in and sort it out, is increasingly being called into question in the contemporary world. This is a new dimension of political activity that is breaking down the barriers that have traditionally confined it.

One of the most vivid expressions of this process lies in the formation of corporate associations totally different from what corporate representation has been here up until quite recently. In the international sphere, the World Business Council on Sustainable Development is probably largely responsible for the introduction of the term 'eco-efficiency' into contemporary corporate culture.[19] More than that, it is an organization that congregates prominent global organizations like Alcoa, PricewaterhouseCoopers and Syngenta International to elaborate the strategic horizons for sustainable development. Each of the documents it produces is the result of an intense discussion process, involving the participation of leading specialists, of course, but the contents produced become part of the culture of those companies that supported their elaboration.

In 1987, a group of young businessmen in the state of São Paulo set up the *Pensamento Nacional das Bases Empresariais* (National Thinking on Corporate Fundamentals), with the explicit aim of establishing a counterpoint to the usual forms of corporate representation performance by placing priority on the matter of transparency in relations between state and society, and even more so on the relations between the state and companies.[20] That venture led to a series of outputs and consequences, among which was the founding of the Ethos Institute, to which over a thousand companies have voluntarily associated themselves.[21] Far from being just another mechanism for defending the immediate interests of its associates, Ethos is noted for its efforts to coordinate various segments of civil society with the private sector in a quest to find ways in which corporate actions can contribute towards sustainable development. Ethos has played a decisive protagonist role, for example in the Sustainable Amazon Forum, given that Brazil's richest regions, basically in the state of São Paulo, consume various products that are part of the explanation for the devastation of different parts of the Amazon biome, above all meat and wood. Furthermore, Ethos has a Climate Forum in which companies discuss mitigation and adaptation goals and mechanisms contributing to the formulation of public policies. One of Ethos' most important activities is in the field of 'strategic management for sustainability', a specialized advisory service (including the qualification of company staff on the various subjects offered by the UNIETHOS, a kind of corporate university run by the Institute)[22] that seeks to interfere in the very planning processes of its associate companies. The Brazilian Corporate Council for Sustainable Development also offers advisory services in strategic planning to companies to enable them to make better use of the resources on which their corporate activities are based.[23] These are just a few of the wide range of examples that could be given in which companies dedicate themselves to a greater or lesser degree to rethinking their roles and practices in the context of contemporary society and that serve to corroborate the idea that the contents of the market should not be pre-judged as being merely the result of the 'mechanics of interests' but actually result from the way in which a variety of social forces contribute to its construction.

Traceability, certification and new parameters for social organizations

International initiatives directed at socioenvironmental tracking and socioenvironmental certification first began to take hold effectively at the beginning of the 1990s. Forest products, clothing and accessories industries, the fisheries and marine sector, construction and civil engineering, tourism, the chemical industry, mining, transport and various agricultural segments responded, formally at least, to protocols involving tracking their activities and to certification processes for their products.

Obviously there is notable inequality among the certification practices. In many cases (like the use of charcoal produced from native vegetation in the steel mills, for example)[24] the tracking has resulted in some progress in spite of the continued existence of unacceptable procedures. Another point is that certification involves costs so high that eventually they may severely restrict access to the markets for producers with little economic clout.

Social movements and organizations have done far more than just pressure and organize public demonstrations to denounce situations that they feel are unfair. They have been capable of mobilizing and forming a group of institutional entrepreneurs which today is interfering decisively in the elements that make up the traceability and certification processes of the products. The certification of forest products, for example, has been strongly influenced by civil society organizations (Bartley, 2007). In the case of textiles, the interference of the American government helped to establish more demanding standards for running the market. A supposedly 'private' transnational regulation of economic organization actually involves a decisive public dimension – and more than that, *for as long as the discussions and initiatives were restricted to the corporate sphere, certification failed to be consolidated*. It only really became an effective regulatory norm on the basis of the performance of institutional entrepreneurs connected to NGOs and government bodies. So the market does not solely depend on the corporate businessmen's ability to coordinate issues so well known to institutional economists such as opportunism, the hitchhiker effect or adverse selection. Its construction involves the eminently political and conflictive dimension associated with the values that should guide certification.

In an effort to demonstrate that idea more clearly, Reginaldo Magalhães studied Greenpeace's activities over the last 30 years. Figure 3.1 illustrates the importance that demands and pressures on the private sector have in its organizational strategy.

In the 1970s the organization dedicated most of its efforts to campaigns targeting national governments, protesting above all against the expansion of nuclear power plants and predatory whale hunting. In the 1980s, pressure was also directed at multilateral organizations like the World Bank. In the 1990s the issue became more diversified and included toxic waste, tropical forests and climate change, and at the same time the campaigns against big multinational corporations were launched. However, it was only in the 2000s that the campaigns explicitly directed against the destructive performance of parts of the private sector were intensified. Global brands and companies are now the targets of campaigns, naming them publicly. That usually obliges them to respond to their critics, set up departments

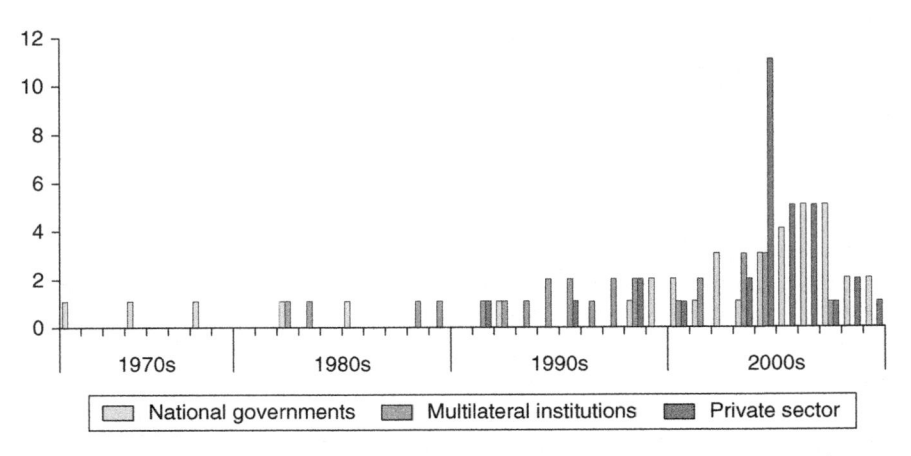

FIGURE 3.1 Targeting the corporate sector. Greenpeace campaigns between 1970 and 2010

Source: Magalhães (2010).

to handle their relations with civil society and even alter the methods used to evaluate their business activities. Nowadays there are companies specializing specifically in private sector consultancy services offering guidance on its relations with stakeholders that are not restricted to occasional inter-occurrences at times of crisis but are part of the companies' strategies. The area itself is undergoing a professionalization process, and many corporations are forming teams specially dedicated to it. There is a surprising variety of sectors where relations with stakeholders are intensifying, ranging from mining to furniture manufacturing and including agrofood and transport.[25]

The time has passed when only certain product niches in specialized high-income markets needed to offer attributes that went beyond the limits of each country's legal requirements. Nowadays product qualification is becoming increasingly widespread and intense. It is impossible to conceive of a single indicator to cover all those results. There is not, and probably never will be, a synthetic parameter capable of measuring the state of relations between society and nature in the way that GDP serves to represent economic growth. Even so, it is important to take note of the improvement in the field of indicators of the relations between the economy and the ecosystems. In the Carbon Disclosure Project's fifth report published in 2008, the 500 participating corporations not only measured their own emissions but also the indirect emissions involved in business trips, transporting employees, the functioning of their supply chains and even the life cycle of their products.[26]

Such indicators function as a kind of compass serving to orientate corporate practices, and they are much more than the results of indispensable ecological engineering. They are formed as a consequence of social conflicts that occur in governmental regulatory agencies, inside the companies themselves and in relations of both of them with the various segments of organized civil society. Some of them have been established by long negotiating processes like those obtained by the various multistakeholder roundtables (soybean, palm oil, biofuels, cocoa, beef cattle, etc.) or those that have been consolidated under the aegis of the Forest Stewardship Council (FSC), which congregates over a thousand forestry companies in 81 countries, representing 40% of the world's productive forests.[27]

These processes involve two-way changes. On the one hand, companies and corporate associations begin to identify parameters for judging their activities that go far beyond the balance of accounts or the dividends paid out to shareholders. This involves establishing various indicators such as material and energy use, the net emissions of greenhouse gases and information on the impacts of companies' activities on both biodiversity and the populations involved in their respective supply and production chains. On the other hand, NGOs also alter their procedures. They become protagonists of direct negotiations with the private sector, and that calls for their technical qualification and a kind of agenda that did not exist for them just a few years ago. On both sides there are increasing risks to reputation involved. Companies need to know how to select the stakeholders they will be dialoguing with, delineate the relevant issues, make use of suitable interlocution channels and show genuine commitment, visibility and openness in all they do, and each one of those aspects brings with it immense risks and conflicts. As an example, they need to choose stakeholders sufficiently well qualified to have a technical understanding of the outreach and limits of the activities undertaken while at the same time not ignoring those stakeholders whose expectations regarding the company will not be based on specialized knowledge. Involving stakeholders in the life of the company is no longer restricted to the communication sector but lies at the heart of the company and is part of its long-term strategy.

Yale University Professor Benjamin Cashore has coined the phrase 'non-state market-driven governance' for one of the results of those double changes.[28] It goes far beyond signifying a mere opportunistic and occasional attitude and actually creates a set of norms and values that the protagonists (companies, NGOs, consumer organizations and governments themselves) are increasingly adopting. A kind of NGO/industry complex is forming, embodying the new standard of private transnational regulation. The chain of requirements and guarantees embedded in the companies' licences to operate involves much more than what has habitually been negotiated in supply chains. It is not just a case of directly accusing certain sectors or companies that have outstandingly damaging conduct; it actually means organizing the markets on the basis of a public exposition of their main socioenvironmental impacts.

Recent surveys investigating certification and socioenvironmental traceability have revealed at least four important features of these new forms of market organization. First, even though they were initially inspired by market niche products (organic agriculture, fair trade coffee and cocoa, among others),[29] commitments to maintaining determined production standards are now entering the sphere of undifferentiated products, namely commodities, at a surprising rate. Due observance of the Better Sugar Initiative parameters, for example, will undoubtedly be a decisive factor in enabling Brazilian ethanol to participate in the decarbonization of the European Union transport energy matrix. Socioenvironmental standards now tend to function as parameters governing the conduct of sectors as a whole and not just as special features of certain products in particular.

The second fundamental feature of the new forms of certification is that they show a tendency to affect very highly internationalized segments: global markets' liability to social pressure increases, and so do the risks of damaged corporate reputations in the case of denunciations, with wide repercussions in the media.

Nevertheless it would be a flight of technocratic imagination to visualize certifications as capable of arriving at a single definitive set of coherent best practice requirements for each sector. Precisely because the process involved is one of tense conflict-riddled social construction, the appropriate indicators of adequate socioenvironmental conduct are subject to great variations, and that is the third major feature resulting from the strong presence of social organizations deep inside contemporary markets.

A fourth feature is due to the fact that socioenvironmental standard demands are less and less restricted to market niche products, and so, if they are to be applied with any semblance of efficiency, they must involve constructive interaction with the state itself. Whether what is at stake is land tenure regularization in the Amazon and Indonesia or enforcement of environmental and labour legislation, socioenvironmental requirements directed at the private sector are unlikely to be complied with unless there is an appropriate legal framework and also a minimally efficient state administrative body duly installed.

In economic growth lurks the scorpion's sting

Corporate initiatives designed to break away from "business as usual" in conducting their affairs are becoming increasingly ambitious. That shows itself in two basic ways. On one side, global corporations set themselves ambitious socioenvironmental goals with clearly defined dates for them to be achieved by. On the other, corporate organizations are emerging whose purpose goes far beyond the effort to correct the socioenvironmental damage of economic activities. The aim of the circular economy propagated by the Ellen MacArthur Foundation is to make sure that, from the outset, the products and services on offer should be conceived with the objective of ensuring that the materials and energy that they depend on are permanently reused and, more importantly, revalued. It is not just a question of applying the famous three 'r's: 'redesign, renew, regenerate'. The report on the circular economy published by the World Economic Forum in 2014 recommends that the concept should orient global value chains and foresees that internet of things, the theme of the next chapter, will have a decisive role to play in that direction.

Another example is the B team.[30] It is an initiative headed by well-known big businessmen: Richard Branson (creator of Virgin Stores), Jochen Zeitz (PUMA), Guilherme Leal (Natura), Arianna Huffington, Paul Polman (Unilever), Muhammad Yunus and Gro Harlem Brundtland, among others. Up until now, "companies have been driven by the profit motive alone and this is no longer acceptable". One of the group's main initiatives is designed to show how companies' real operating costs are opaque and how global corporation profits are based on prices that are lies. PUMA, for example, operates in 120 countries and employs more than 9,000 people. Its turnover in 2010 was 2.7 billion euros and its liquid gains totalled 202.2 million euros. PUMA called in the global consultants Trucost to calculate the hidden costs (those that are not paid) associated with greenhouse gas emissions, water use, soil use, pollution of the atmosphere and waste production. The costs of these items amounted to 145 million euros. That means the environmental costs of the PUMA value chain correspond to more than 70% of its profits. Those unrevealed costs in the price system are by no means restricted to PUMA but are actually a feature of the global economy.

If the 1,600 larger global companies were to pay the costs associated with the use of the ecosystem resources on which they depend, all their profit would vanish. In the US economy, these costs would go beyond 6 percent of GDP, according to the work done by KPMG for the State of Green Business 2015 (https://www.greenbiz.com/report/state-green-business-report-2015, consulted on 23 June 2015).

It is not just the contents of the information published that is important here but also the fact that they were publicized and disseminated by some of the most prestigious global corporate organizations. And it cannot be said that those companies were merely contemplating the costs and not trying to reduce them. In fact, what can be said is that sustainability has been appropriated not only by the discourse but by the practices of the major global brands.

In the last five to ten years, Coca-Cola, Nestlé, Procter&Gamble, Unilever, Walmart, McDonald's, Nike, IBM, Google, Siemens and General Electric have each launched ambitious programmes by means of which they have migrated to accredited supply sources, cut down on greenhouse gas emissions or reduced their water footprints.

Cosmetic changes, false advertising, makeup? Quite often, yes. But it would be taking a risk incompatible with the size of their businesses if such global companies were to promise water neutrality, supply from certified producers only, elimination of toxic waste or a transition to renewable energies and imagine that it would not be noticed if they failed to fulfil their commitments.

That fact obviously raises a question that is crucial for the theme being discussed in this chapter: will the transition of global capitalism's biggest corporations to ecobusiness be capable of interrupting the ecosystem losses that global economic growth has led to? Peter Dauvergne and Jane Lister answer with a resounding no in their important but little publicized book published by the Massachusetts Institute of Technology Press in 2013.

Possibly the biggest current challenge facing human societies can be found in the contradiction between improved performance in the use of natural, energetic and biotic resources and environmental deterioration. Why are major global companies making sustainability a strategic objective? Why, in spite of that, does the destruction continue? What are the best ways to overcome this impasse?

Obviously pressure from civil society and the increasing exposure of big brands to reputational risks can help to explain their involvement with socioenvironmental issues. That is precisely what this chapter has been trying to show. Dauvergne and Lister, however, call attention to other factors involved in this conversion. What is at the heart of it is that the organizational axis of modern capitalism is no longer the factory operating in a fixed location and gathering thousands of people to participate in an activity that is clearly managed and hierarchic.

On the contrary, what predominate today are value chains that function on the basis of thousands of suppliers. Walmart, for example, has over 100,000 suppliers, of which 20,000 are in China alone. The offer of industrial products, whether they be textiles, shoes or electronic equipment, is supported on a pulverization of product manufacturers and, in coordinating them, improved water and energy use, and a reduction of waste and emissions is indispensable.

Furthermore, these big global brands take steps to protect themselves against the volatility of the commodities markets. Coca-Cola is the world's leading purchaser of aluminium and sugar, the third biggest purchaser of citric products and the fifth of coffee. Obviously the company is highly concerned not only to organize its supplies of those products but also to stimulate the reuse of everything it utilizes. It was not for nothing that in 2013 the WWF celebrated an agreement with Coca-Cola for it to reduce greenhouse gas emissions, make better use of water and recover packaging.

There have been many such agreements between big NGOs and big brands. The influence of these big corporations on economic agents is often greater than that of governments and multilateral organizations. The big brands have become private authorities regulating the use of ecosystem resources in a kind of corporatization process affecting the global political arena. What they decide has a much faster effect on suppliers than any government decisions. The 'non-state market-driven governance' mentioned above is actually a kind of corporate/NGO governance.

But if that is the case, and these companies are making an effort to use less water, make the transition to renewable energy sources and recycle more and more, why is that not reflected globally in the form of improved environmental indicators?

The reason put forward by Dauvergne and Lister corroborates the point of view set out in Chapter 2 of this book. At the same time as they seek to reduce the material, energetic and biotic support bases of the products they offer, the corporations carry on launching more and more products in the market, a counterweight to the fact that each one has been elaborated in a more efficient manner.

Considering that each company's manufacture does not stop growing, the reduction in resource use is insufficient to ensure that the company keeps within the bounds of the ecosystem limits in spite of the huge corporate effort to improve the socioenvironmental performance of the global value chains.

The individual automobile mentioned in Chapters 1 and 2 continues to be a glaring example of this paradox. In spite of the improvements of its efficiency, in a report published in 2013, the International Energy Agency forecast that annual emissions of the transport sector will double by 2025. However efficient they may be, private automobiles will be responsible for 90% of that increase. The greater numbers of cars will counterbalance their improved performance.

Another example is cement production: from 1990 to 2011, each ton of product was manufactured emitting 17% less greenhouse gases, but production itself increased so much that total emissions increased by 44% over the same period.[31]

The world's most expressive business organizations recognize the impasse. Shortly before the Rio+20 conference, the World Economic Forum published a report showing the urgent need to rethink economic growth and the collective meaning of consumption, whose expansions have not proved to be capable of providing true well-being to human societies.

Stimulating the shared use of goods (and not individual proprietorship), setting a higher value on people's spare time and recovering urban spaces for society are decisive values, as the World Economic Forum has recognized.

That recognition is admittedly important, but one essential thing is lacking: the willingness of the major global brands to orient their activities not by economic growth goals but by their ability to meet and satisfy real human needs.

If the big NGOs could manage to establish a dialogue with the big global brands that was not just about reducing harmful aspects but instead about the purpose and usefulness for social life of all that is being offered, it would be a relevant step towards solving the current impasse.

Conclusions

The major difficulty facing the transition that is the subject of this book – in which growth is not the only purpose of economic life but is submitted to the greater objective of expanding people's substantive freedoms and is limited by the possibilities of the ecosystems – consists of carrying it out in the context of a decentralized economy in which the non-state actors (consumers, companies and NGOs) have huge powers of decision. Fundamental proposals of the economic system (meet basic needs, expand human capabilities and promote regeneration of the degraded ecosystems) can only be mere aggregated products of those decentralized decisions. It is essential to orientate them by means of public policies, but the latter are insufficient on their own.

This chapter has endeavoured to portray what is undeniably an incipient and minority process, but one that needs to be imbued with contents, depth and velocity by means of intense social participation in spheres that are usually not present on the agendas of civil society organizations. Markets must not be viewed as the exclusive domain of private life, as opposed to that of the civil society or the state in which the public sphere has exclusive rights of expression. Companies are increasingly organizing themselves to handle the social pressures stemming from the activities of their value chains, in a more professional manner. It is equally important that civil society organizations should expand their participation in that field, and such interaction will have a decisive role to play in the emergence of a new economy.

A hundred and fifty years ago, when capitalist markets as we know them were in their infancy, Marx contrasted the intelligence of manufacturing organizations and the anarchic forms of social production and recommended something like a form of centralized planning that would make social needs the central axis of economic life. The current development of contemporary markets and their salutary mixing with social organization may have made them a privileged arena in which fundamental objectives like justice, solidarity, social participation and valuing biodiversity are increasingly exposed. It is indeed a field of conflicts and disputes around determined interests and visions of the world, not a complete, ready-made project for organizing the world. That is precisely what makes the markets one of the most interesting expressions of contemporary cultural and political struggles. All the more so in an information networks society where the markets no longer express, exclusively, the participation of actors motivated by economic interests alone but are being made up of a surprising mixture of public and private, individual and cooperative, gain-motivated and non-economically motivated elements, as we shall see in the next chapter. The big doubt is whether the information

networks society will open the way that will enable the increasing socioenvironmental commitments of the global corporations to make their products and
processes compatible with the limitations of the ecosystems.

Notes

1 This is the central idea of Reginaldo Magalhães' important work: his doctoral thesis
contains a rich analysis of the socioenvironmental responsibility of the financial sector.
See Magalhães (2010).
2 In 1970, Milton Friedman, who was later to be awarded the Nobel Prize for Economics,
wrote in the *New York Review of Books* that companies that seek to go one step further
than they have to by law in regard to their socioenvironmental responsibility are in fact
indulging in 'pure and simple socialism'.
3 John Kenney's *New York Times* article analyses Beyond Oil under the heading 'Beyond
Propaganda'. See Kenney (2006).
4 Auden Schendler's trajectory can be found in *Business Week* (Elgin, 2007).
5 The already-mentioned Benefit Corporation shows the efforts being made to change the
US legislation so that companies can be defined legally in a way that takes into account
other interests than those of their shareholders alone (http://www.benefitcorp.net/state-
by-state-legislative-status, consulted on 23 June 2015). Sukhdev's (2012) book contains
an interesting historical explanation of this point.
6 In microeconomics and some segments of political science, it is common to refer to what
specialists call the agent/principal relation. In the case of a firm, for example, the principal
is the body of shareholders and the agents are those that actually run the firm and are
supposed to act in the name of the shareholders. As the principal cannot exercise total
control over the actions of the agents, there are sets of incentive mechanisms (contracts and
remunerations) that serve to adjust and align the interests of both. The Wikipedia entry on
this subject is excellent (https://en.wikipedia.org/wiki/Principal%E2%80%93agent_
problem, consulted on 23 June 2015).
7 The academic and corporate literature on this issue is vast. One of the most emblematic
texts is that of Sundaram and Inken (2004). The debate among specialists published in
the review in which their article appeared is particularly interesting and perfectly suitable
reading for non-specialists.
8 Karl Polanyi (1886–1964), a Hungarian thinker, is the author of one of the most notable
and critical books addressing the outreach and the limitations of the market economy
in the formation of contemporary societies (Polanyi, 1980).
9 The work of Douglass North, winner of the Nobel Prize for Economics, is directed at
thinking on the role of institutions in the development process. See North (1977).
10 The contribution of Ronald Coase is, like that of Douglass North, fundamental in
regard to the role of institutions in economic life, especially to the question of transaction
costs that are unavoidable in a market-based economy. See Coase (1988: 81).
11 The best reference on this question is French researcher Thierry Hommel's (2004) book.
12 http://www.abiove.com.br/sustent/relatorio09/moratoria09_relatorio_jul10_br.pdf
(consulted on 26 March 2012).
13 The source for this information is Washington Novaes (2010), one of the most knowledge-
able individuals in regard to Brazilian socioenvironmental problems, especially in connection
with the Cerrado savannahs.
14 The Greenpeace report can be accessed at http://www.greenpeace.org/brasil/Global/
brasil/report/2007/7/comendo-a-amaz-nia.pdf (consulted on 23 June 2015).
15 http://www.socioambiental.org/pt-br/campanha/forum-amazonia-sustentavel-fas
(consulted on 23 June 2015).
16 The TEDx held with the mayor of Paragominas, Adnan Demachki, is very interesting
(https://www.youtube.com/watch?v=9chjbWtBx3w, consulted on 26 March 2012, page 84).

17 http://www.yikatuxingu.org.br (consulted on 26 March 2012).

18 See http://www.accesstomedicineindex.org (consulted on 26 March 2012).

19 See http://www.wbcsd.org/home.aspx (consulted on 23 June 2015).

20 See http://www.pnbe.org.br (consulted on 23 June 2015).

21 See http://www3.ethos.org.br/ (consulted on 23 June 2015).

22 See http://www.siteuniethos.org.br (consulted on 23 June 2015).

23 See http://www.cebds.org.br (consulted on 23 June 2015).

24 The main reference on this subject is the Social Observatory Institute, which alongside the Ethos Institute and with support from various other entities (among them, the Fondación Avina) endeavours to eliminate the use of natural vegetation as a source of charcoal for use in smelting iron ore and producing steel, and at the same time seeks to stamp out degrading working conditions, which, even today, are common in this activity. See http://issuu.com/papel_social/docs/steel_devastation/16, consulted on 23 June 2015.

25 See for example the advice given by Harvey (2011) of Manager Corporate Programs, part of the Ceres global consultancy.

26 This is one of the most important global corporate organizations dedicated to modifying contemporary production patterns in the light of reducing greenhouse gas emissions and damage to biodiversity. Nowadays it is active in areas that range from business chains to water resources, embracing such aspects as sustainable cities and the discussion of a variety of government policies (https://www.cdp.net/en-US/Pages/About-Us.aspx, consulted on 23 June 2015.).

27 In regard to FSC governance, see the important work of Voivodic (2010).

28 Cashore, together with his co-author Bernstein, are researchers at Yale University and the University of Toronto, respectively (Bernstein and Cashore, 2007).

29 Regarding fair trade, see http://www.fairtrade.net/, consulted on 23 June 2015.

30 See http://bteam.org/, consulted on 23 June 2015.

31 See https://www.environmentalleader.com/2013/07/16/cement-industry-cuts-carbon-emissions-17 (consulted on 19 November 2014).

4

THE INFORMATION NETWORK ECONOMY EXPANDS SOCIAL COOPERATION

Introduction

It would seem that the information network society has the opposite qualities to those needed to establish a new economy in which ethics and respect for the limits of the ecosystems are at the heart of decision making. The digital media are unceasingly expanding, and in many countries the number of mobile phones is greater than the number of inhabitants.[1] Being the owner of the latest model has now become an obsession, and the result is a frightening increase in the quantities of electronic waste.[2] At the same time electronic commerce has become one of the fundamental elements of a generalized expansion of consumption and, accordingly, of economic growth itself. Daniel Bell's hopes back in 1973 for a post-industrial society associated with a dematerialization process and decisive changes in production processes have been almost entirely frustrated, as was shown in Chapter 2.[3] The efficiency introduced by new digital technology has not been sufficient in itself to promote the decoupling of economic life from the ever-growing consumption of materials and energy. Worse, as Daniel Sieberg shows, in the first decade of the new millennium, the contemporary world went from being "a culture that makes use of technology to another that is completely absorbed by technology" (see Sieberg, 2011).

Furthermore, the business model of the giants of the Internet threatens the privacy of people (Balkan, 2014) and gives room to severe forms of wealth concentration (Brynjolfsson and McAfee, 2014). That portrayal and the risks that it highlights are certainly true. However, it fails to take into account a more important aspect, which is *the social, cultural and political bases of the wealth that is generated in the social networks*. Digital media promote and open the way for unprecedented forms of human cooperation, or, as one of the most important thinkers on this issue, Michel Bauwens, puts it, a new economic ethics that brings with it decisive consequences for the organization of civil society.[4] Furthermore, digital media-based collaboration is not restricted to what takes place in limited circles of intercommunication, such as family groups or groups of friends, but, rather, to an anonymous form of collaboration in public spheres whose regulation does not stem exclusively from price systems or from any hierarchically regulated entity. They are decentralized modes of creating wealth but they are not governed by a strictly market logic. This kind of social cooperation does not repudiate the market. Instead, in spite of the overwhelmingly prevalent tradition in the social sciences that views this assignment as something entirely incompatible with the market's workings, it introduces into it community support initiatives; missions and gains that derive from the capacity to create value, not only for the entrepreneurs but for the entire set of those they have relations with. The information network society opens the way to overcoming the antagonism that has always marked the relations between the market and social cooperation. What is involved here is not the colonization of associative life by the coldness of the world of interests, but the orientation of those organizations that compose the market towards finalities that have their roots in social cooperation and may involve the practices and the ways in which the decentralized units that make up the economic system orientate their actions. That is applicable not only to those sectors that currently operate on the basis of direct social cooperation (like waste pickers, or business units under collective management, of which the Basque corporation Mondragon is the most emblematic example)[5] but also, increasingly, to some of the dominant industrial segments, albeit they are still a minority. The connectivity of the cars on show was the outstanding feature at the 2011 Tokyo Motor Show (see Olmos, 2011). From now on, in addition to the vehicle concept, the automobile industry's designers will have to participate in the planning of housing, garage spaces, roads, highways and cities. Car production will continue to be under the aegis of a corporation but its planning, based on the devices and forms of social cooperation offered by the information network society, will have to go far beyond what has typified private sector management since capitalism itself began. Interaction with consumers can no longer be restricted to what the price system can offer but must take into account social needs that express themselves in public planning. The current schism whereby the production of cars is a private autonomous activity, and urban mobility is the object of concern of the public powers and that the automobile industry has nothing to do with it (after all it merely produces cars – traffic jams are the city authorities' problem), is now strongly negated by the possibility of open, social cooperation stemming from the strengthening of the information networks society. Though the car was still the star, the great novelty at the Tokyo Motor Show in 2011 was the fact that the car is no longer the exclusive owner of that space; the show included housing and parking proposals and showed that manufacturers are allying themselves with architects to present designs for houses that interact with the automobile. Bill Ford, great grandson of Henry Ford and executive chairman of Ford Motors, recognizes, in an interview to the McKinsey newsletter, that "we now have disruption coming from every angle, from the potential ways we fuel our vehicles to the ownership model".[6]

The access to new digital technologies places in the hands of people something that ever since the Industrial Revolution has always been concentrated in the hands of the few, namely the means of producing social wealth. In that sense, the information networks economy questions, at least in part, one of the pillars of capitalist society itself: the radical separation of the producer from the objective conditions of production. Obviously, banks, factories, laboratories, investment funds, supermarkets and even digital media are owned by companies and, above all, by large corporations. The novelty is that, nowadays, interconnected individuals can not only gain access but actually create some of the most relevant modalities of wealth. By 2011, the mobile phone had greater computing power than the entire Apollo space programme had in 1969 (see Thiel, 2011). It has a decisive effect on the production of knowledge, information and culture, but it also reaches out to the entire gamut of social production, which tends to base itself on methods that involve an increasing degree of social participation. A significant part of the prosperity, goods and services that individuals place the highest value on today is offered by collaborative, non-remunerated platforms. A similar observation can be made in regard to the use of materials, and it is based on an explicit concern with reducing impacts on the eco-systems. Examples are: sharing office space, sharing vehicles and even clothes, and also the recycling of electronic goods and their reuse in strengthening social networks, as in the case of the Brazilian organization *metareciclagem* (meta-recycling).[7] The world of energy could be entirely transformed based on the dynamics of such unprecedented interaction between communication and energy. That is the central theme of Jeremy Rifkin's important book mentioned earlier: "internet technology and renewable energy are on the verge of a fusion that will create a powerful new infrastructure for a Third Industrial Revolution, which will change the world. In the new era, millions of people will produce their own green energy in their homes, offices, and factories and share it with others by means of an "energy internet" in the same way that, today, we share information on line."

Far from limiting itself to any one specific domain, a kind of fortress where it is protected, this form of non-market cooperation mixes itself in the field of remunerated activities to the point of actually altering the very idea of what markets consist of in contemporary societies. The image of free software as the fruit of spontaneous, voluntary activities based entirely on the logic of the spontaneous gift does not correspond to the facts. Seventy-five per cent of the development of the Linux kernel during 2009 came from people paid to carry out the work (see Kidman, 2010). What is interesting is that its results continue to be freely accessible. Big corporations like Google and IBM, for example, invest increasingly in open source software. Far from representing any threat to the importance of free software, the fact is that in 2005 only 30% of computer programs were sold as private property (see Perens, 2005). The rest were the object of non-market exchanges, even though they were widely appropriated and used by the private sector, especially the big corporations.

Large corporations now support open, collaborative innovation systems where paid professionals find themselves in the company of volunteer contributors. Why do they do it? Because they realize that the organizations are unable to control the knowledge needed for their own performance and so the most important challenge to be addressed, from the innovation angle, is extrapolating their own boundaries. Harvard University's John Hagel, creator of the Shift Index,[8] is one of the most important researchers in this area, and he has shown that protecting a given stock of knowledge and trying to extract value from it is now being substituted by a participation in diffuse innovation flows. If the information the company needs to function no longer belongs to it, then the days of the closed innovation model are numbered. That argument is proffered by Karim Lakhani and Jill Panetta of Harvard's Law Faculty: "the achievements of the open source software (OSS) communities have imbued the distributed innovation model with visibility and today this model involves sectors as varied as clothing, encyclopedias, biotechnology, the pharmaceutical industry, music and entertainment" (see Lakhani and Panetta, 2007). The Third Industrial Revolution, analysed by Jeremy Rifkin and converted into a public policy by various bodies in the European Union and in several cities where Rifkin and his team were active, is based above all on the fact that residential and commercial buildings and various kinds of equipment and installations need not be just energy consumers but have the potential to produce energy that can be shared by means of intelligent networks and in that way begin to overcome the extreme centralization that was the hallmark of energy production and distribution in the industrial revolutions powered by coal in the nineteenth century and oil in the twentieth. The most important feature of this connection between energy and communication is that digital culture does not refer to the virtual and immaterial only; in this transition to a new economy, the devices available to the information network society based on large-scale social cooperation open the way for making better use of those materials and forms of energy on which social reproduction as a whole is based. That, however, requires that the hierarchic, centralized command control organization so typical of the kind of corporate organization dominated by the energy giants of the nineteenth and twentieth centuries must be replaced by cooperative mechanisms, and the latter can only emerge as a result of decentralization of that very power over natural resources and how they are used. If that were to happen then a new orientation for private business transactions themselves could emerge where the typical figures of producer and consumer, buyer and seller become mixed and less distinct. As Rifkin puts it, "self interest is subsumed by shared interest", and that is reflected in the way the network functions, making use of energy distributed in the equipment and the households, enabling it to be used, sold, conceded and obtained according to the circumstances and not on a centralized authority. Information about such energy needs to be shared to make efficient distribution feasible and that presupposes the existence of transparency, not secrecy about energy availability.

It is true that, within the very same digital culture, interests that base themselves on blocking open use and sharing are extremely powerful, and perhaps no group represents a better expression of such efforts to exercise control as Apple and its late iconic leader Steven Jobs. However, Ronaldo Lemos, who is running one of the most promising study programmes on this very issue (Instituto Tecnologia e Sociedade in Rio de Janeiro),[9] shows how products very similar to those of Apple are being sold for just R\$ 160.00 and not for over R\$ 1,000.00. They are devices manufactured in

China based on free software produced by Google. Such products have tremendous chances of occupying spaces in low-income markets around the world. Ronaldo Lemos is critical of the agreement between Brazil and the Foxconn company whereby the country would receive investments of R\$ 12 billion for the production of the iPad: "The Brazilian technology sector needs to learn from the Chinese companies that operate in clusters based on policies embracing opening hardware and sharing designs and circuits" (see Lemos, 2011). The image of Chinese companies as being incapable of autonomous technological conception and development is a mere caricature: in fact they innovate, and often do so with the explicit intention of addressing the demands of publics that share their use of goods and services that the Chinese companies create.

In an impressive manner, digital technologies have accelerated and disseminated wealth based on the *sharing economy*.[10] New electronic devices, typified by declining prices and increasing mobility, make it possible to track economic life, its material and energy bases and its social consequences to an extent that, ever since the Industrial Revolution and throughout the twentieth century, had seemed to be incompatible with the functioning of a decentralized economy in which the markets were the central players. New information and communication technologies make it possible to reduce the markets' opacity and analyse more profoundly the life cycles and flows of materials and energy involved in social production. The Soybean Moratorium referred to in the preceding chapter presupposes the existence of cooperation among social and political forces whose reciprocal relations prior to the initiative were limited to confrontation. The moratorium, however, could never have existed without the existence of geo-referencing devices that have now endowed land use patterns with an unprecedented visibility. The same goes for the systems that monitor the pact whereby large retailers have agreed to stop selling any meat produced in recently deforested areas of the Amazon outlets. Such equipment has the extraordinary potential power of transforming products into services, that is to say, to reduce their use to a minimum in accordance with people's demands and frequently, according to characteristics that can be detected and processed by digital means. The impacts on material consumption and on the very planning processes can be extraordinary. In his fascinating book, a true epic, Ignacy Sachs shows that the elaboration of economic plans in Poland relied heavily on the use of the abacus.[11]

Greater chances of accessing qualified information based on increasingly available devices also increases the opportunities for doing business in the grassroots and solidarity area of the economy: solid waste pickers can obtain precise information on the location and destination of the materials they collect while, at the same time, new forms of financing have the virtue of facilitating access to the markets.

The information network society expands the possibilities for rethinking the outreach and limits of the ethical base on which a decentralized economy is founded. The fact that an ever-growing portion of the transactions in the contemporary economy are no longer mediated by the markets, but by the social networks, and that the latter actually influence the way the markets function, opens up extraordinarily fertile possibilities for enabling ethics and respect for the limitations of the ecosystems to occupy a central position in the decision-making processes of agencies that are essentially private but operate on an increasingly cooperative basis. Herein lies one of the most important *objective foundations for the emergence of a new economy*.

Prosperity that emerges from cooperation

The rich contents of Wikipedia, free software, platforms for sharing music or YouTube are not exclusively due to the extraordinary technical means available in the form of connections to computer networks and devices like smartphones and tablets, which are increasingly powerful and cheap. In the year 2000, there were 720 million mobile phone accounts in existence.[12] In 2012 that number was applicable to the number of mobile phones in China alone. The global total had already gone beyond the amazing figure of 6.8 billion by the end of 2014, and every day there are an additional 2 million new subscribers.[13] Internet access via mobile phone, which in 2009 corresponded to a mere 360 million accounts, was expected to hit the mark of 3.4 billion subscribers by the year 2015. Facebook was only launched in 2004 but in 2011 it already had 800 million active users.[14] In Brazil alone, by January 2012, more than 40 million people were participating in social networks, forums, blogs or micro-blogs.

Far more important than this impressive expansion of devices, their mobility and the decline in their prices are their social bases, which, in turn, cannot be dissociated from the cultural habits/norms that sustain them. Far from being a form of traditionalist parochialism or an alternative movement invariably confined to minority groups and sects, this cooperation is at the root of the most interesting and promising forms of producing prosperity in the contemporary world. At the root of this cooperation, making their presence felt with increasing force in the private sphere, in public affairs and in the relations between the state and its citizens, there are genuine, comprehensive, significant human bonds endowed with the power of communication and creating mutual trust among people.

Wikipedia, for example, so often disdained by the academic world as producing knowledge of an inferior quality, at the end of 2014, in its English language version, had over 4.6 million articles and is the Internet's seventh most visited site: 300 million visits a month or 13% of all the daily visits made to the Internet.[15] Its contents (50 times bigger than the Encyclopaedia Britannica) stem entirely from the voluntary contributions of its 31,000 participants, each one contributing an average of ten changes to the articles published. The mediation between its contributors is conducted exclusively by means of a computer. Even so there is a powerful feeling of community, of participating in a common venture motivated by shared values, pervading its contributors. The explanation for such feelings of identity in a group of participants that, by definition, is anonymous is the permanent stimulus to communicate among those who are active participants in this platform. Each article published is supported by a discussion channel, an open forum where the authors and readers can point out mistakes or other flaws in what has been posted. The results are highly impressive: according to a survey published by *Nature* in 2005, the errors to be found in Wikipedia are not significantly greater than those found in the famous Encyclopaedia Britannica.[16] Obviously what is important here is not a matter of the superiority of knowledge produced by people as compared to specialized scientific knowledge. The fundamental aspect of the richness of the innovation and knowledge platforms based on sharing and cooperation is their ability to expand the limits of human communication far beyond the limits of purely personal relations. Furthermore, the exposure of ideas to public discussion on the basis of agile platforms that are easy to access opens the way for exchanges of information and ideas and, above all, for ensuring that any mistakes are contested and corrected.

Another self-organized community has formed around free/open software, a group that interacts on the basis of shared rules, observing a certain conduct code but not governed by the usual price mechanisms, in spite of being entirely decentralized. Linux began in 1991 when 22-year-old Linus Torvalds posted an appeal on the Internet saying, "I am creating a (free) operational system, it is just a hobby, nothing great, not even professional. I would like to hear from people what they like and dislike. This is a program for hackers, made by a hacker. I have enjoyed making it and maybe someone would like to take a look at it and adopt it to their own needs. Drop me a line if you would agree to let me use your code."[17] From there the Linux kernel was born, initially with a mere 10,000 lines of code, but by 2007 it already had over 4 million lines contributed by thousands of individuals.

It would be very surprising if all that creativity were to be confined to the non-market world. In 2008, the commercial system associated with Linux had reached the value of no less than 35 billion dollars, with its programs installed in more than 43 million devices like computers, mobile phones, GPS programs and others.[18] In 2003, IBM was registering a higher turnover with sales of services constructed using free software than from the entire set of its patented activities, in spite of the fact that it was the United States' leading patent holder. In the 1990s IBM began to abandon the computer and printer sides of its business and to concentrate on software and services that have come to represent 80% of their 100 billion dollar global revenues. That is where the collaborative platforms have a fundamental role to play. Collaboration not only takes place between companies and autonomous individuals, but it is also operated on the basis of corporate innovation networks. One example is the open innovation that has progressed on the basis of the collaboration between IBM and new partners such as universities and even including its competitors, Sony and Toshiba. The Eclipse Foundation, for example, is an "open source community" that brings together 200 open software projects. Voluntary creative processes supported by social networks and affecting market functioning is not restricted to information and communication technology producers. The world's most important pharmaceutical company, Roche, has been practising open innovation since the end of the 1990s.[19] In 2011 the company made an agreement with a non-governmental, non-profit organization in Sweden that congregates researchers working from open research platforms. It also acts by means of the already-mentioned Innocentive platform (see Introduction).

Threadless.com is an on-line T-shirt factory that bases itself on proposals made by its community of T-shirt users. Clothing and fashion companies face two major challenges: how to attract the best designers at the moment when new fashion trends emerge, and how to forecast sales in order to adapt to market oscillations (see Lakhani and Panetta, 2007). Threadless used the international community it maintains relations with to address both of them. The company's online platform selects from six to ten new designs every week, and their authors receive a US$ 2,500 reward in addition to a reward in the form of enhanced reputation stemming from the posting of their work on the company website. In 2006 the company sold more than 1.5 million T-shirts, and its active community consisted of 600,000 members who elaborate more than 800 designs a week. Each new design is evaluated and the community gives it a score. Furthermore, production is tailored according to the registered purchasing intentions of at least 500 people a week, and planning on that basis has meant that storage and stock expenses are almost non-existent. Posts on the site run to 1,000 a day and include videos, submission of work for evaluation by the community and discussions on design and art. Success has been so great that, up until recently, the company had been systematically turning down offers for launching its products in conventional retail outlets. It is a true form of supply planning but highly decentralized and supported by powerful digital devices.

There is another initiative that not only bases itself on a community of participants but has an openly declared socioenvironmental orientation. The aim of the Patagonia Company's Common Threads Initiative is to reduce clients' clothing consumption. The programme first requests clients do not buy anything they do not really need, and if they do need something, to buy an item that will last a long time, to repair it if it breaks and to re-use or re-sell whatever they are not using any more. "We are the first company ever to make such a formal request and propose a partnership with consumers to reduce consumption and maintain products far from the incinerators and solid waste dumps," stated the company's founder and president Yvon Chouinard. The Common Threads Initiative, headed by Patagonia, is using the eBay platform to stimulate clients to transact their used clothes. One of its advertising pieces actually recommends clients "buy less, buy used clothes" (Aston, 2011).

The expression 'crowdsourcing' synthesizes the most important aspects of this emerging production model. It evokes the idea that cooperative networking, that is, the crowd, is a decisive source of prosperity and seeks to solve problems using collective intelligence and, at the same time, to improve the quality of goods and services being offered. Donations and funding, platforms that seek to give visibility to public data, and scientific and technical knowledge, to stimulate community life, open innovation and access to products that could formerly only be acquired through individual purchasing, are just some of the areas in which these forms of collective collaboration to create prosperity are springing into being. The crucial element is the use of collective creativity, admittedly diffuse, but capable of being brought together in a practical and operational manner.

Also undergoing a process of rapid diffusion is the process of crowdfunding: donations and philanthropy, and loans and investments, are just a few of the sub-areas that often seek to occupy spaces where conventional financing organizations are absent and that seek, above all, to associate their organization's growth with ethical precepts that not only encompass innovation but also attempt to be part of the struggle against other forms of injustice and inequality. It must be noted that crowdfunding does not involve philanthropy alone: one of the outstanding features of these forms of decentralized common action is that they are almost always a mixture of cooperation and competition. The amounts that may eventually be received depend on the ability to persuade and interest a given target public in regard to the project being put forward. They are always high-risk projects even when their overall purpose is not directly market driven. In April 2012 there were 21 crowdfunding platforms in Brazil.[20]

Biciescola (school bike), *carona social* (social ride), *reciclar sempre* (always recycle), *meu carrinho minha vida* (my wheelbarrow, my life) (for waste pickers), *moeda bike* (bike currency), *rode menos e ganhe mais* (drive less and earn more) and *torpedo de aviso* (torpedo warning – urban catastrophe alerts) are all initiatives that are part of a festival of ideas promoted by the Ruth Cardoso Center (and various other organizations) in São Paulo, which in a three-week period registered 346 suggestions. While it is true that the best three selected by an independent jury were each awarded a R$ 10,000 prize, the rules of the competition are more interesting insofar as they integrate the proposals into a network where they are submitted to criticisms and receive suggestions and where their multiplication is strongly stimulated: "Any network user can make comments, suggest details and, if necessary, appropriate, modify and republish the idea. Remember: it is good to be copied. What is important is networking."

Social networks can play a revolutionary role in addressing urban mobility problems aggravated by the prospect of the expanded production of individual automobiles, as was shown in Chapter 2. In the United States, for example, in addition to Zipcar mentioned above, there are a number of other companies based on sharing automobile use. In the case of I-Go in Chicago, as Jeremy Rifkin points out, there are multi-modal devices that make it possible for the user to opt for using a car, collective transport, a bicycle or going on foot at his or her convenience and based on information the person receives about which is the best option at that moment in terms of the ratio between cost and the time taken to get to the destination. It is estimated that each vehicle available for hire in that kind of arrangement represents the equivalent of 20 private cars fewer on the streets. Furthermore, a user survey has shown that distances travelled fell by 44% in the case using the hire scheme. In Europe a survey of shared car hire schemes detected a 50% drop in greenhouse gas emissions associated with each user. The success of this kind of business is impressive. Zipcar, which began operations in 2000, had a turnover of US$ 130 million by 2009 and was growing at a rate of 30% a year. At the beginning of 2012 an association was formed initially by 18 organizations engaged in the shared use of cars in various countries.[21]

In short, the prosperity that emerges from collaborating in networks goes far beyond the limits of the virtual economy and actually reaches out to areas that are enormous consumers of materials and energy, as in the case of the textile and automobile industries. The counterpoint to all those examples (which Chapter 2 took pains to portray) is the predominant way of using the resources on which the overwhelming majority of the goods and services supply depends. The examples cited here compose a very small minority. They do show, however, that it is at least possible for social cooperation, and with it ethics and respect for ecosystem limitations, to be organically integrated into running the markets. The next section will examine what that possibility rests on.

New microeconomic bases for efficiency

The triumph of cooperation over self-interest, used as the sub-title of Yochai Benkler's book of 2011, challenges what has been one of the social sciences' most ingrained ideas since the 18th century, namely that the more individuals concentrate on looking out for their own interests and objectives and limit their cooperation to the minimum necessary to achieve them, the better economic life functions. As we saw in Chapter 3, Friedrich von Hayek was the most sophisticated defender of this idea. In his view, given that no one is capable of bringing together all the information needed to fully portray social aspirations, and there is no computing capacity available for bringing together such information, and even less to respond to the demands that emerge from them, then the price system, better than any kind of planning system, is what can best perform that role. The underlying presupposition is that by dedicating themselves to what they know best without any need to consider the social consequences of their acts (within the sphere of legal activities, obviously), individuals will be making their best contribution to society at large. In that light, the domain of free voluntary collaboration in economic life is infinitesimal. Efficiency in allocating resources that social life depends on is conditioned to individuals concentrating their very best efforts, in a rational and self-interested manner, to getting the best possible remuneration for themselves. The emergence of the information networks society constitutes a concrete refutation of those premises.

The growing importance of science, information, culture and of symbols and brands in the prosperity of contemporary societies swamps the microeconomic foundations that are usually the basis for the defence of the habitually strict protection afforded to closed innovation systems. There is a crucial difference between this type of wealth and that which has been the typical feature of the industrial era. Microeconomics teaches us that cultural goods (information, knowledge and science) are non-rivals. That means that their being consumed by one person in no way jeopardizes their simultaneous or later consumption by another. Apples and oranges are rival goods. After someone has consumed them, new resources need to be allocated to their production to meet the needs of any new consumer. That is not the case with science or information, and accordingly, they are strong candidates for production outside the sphere of the laws of the market. The fact that non-rival goods are not being destroyed by their consumption completely alters the nature of incentives to their production and use in comparison to the rules that govern the supply of rival goods. The very definition of 'economy' to be found in manuals on economics (the allocation of scarce resources among alternative ends) is weakened by the existence of goods whose basic economic nature is not associated with scarcity.

There are only two possible reasons for any restrictions on the consumption of non-rival goods. First, to guarantee the rights that will enable the diffusion of culture on the part of those that are engaged in such diffusion: for almost two centuries, printing presses, television antennas and cinema studios were the indispensable means of disseminating at least part of the cultural production. If they had not been remunerated (and profitable, considering that they were the object of corporate investments), then they would have been unable to meet cultural diffusion needs. Payment for consumption of cultural goods is justified from the microeconomic standpoint as being necessary to guarantee the investments needed for their dissemination. While it is true that knowledge is not destroyed if more than one person reads a given book or journal or goes to a concert, the fact is that the diffusion of such cultural contents requires raw materials, projector equipment, cinemas and distribution systems which could not exist unless the production of the cultural goods remunerated all those factors. Therein lies the microeconomic justification for payment for knowledge in an industrial economy of information.

The second reason is that collecting copyright fees on the production of non-rival goods, such as knowledge, culture and science, ensures that authors are remunerated, thereby guaranteeing the continued creation of the said goods.

Computers, the Internet and mobile devices with access to the networks and their underlying social collaboration are all part of institutional changes that effectively nullify those two justifications. The digital media and their almost unlimited possibilities for reproducing contents at extremely low cost have stripped cultural and scientific goods and information of any vestige of scarcity they once possessed and that were the hallmark of the industrial society. If printed newspapers and journals, movies in the cinemas and shows at the theatres are paid for and that payment opens the way to business based on restricted (paid) access to those contents, in the information networks society that situation is radically altered. Diffusion of cultural goods now takes place through social networks, and payment for their functioning cannot be effectuated under the aegis of the rules governing the industrial economy. The dominant patterns of cultural production in the course of the twentieth century materialized in the form of the Hollywood studios; and the big networks of recording, telecommunications and newspaper companies (of which *Citizen Kane* is an emblematic example) worked on the basis of manufacturing relatively few products but making extraordinary gains through their mass distribution. Cultural diffusion in its industrial information economy version tends to be restricted and undiversified, given that the objective is to maximize gains stemming from a small number of products through a process of massification. That is largely what has led to the scepticism with which some of the twentieth century's most important intellectuals viewed mass culture, deeming it to be synonymous with alienation, passivity and the docile reception of values which society actually had very little power over.

As for the protection of authors' copyright, there exists a counterpart to it identified by a research survey of changes in intellectual property rights in 60 countries over the course of the last 150 years (see Lerner and Tirole, 2002). The results are highly disconcerting for those that embrace the idea that without the protection of intellectual property rights, there can be no innovation: in fact, the protection offered by patents fails to increase countries' levels of innovation. Another study reported in abridged form by the German magazine *Der Spiegel* revealed very similar results (see Thadeusz, 2010). A comparison of the intellectual panoramas of England and Germany in the course of the nineteenth century contradicts the theory that intellectual property rights are the indispensable pillars that support the progress of innovation. The most remarkable effect of the absence of such rights in Germany was an explosive expansion of the publishing market, and the unrestricted reproduction of copies led to an increase in readership. What is even more interesting is that the publications were not the usual classical works but scientific literature. At the same time, in England, important discoveries were published in expensive book form and printed in small numbers. In Germany the habit of printing refined editions for clients who can afford to pay and publishing very cheap editions for the masses (a practice adopted by the contemporary publishing market) dates back to the nineteenth century. Thus academic, scientific and especially technological books were popularized in Germany at that time on the basis of their low prices, which was not the case in England.

There are two basic reasons underlying that paradox (at least in the light of conventional economic wisdom), explaining why prosperity is not based on strict protection for authors' property rights. The first lies in the so-called 'shoulders of giants' effect, as referred to by Newton when he declared that he could not have written his theories without the support of the works of Copernicus and Galileo. The second reason questions the social utility of privatizing knowledge, information and culture and refers to the aspect of non-rivalry. Often the costs of gaining access to protected information are higher than the value of the benefits that are hoped to stem from their use. In other words, what is worse than not providing protection to those who write, invent, compose or create is to restrict the access of interested parties to their production.

If that is the case, then how can the creators of culture and knowledge survive in this world in which production, shared with and certified and evaluated by peers, devoid of any protection or any possibility of direct commercialization, is increasingly important and even part of the strategies of huge economic groups like IBM? Won't the suppression of copyright and intellectual property rights lead to the annihilation of creative energy that some individuals are especially endowed with? The answer is that the information network economy actually strengthens the mixture of market and non-market relations. A cultural promoter who stimulates the sale of his work in CD form will expand his chances of remuneration at shows, festivals or conferences or of gains from advertising (Benkler, 2006). IBM itself registered 29,000 patents in the period 1993 to 2004, and in the year 2000 almost all its revenue was from patents (see Benkler, 2011). Today, the Linux-based services it offers bring in more than twice the revenues stemming from those protected by patents or copyright.

The fecundity of artistic creation in the popular sphere does not stem from any monetary incentives paid to the creators but rather from the fact that the works of art in question are part of people's daily lives, irrespective of any eventual remuneration. The statements of many leading popular artistes corroborate that. Obviously that does not mean that artistes should not be remunerated for their work, but that remuneration is far from being guaranteed by privatizing the rights to their diffusion, except in the case of a very small number of artistes. Furthermore, widespread diffusion opens up the possibility of other forms of remuneration coming from public presentations in shows and conferences. The most important artistes of the 'brega' genre in the state of Pará, Brazil, for example, usually distribute or encourage the sale of their songs in CDs at their shows for prices that are so low they are almost symbolic (see Favareto *et al.*, 2007). On the other hand, their shows usually draw huge crowds in the state for which they receive payment and that provides the income they need to carry on their artistic lives as professionals. Thus, from the social standpoint, restricting access to information, knowledge and culture through the practice of copyright may actually threaten the vigour of innovating processes. Similarly, some performers display their work on the Internet under a voluntary payment regime, and there are several examples of their receiving considerable sums.[22]

That is what the large corporations that have launched innovation platforms in recent years based on voluntary social participation have increasingly perceived. Those platforms may be offered by private companies or by associations and they may also be either entirely voluntary or involve some form of remuneration. Their most important feature is that they operate on the basis of cooperation and open public debate and more than that, on the basis of mixing and remixing, the generalized use of what others can offer as the basis for an individual's new creative effort. One of the most fecund thinkers on this aspect is Lawrence Lessig, creator and current director of Creative Commons, a non-governmental organization dedicated to expanding the offer of creative works whose authors permit them to be shared in various modalities on the basis of legal licensing. In 2008 Lessig published a book entitled *Remix*, in which he shows how one of the most fertile tendencies in knowledge, culture and science in today's world is mixture and re-mixing, not only being supported on the shoulders of giants with the conventional explicit and respectful citations of the same but sharing the very basis for cultural production. One of the great challenges facing school life today, at all levels, is to substitute the myth of originality and the value of individual work with the value of the fecundity embedded in cooperation and permanent consultation and elaboration based on already-formulated knowledge.

The antagonisms of free production and patented production and of market and direct cooperation are becoming weaker.[23] In the first decade of the twenty-first century, the number of patents registered in the United States doubled. There were more than 1 million people awaiting decisions of the US Patent & Trademark Office (USPTO). Each patent consumes at least 20 hours of work on the part of a trained technical person. At the same time, legal actions involving patents are becoming increasingly costly for companies. In 2005, a New York Law School researcher proposed that the USPTO should adopt a system of peer-to-peer review to determine patent concessions. The process is backed by prestigious philanthropic foundations like IBM and Hewlett-Packard. What is interesting is that it is a participative process involving not only the scientific community, but also protagonists that may have an interest in denying the patent because of its possible non-originality.

But the emergence of a collaborative economy is not restricted to the immaterial domain alone. In his 2011 book Jeremy Rifkin gives a persuasive demonstration (and has made efforts to convert his idea into a public policy in several parts of the world) of how residential and commercial buildings can become mini-generating units of alternative forms of energy (basically solar and wind), provided that they are connected in a network. That obviously means that the approach to the construction of buildings must place as much importance on such considerations as on the comfort and functionality they offer to their occupants. In that sense Rifkin defends the idea that an energy/Internet junction achieved by forming intelligent networks is the 'backbone of the new economy'. Here, "new economy" does not mean simply creating value on the basis of intangible assets and the transition to shared and decentralized forms of producing and obtaining energy: at the very heart of this transition process are the ethics of sharing and of respect for ecosystem limitations. That means that, in this kind of functioning, the energy companies depart from their former logic, based fundamentally on their capacity to sell more and more energy, and instead manage a network of energy and information. In that kind of perspective, it is the overall set of society's material life that is highlighted and acquires the visibility needed to enable resource use to be planned, this time on the basis of power that is increasingly within the grasp of the individual units (households and companies) that compose economic life.

It is obviously unrealistic to imagine that the digital media as such will manage to transform the corporate culture typical of an industrial society. What is at stake, as Jeremy Rifkin points out, is not the opposition between fossil fuels and a low carbon economy. What is fundamental is the conflict between the centralized mode of generating energy (including renewable forms) and those that are based on exploiting local sources sustained by the decentralized generation. The Obama government, for example, in spite of the strong association of the president's image with the use of digital media, has not only decided to accelerate programmes for obtaining energy from nuclear sources, and to intensify offshore oil exploration in a bid to reduce the worst effects of coal use, but its investments in the field of renewable energy are still based on models that envisage a high degree of centralization whereby gigantic solar panels or huge wind farms are concentrated in certain regions and the energy is distributed to the rest of the country. Rifkin shows that this way of generating renewable energy has aroused huge opposition from governors of states that the energy would be directed to and also from the energy companies themselves. What is happening is a clash between different corporate cultures.

Conclusions

The examples examined are more representative of an ongoing process than a particular model. The information network economy reinforces an environment favouring forms of collective action no longer bound to price systems or other practices typical of firms and corporations. A new public sphere is coming into being not to be confused with the markets nor with public or private hierarchies, but which nevertheless has an enormous influence over those categories.[24] The penguin in the title of Yochai Benkler's (2011) book symbolizes direct, voluntary, unpaid human cooperation whose main reward lies in the sensation that relations between people involved are fair, stimulate their intelligence, value their participation, broaden their knowledge, are based on communication and open up possibilities for a joint solution of problems.

The assimilation between rationality and egotism is contested, not by any metaphysical considerations concerning human nature, but based on scientific research. Benkler mobilizes fascinating and instructive empirical and experimental evidence from the realms of biology, evolution, neurology, psychology, experimental economics, network sociology and political science to highlight what daily life reveals and specialized knowledge quite often obscures: not only are people far more cooperative than economics and common sense like to admit but also, and more importantly, cooperation processes are far smoother when they are based on real human relations, and the satisfaction of mutual recognition, respect and trust.

There are numerous examples to back that, ranging from the paradox whereby blood donor systems function better when they are non-remunerated, as in Great Britain, than when they are paid for, as in the United States up until the 1970s; to the example of industrial organization whereby huge disparities in salary levels and forms of work organization inhibit worker initiatives, as in the US automobile industry, and lead to disastrous results compared to the innovation typical of the Japanese system where executives earn far less and workers have their say on the factory floor.

The information networks society shows three tendencies of fundamental importance for the transition that is the main subject of this book.

The first is of an ethical nature: all the studies and experiments mentioned above have overthrown the idea that organizations work better when they are supported by incentives of a strictly material nature. Quite the contrary; the feeling of belonging and that business is being conducted on a clearly visible and equitable basis, the enjoyment of socialization, exchanging ideas, the ability to listen and being able to voice an opinion are decisive attributes for any human achievement and at the same time a strong stimulus to obtaining better results in organizations.

From that stems the second aspect of this triumph of cooperation, this time of a political nature: incentive systems based on increasing communication among people, stimulating their initiatives and comprehending the situations they find themselves in function better than reward and punishment systems. Those principles guided Chicago's police and religious leaders, enabling them to improve the quality of life in city neighbourhoods formerly dominated by gang violence by means of social participation.[25]

The third dimension of the triumph of cooperation also lies at the heart of the most important private organizations. Nowadays Linux is used by IBM and a number of other corporations but it continues to be an open system. At the same time, platforms originally intended for public good purposes have become prosperous businesses, but the fact has not led them to abandon the user relations that they were based on when they were created.

The information networks society is based on a scientific revolution, wherein there is convergence of unprecedented human cooperative behaviour, and new forms of organization of the state, business and associative life. Direct, deliberate cooperation based on clear social norms, but not in any way localist or parochial, is the single most important pathway to new relations between economics and ethics.

Notes

1 In 2011 there were 5.6 billion mobile phones, 11% more than in the previous year according to the Gartner Newsroom (http://www.gartner.com/it/page.jsp?id=1759714, consulted on 6 April 2012). In January 2012, Brazil went beyond the mark of 245 million mobile phones, according to the National Telecommunications Regulatory Board – *Agência National de Telecomunicações* (ANATEL) (http://www.infomoney.com.br/comprar-um-celular/noticia/2343572-celulares+numero+novas+linhas+janeiro+maior+dos+ulti mos+anos, consulted on 6 April 2012). These references can be found in the well-documented Wikipedia entry which provides a list of countries ranked according to the numbers of mobile phones in use (http://en.wikipedia.org/wiki/List_of_countries_by_number_of_mobile_phones_in_use#cite_note-12, consulted on 6 April 2012).

2 A United Nations report in 2009 recognized that data is relatively scarce but estimates that more than 40 million tons of electronic waste are being produced in the world every year (UNEP, 2009). An article by Cristiane Prizibisczki (2009) presents some impressive figures in that respect: on average a British citizen produces 3.3 tons of electronic waste in the course of his or her lifetime. While 80% of mobile phone components are suitable for recycling, in 2009 only 3% of mobile phones were actually recycled. The average working life of a mobile phone is 18 months and of a computer 3 years.

3 In 1973, this great US sociologist already foresaw the emergence of what he called a post-industrial society in which economic life would become increasingly dematerialized (see Bell, undated). It is now a fact that the importance of industry in the global economy is decreasing more and more. That, however, as Chapter 2 clearly demonstrates, is far from being a manifestation of any supposed dematerialization of economic life.

4 See in particular http://community.paper.li/2011/11/30/michel-bauwens-a-peer-to-peer-economy (consulted on 4 December 2011).

5 Initiated at the height of the Franco regime in the 1950s, in the little Basque town of Mondragon, the corporation has become a group which today employs over 80,000 people and is the leading economic group in the Basque region and the seventh largest in Spain as a whole. The group competes with other global giants like Hitachi, Mitsubishi, GE and LG and, as reported by Bibby (2012), it maintains 14 research and development centres.

6 See http://www.mckinsey.com/Insights/Innovation/Bill_Ford_charts_a_course_for_the_future?cid=mckq50-eml-alt-mip-mck-oth-1410 (consulted on 19 November 2014).

7 See http://www.metareciclagem.org (consulted on 6 April 2012). See also Dimantas (2010).

8 In 2010, John Hagel, John S. Brown and Lang Davison published an important book on recent changes in contemporary organizations. The Shift Index is a set of parameters elaborated by global consultants Deloitte designed to measure technical and social innovation (http://www2.deloitte.com/us/en/pages/center-for-the-edge/topics/deloitte-shift-index-series.html, consulted on 23 June 2015).

9 See http://www.itsrio.org (consulted on 11 December 2014).

10 The expression is used by Lessig (2008: 99).

11 See Sachs (2010)

12 This information can be found on the Ericsson website (http://www.ericsson.com/thecompany/press/mediakits/lte/information, consulted on 6 April 2012).

13 See http://en.wikipedia.org/wiki/List_of_countries_by_number_of_mobile_phones_in_use (consulted on 11 December 2014).

14 See http://pt.wikipedia.org/wiki/Facebook (consulted on 6 April 2012).

15 See http://en.wikipedia.org/wiki/Wikipedia_community (consulted on 21 December 2014).

16 See http://blogs.nature.com/nascent/2005/12/comparing_wikipedia_and_britan_1.html (consulted on 6 April 2012).

17 Linus Torvalds' story can be found at http://www.cs.cmu.edu/~awb/linux.history.html (consulted on 6 April 2012).

18 See http://en.wikipedia.org/wiki/Linux (consulted on 6 April 2012).

19 There is an interesting report on Roche's success with open innovation. See http://www.innocentive.com/files/node/casestudy/roche-experience-open-innovation.pdf (consulted on 6 April 2012).

20 See http://escoladeredes.net/group/redescolaborativaviacrowdfundingecrowdsourcing/forum/topics/mapeamento-de-plataformas (consulted on 6 April 2012).

21 See http://carsharing.org (consulted on 23 December 2014).

22 Some of the most well known are http://www.kickstarter.com, http://crowdculture.eu/en and, in Brazil, http://catarse.me/pt (the three websites were consulted on 7 April 2012).

23 See Hagel and Brown (2009). The project site in the US Patents Office is: http://peertopatent.tumblr.com/abouttheproject (consulted on 7 April 2012).

24 There is a very interesting description of the emergence of this process in Brazil by Costa (2011).

25 Benkler (2011) refers to this extremely interesting example of using social cooperation as the basis on which to address and solve difficult urban problems.

CONCLUSION

I

Never has so much important progress been made in combating poverty, enhancing eco-efficiency and changing the habits of companies and consumers alike, as has been made in the last 30 years. At the same time, however, there is a widespread feeling that, to use UN Secretary General Ban Ki-moon's expression from his address at Davos in January 2011, "the world's current economic model is a global suicide pact".[1] Why then this contrast between such important achievements and the scepticism that it continues to arouse? If recent progress has been so significant (as the first two chapters of this book have shown), why is there such a feeling of acute uneasiness in civil society, governments, international development organizations and the private sector itself? Two hypotheses can be formulated to answer this question.

The first proposes that we need to accelerate and pursue the same course we are on now. It is most clearly set out in the Brazilian document prepared for the Rio+20 conference.[2] The document defends, quite rightly, the urgent need for a global programme to counter absolute poverty and abolish the hunger that currently affects almost one billion people: a kind of universal '*bolsa familia*'-type allowance scheme.[3] Such an initiative, it says, would be a decisive contribution to the fight against poverty in the world and, to some extent, against inequality. Its cost would lie within the reach of current possibilities. The Brazilian document also insists on the urgency of expanding the traceability of the environmental impacts of the goods and services supply and, accordingly, of the private sector's socioenvironmental responsibility.[4] It is in that setting that the Brazilian document for Rio+20 and the various UN texts used in this book defend the idea of a green economy directed at conciliating economic growth and combating poverty by reducing the use of energy and materials and, in so doing, reducing the impacts on biodiversity stemming from economic life.

Why then this great contrast between such important achievements and the scepticism that it continues to arouse? The first hypothesis is that not enough progress has been made and so the way to go is stepping hard on the accelerator heading in the same direction we are headed in today, but with greater transferral of income to the poor, greater economic growth and more eco-efficiency.

The main aim of this book is to show how that hypothesis, that route and that strategy leaves aside at least two central issues and therefore cannot offer any escape from the 'suicide pact' referred to by Ban Ki-moon in Davos. The first of those two issues is inequality. Meeting basic needs and expanding the capabilities of those who find themselves living in poverty today is incompatible with maintaining the high consumption patterns that predominate among those at the top of the social pyramid. Public policies to increase the income of the poor, either by direct transfer or as a result of the expansion of the labour market, are not sufficient, neither are policies directed at fostering innovation to ensure that less energy, less material and less pollution accompany the expansion of the goods and services on offer. Clearly those policies are fundamental, and the construction of innovation systems designed to ensure sustainability is one of the most important premises of an economy in which ethics and respect for the ecosystems' limitations are at the centre of all decision making.

But, however much innovation advances, and however generous the programmes to transfer income to the poor may come to be, if no limits are set for income inequality and inequality in access to goods and services and, above all, limits to the inequalities that are typically associated with the use of natural resources and energy and the occupation of carbon space, and if those limits are not effectively imposed on those segments with the highest income and greatest power, then advancing in the fight against poverty and, at the same time, maintaining and regenerating ecosystem services that human societies depend on will be impossible. Nobody doubts that the pressure on the ecosystems stemming from the three billion people that will be entering the consumer market in the next 30 years will be immense and will continue to grow, as the previous chapter clearly shows. It is equally true that democratic family planning policies that emphasize respect for the rights of women and their ready access to public health services and modern means of contraception could reduce that pressure considerably without needing to involve any authoritative forms of birth control. The World Bank's 2012 report shows how urgent it is to expand women's ability to "voice their preferences in regard to the number and spacing of children to have" in the domestic environment.[5]

But none of that is enough to attenuate the crucial importance of inequality among nations, and within each one of them, in the use of resources and in the occupation of the carbon space. The struggle against inequality is not just a question of emancipating those that find themselves in situations of poverty or destitution. In a strategic manner, it presupposes limits and transformations in ways of life, above all for those that make the greatest use of resources; and they are neither the very poor, nor those that are currently emerging from a situation of poverty, albeit those two categories are undeniably important in this respect. It is true that the emissions of the developing countries (basically China and India) have already surpassed those of the developed world (see Peters *et al.*, 2012). However, when consumption is taken into account rather than production, and even more so when the calculations are made per capita and not by countries, the huge abyss that separates those responsible for the greatest pressures on the ecosystems and the vast majority of the world population becomes very clear, however welcome the achievements at the base of the pyramid may be.

One of the greatest challenges to be faced by the transition process this book is dedicated to is that contemporary societies have more efficient instruments at hand to combat poverty than ever before, but the same cannot be said for combating inequality. That is one of the explanations for the illusion whereby it would be possible to reduce inequality while only slightly affecting the interests and living standards of those who currently consume most of the resources and services the ecosystems offer to human societies. The last 20 years of the twentieth century taught us some precious lessons on how to combat absolute destitution – even though the millennium goals mentioned in Chapter 1 have not been fully achieved, especially those referring to sanitation and access to good-quality education. In the case of inequality, however (with the exception of some Latin American countries, Brazil among them, where there was deconcentration of incomes), the situation has grown worse and, what is more, the instruments contemporary societies have available to handle the issue are astonishingly precarious.

That leads to the second central issue left aside by this strategy for addressing contemporary socioenvironmental problems, which consists of intensifying and expanding the fight against poverty and enhancing eco-efficiency and corporate socioenvironmental responsibility. It concerns the very meaning of economic life: produce – and produce more and more – to what end? In the world of the nineteenth century and the first half of the twentieth century when material and energy sources appeared to be infinite (or at least infinitely substitutable), that question was almost irrelevant; but in a situation where increasing the goods and services on offer represents an increasingly obvious threat to the existence of the human species because of its effects on biodiversity, on the climate and on the great geochemical equilibriums which life itself depends on, the question becomes absolutely central.

The first and second chapters of this book discuss the real meaning, sense and usefulness of wealth to contemporary societies. The food and automobile industries are emblematic examples of the distance that can exist between wealth and prosperity, as Tim Jackson puts it. Extrapolating even their weight in economic terms, a decisive part of twentieth-century culture was formed around the automobile and processed food industries. However much they may be products that emergent populations aspire to, their nefarious effects on people's health, on territorial dynamics and on the very cohesion of communities are becoming increasingly obvious.

Chapter 2 shows that the American automobile industry (naturally accompanied by fossil fuel interests) concentrated its innovation efforts on the most destructive aspects of the car: greater speed and greater weight, and the consequent relative increase in the use of fossil fuels in vehicles whose degree of inefficiency in the use of materials and consumption of energy is almost beyond belief, as shown in a 2014 article by Vaclav Smil.[6] It marks the union of the Iron Age with the Oil Age. In the food industry there is also a visible gap between the commercial success registered and authentic human health needs. The gap is present when fast food is associated with an offer of toys for children, in the sugar and fat levels in processed foods and in the generalized inability to address the global epidemic of obesity as having its origins in the way that food culture is disseminated today, with disastrous consequences for human health and the use of resources.

Global livestock production is the second largest emitter of greenhouse gases, second only to homes and ahead of individual transport (see FAO, 2010). At the beginning of the twenty-first century, non-communicable diseases, among which obesity is one of the most important, are responsible for more than half the deaths in low- and middle-income countries, according to the WHO (see Stuckler *et al.*, 2011). What is in play in the case of the two examples above is something that is usually far removed from social sciences' (and particularly economics') preoccupations and that is examining the merit, the value of the goods and services the economic system produces and their capacity to create well-being. The issue is treated as if the fundamental contributions of goods and services production were creating jobs, levying taxes and stimulating innovation as a result of the competitive environment. However, fundamental questions – e.g. What use will society make of the things it produces? Will using them enhance well-being? Is the offer compatible with the limits of the ecosystems? – are avoided. It is of crucial importance to evaluate economic life from an ethical standpoint and not merely view it as a mechanism capable of reacting to stimuli stemming from consumers' demands by producing a supply of goods and services.

This book has attempted to show (particularly in Chapters 3 and 4) that such an evaluation goes well beyond being an abstract, pious wish with negligible practical results: the reinsertion of ethics into the economy is one of the most vigorous movements of the social sciences at the end of the twentieth century, and its most important expression can be found in the works of Nobel Prize winner Amartya Sen and in the vast intellectual production of the 'capabilities' school. That cultural change is also increasingly present in corporate administration theories about the attribution of societal purposes and the capability to imbue corporate activity with meaning beyond that expressed in the balance sheets and payrolls. Far from being a purely intellectual movement, this reinsertion is now part of the business world, as can be seen in the contents of manifestations of corporate associations like the Benefit Corporation and the World Business Council on Sustainable Development, and also in the new corporate strategies whereby the consequences for people, communities and territories are becoming a part of corporate planning processes.

It is not just a question of abiding by the law and guaranteeing the interests of the different protagonists involved in business transactions, nor is it a question of introducing whatever technical innovations are necessary to reduce the impacts of economic life on the environment. It is much more a question of going beyond the green economy and questioning whether the economy is contributing towards achieving a better society in which human beings' substantive freedoms are expanding and in which the permanence and regeneration of the ecosystems we all depend on are guaranteed. However great the strides that have been made in the fight against poverty, in the conquest of eco-efficiency and in obtaining changes in corporate behaviour, there is tremendously strong evidence that the contemporary economic system is far from being able to meet the requirements of a world that will probably have a population approaching 10 billion people during the twenty-first century.

The first two chapters of this work show that there is little or no chance that a green economy will be capable of addressing this problem constructively, and that is all the more true in the case of 'green growth'. Facing up to it does not call for innovation alone, however decisive it may be; it calls above all for limits. There can be no doubt about the need to improve governance in innovation systems, and above all to base them on the principle that technological and scientific knowledge are a common human asset, and using them to accelerate the transition to a low carbon economy cannot be subjected to the conventional mechanisms of payment for intellectual property rights. Although scientific and technological cooperation (not transferral) is a crucial aspect of sustainable development itself, the first two chapters of this book make it very clear that unless limits are being set for those who most make use of ecosystem resources, the innovations associated with the green economy will be unable to make the size of the economic system compatible with the maintenance and regeneration of the ecosystem services.

II

The great challenge facing any bid to achieve an economic life in which ethics and respect for the ecosystems' limitations lie at the heart of the decision-making process is best expressed by the word 'emergence'. It is employed by various fields of knowledge but particularly in biology when attempts are made to describe the complexities of the evolution process. One of the twentieth century's greatest biologists, Ernst Mayr, states that even though the biology of evolution is a natural science, it has much more in common with the humanities (especially history) than with the so-called 'hard' sciences (Mayr, 1997). It is not a science that offers predictions. It is especially remote from Newtonian physics. It works largely with concepts (mutation, adaptation and niches, for example) that explain how certain processes occur, bringing together empirical elements specifically associated with the event in question but avoids formulating supposedly universal scientific laws of evolution. In that sense, the emergence of different forms of life does not follow any identifiable direction; it does not respond to any kind of orientation or meaning, much less any intention. Natural phenomena emerge as a result of innumerable circumstances and not as the inevitable product of an intentional process.

In that sense, the term 'new economy' brings with it an undeniable ambiguity. On the one hand, the economic life resulting from the end of the oil era, of the social pressure against inequality and the progress of cooperation that the information networks society is making possible, will be the product of emergent objective factors and social dispositions which have been partially analysed in earlier pages. At the same time, unlike the natural processes analysed by the biology of evolution, overcoming the deadlock that economic life is leading the contemporary world into depends on the conscious, deliberate, voluntary intervention, not of some centralized sphere of authority but instead of an immense multiplicity of civil society and private sector actors and actors from various spheres of government.

The idea that the economy is the product that emerges from the interaction of millions of actors and from it, globally, stems the satisfaction of the interests of all necessarily implies that the purposes of economic life cannot be conceived in any other way than through the narrow viewpoints of each one of its components. That being so, it makes no sense to talk about the economy's mission, function, purpose or objective. Trying to imprint intention onto such a complex set of relations as the economic life of a modern society would be a display of ingenuousness or, even worse, of authoritarianism. It was on the basis of such considerations that, at the moment it consolidated itself as a social science, economics separated itself from ethics, as we saw in Chapter 1. That separation is correlated with the idea that has dominated the formation of the social sciences ever since the 18th century and makes society itself an object for science insofar as it sees it as separate from nature. Reuniting ethics and economics, society and nature, there can be no more important mission for the social sciences in the twenty-first century, and the new economy is the process that effectuates that double reunion.

III

Very little contribution towards the emergence of a new economic life dedicated to sustainable development could be derived from elaborating lists of proposals and recommendations to be applied by states, as is done by international organizations and by private and associative actors. Ignacy Sachs is right when he insists on the urgent need to salvage planning and the use of the state's legislative and persuasive powers to signal to the economic agents the best ways to make use of the resources available (see in particular Sachs, 2012). Substituting the abacus with devices that have increasingly great computing powers is one of the premises for ensuring that such planning is efficient. Even more important, however, than the computing powers of the latest devices is the fact that they can function in networks and be accessible to billions of people. That in itself completely alters the meaning of planning and the democratization of public policies without which the planning would merely mean uniting inefficiency with authoritarianism. The information network society does much more than concentrate signals received from society at large in a single sphere and reissue them in the form of laws, regulations and incentives for the actors in the private sector. It opens the way for an era in which the distribution of resources, social sharing and cooperation can form the basis for changes so significant that Jeremy Rifkin has been inspired to call them the Third Industrial Revolution.

The information network society makes it possible to decentralize what, up until quite recently, could only be made available in an economically efficient form on the basis of concentration. It makes it possible to share, in an equally efficient manner from the allocating point of view, what could previously only have a social existence under a regime of private goods, exclusive production and exclusive use. It makes cooperation, not individualized interests, the social basis for prosperity, as was shown in Chapter 4.

Having direct, deliberate, voluntary, largely non-market social cooperation as the basis for prosperity is exactly the opposite of what, since the appearance of Adam Smith's work and particularly since the nineteenth century, the social sciences have perceived to be the appropriate characteristics of an economy in which the markets play a crucial role in allocating resources. That point of view, which places efficiency and cooperation on opposite sides, fostered a kind of intellectual and cultural abyss, on one side of which was all the warmth of the world of civil society, politics, values and ethics (what Jurgen Habermas calls the world of life), and on the other the glacial coldness of money, the market, capital and technical and corporate organizations that only understand the language of vested interests and that seek to permanently subjugate and colonize the world of life (see Habermas, 1987).

Chapter 3 of this book sought to show that those two hostile worlds are starting to mix, a process that is still incipient but vigorous, nevertheless. There can no longer be any doubt — and it was very clear not only in the 2008 crisis but in the fact that none of the actors directly responsible for unleashing it lost any of their political or economic power — that the behaviour of the vast majority of contemporary corporations involved in finance, industry and distribution activities are typified by their predatory practices in relation to the environment. Inequality and destruction of the ecosystems are not generic traits that emerge as a result of the way certain markets are organized: they are the results of the actions of those actors that are responsible for the control of the overwhelming majority of resources that support the process of social reproduction. The examples are not limited to the financial market's obscene profits (to use President Barak Obama's expression) which have entirely lost any connection with what economists refer to as the marginal productivity of production factors, but also in the desperate efforts to obtain oil from the tar sands in Canada, in vigorous efforts to perpetuate eating habits that are harmful to health or in the incessant growth of the production of individual automobiles based on the large-scale use of fossil fuels.[7]

At the same time the force of the social movement that has formed around corporate socioenvironmental responsibility attracts attention even though the deceitful practices of 'greenwashing' still prevail. Just as important as denouncing the inadequacy and often the cynicism that underlies the presentation of irrelevant initiatives as if they were significant is understanding that markets and companies are not impermeable entities, are not autonomous units isolated from one another, that limit their relationships with the social world to what they buy from it and what they sell to it. In the information network society, a company's reputation-related capital gains ever-increasing importance, and civil society organizations clearly perceive that and start to demand non-predatory behaviour on the part of companies in situations as diverse as the exploitation of palm oil in Indonesia or cattle raising in the Amazon.

But companies are doing much more than just avoiding damaging their reputations or reacting to sporadic local protests. They are units that are managed in a strategic perspective, and internal disputes bring to the surface differing conceptions of control over the management of the resources they hold. Up until the end of the 1960s, in the United States environmental issues were treated by the chemical and oil industries as areas to be handled by specialized engineers who responded to occasional problems based on predominantly technical considerations alone (see Hoffman, 2001). Nowadays, however, those issues have gained power and organizational structure within the companies, and more than that they have become a decisive part of the firms' strategic elaborations and competitive insertion, and quite often they are at the centre of innovation itself.

This tendency of corporate strategic administration to evolve opens the way to enabling the meaning of the goods and services supply and the limitations of the ecosystems to become central issues for the private sector itself. Obviously there is tremendous resistance and nobody can guarantee that such involvement will bring in real results. Nevertheless, the influence of international corporate associations like the World Business Council for Sustainable Development, the Benefit Corporation, the Global Reporting Initiative, the B Team, The Ellen McArthur Foundation and, in Brazil, Ethos and the CEBDS is a decisive factor in changing contemporary corporate culture, as seen in Chapter 3. Another outstanding fact is the initiatives of some private companies to incorporate ethics and the limitations of the ecosystems into their management strategies. The Audi Urban Initiative mentioned in Chapter 1 is not a forum seeking to improve quality, performance and the automobile market, but rather a sphere for reflecting on the question of mobility in the world's megacities. The company's recognition that the image of the individual car is increasingly negative in the eyes of the younger generation led one of the participants in the 2011 meeting it organized to trace a parallel with the 'Tobacco problem', referring to an industry that still resists in spite of the abundant evidence that it offers society goods that jeopardize the quality of public health. The fact that problems associated with the individual automobile should be the focus of discussion at a seminar that brought together the world's five largest groups of architects and renowned sociologists like Saskia Sassen and Richard Sennet is impressive but, even more so, is the fact that the discussion was called for by one of the world's biggest automobile manufacturing corporations. Obviously philanthropic considerations are not behind Audi's move. It is no way similar to what some soft drink industries do when they continue to offer the market products that notoriously contribute to the world obesity epidemic but try to attenuate the negative aspect by linking their images to social work in the form of multi-sport courts constructed in poor neighbourhoods. What is important about the Audi initiative, and that of Unilever mentioned in Chapter 3, the Patagonia initiative cited in Chapter 4 and that of the Benefit Corporation, is that at the heart of their corporate strategies and their competitiveness lies their capability to use the markets to solve great socioenvironmental problems. Stating that the markets are blind by nature – as if state planning spheres were clairvoyant and socially less interested than those of the companies – ignores the fact that they are in fact socially immersed, to use the phrase of the new economic sociology, and therefore subject not only to the influence of vested interests but also of social relations, pressures and concepts of control by a culture that far transcends the kind of mechanical response to stimuli represented by prices (see Smelser and Swedberg, 2005). Could it be that in the same way that IBM transformed itself from a computer-producing company into a service provider (supported to a large extent by free software, as was shown in Chapter 4), the big car manufacturers of today will still be manufacturing cars in a future where traffic and pollution are already at saturation points and cities continue to rely on individual transport? Or will they turn to the business of mobility, in which the car (especially the car powered by an internal combustion engine) will become merely an increasingly irrelevant product of theirs?

All these issues doubtlessly belong to the realm of public policies and they involve local, regional, national and global spheres of authority. However, to imagine that states are the only spheres where this planning process occurs is to underestimate not only the companies' strategy-formulating capabilities but also the potential participation of each individual citizen in decision making on resource use conferred by the information networks society. The forces arraigned against a new economy in which decision making in the public and private spheres and in the sphere of associative organizations is guided by ethical considerations and respect for the ecosystems are immense. Nevertheless, there have never been such promising opportunities for the emergence of an economic system in which sharing, cooperation and the distribution of resources are placed at the service of sustainable development.

Chapter 3 of this book leans heavily on a segment of sociology that began to form in the United States and Europe in the 1980s and from then on to spread to the rest of the world, namely economic sociology, which seeks to dismantle the myth whereby the economic sphere is autonomous in relation to social life. Markets, companies and corporate organizations are moulded by factors which, far from being imbued with an immutable essence (like the scorpion's venom), actually reflect historical circumstances that are susceptible to transformation through human intervention. That is the reason behind the title of the forthcoming work of one of the new economic sociology's most important researchers Mark Granovetter, *Society and Economy*, in allusion to Max Weber's classic *Economy and Society*.[8]

However important that inversion may be, it is insufficient: placing conscious, voluntary and intentional human action firmly at the centre of corporate decisions and reinserting ethics into the economy and society at the heart of business decisions are all essential but they are not enough. What is also needed is to reinsert society into nature, to go beyond the conventional separation of nature from culture and, instead of viewing the ecosystems as externalities, view them for what they are – the material, energetic and biotic base on which all human societies depend. That is the greatest theoretical and methodological challenge that contemporary social sciences have to address.

IV

Thin, with a keen eye and anxiously waiting for the microphone to be passed, a student apprehensively asks her question: "Is there going to be enough time?" It is a crucial question but it must be better understood: enough time for what? The answer lies in the great contradiction of our time that underlies this need to go beyond the green economy. *Will there be enough time to do less?* Doing things better is the green economy's major ambition and it is indeed crucial, but it is insufficient. Contemporary societies have learned how to step on the accelerator and there is no doubt that the resulting economic growth has made it possible to strengthen decisive aspects of the development process; it has enhanced longevity and provided access to health and medicines capable of avoiding diseases and deaths, which until recently limited the possibility of "living a full and worthwhile life", to borrow a phrase from the 'capabilities' school of thought.

However, contemporary society's ability to step on the brakes is not so good and that has been clearly underscored by the successive failures to conclude a global agreement to limit greenhouse gas emissions. At the beginning of 2012, 21 scientists, awarded a kind of environmental Nobel Prize, published a manifesto that begins with a paraphrase of Martin Luther King's famous phrase "We have a dream".[9] Their diagnosis is implacable: the human ability to 'do and to make' has gone beyond human capacity to understand; contemporary civilization is living with an explosive combination of rapid technological evolution and very slow social-ethical evolution.

The need to go far beyond the green economy is precisely because it is impossible to carry on stepping on the accelerator and hoping that technological innovation will avoid a situation where the frontiers of the ecosystems, which we have already crossed in some aspects, are totally destroyed, leading to catastrophic consequences for social life. This book has sought to show that contemporary societies are living in what Marina Silva often refers to as a "crisis of excess" rather than a crisis of scarcity. Admittedly there is still a lack of food for the starving, health for the sick, shelter for the homeless and citizenship for those who are humiliated by others or by the state. But to ensure that such goods and services, such social utilities, reach those who need them, we need to make much less than we are making at the moment: fewer cars with their low energy efficiency and destructive effects on the landscapes and social cohesion of the cities, less foodstuff of the kind that leads to obesity, less greenhouse gas emissions and less consumption of material and energy.

That does not mean paralysis or the diffusion of fear. Technical innovations to extract more usefulness from material and energy through better use open up extraordinarily promising opportunities for economic activity, especially in those countries where people's basic needs have still not been met. Expanding human capabilities obviously calls for economic activity – not for the production of anything and everything provided it creates jobs, taxes and brings with it some form of innovation, but, instead, for the supply of what creates long-term value, of whatever increases society's state of well-being, enhances the bonds among people, brings about cities planned with people in mind and not cars, and stimulates rural and coastal landscapes to regenerate degraded ecosystems. In that regard, at the end of 2011, a company founded by no less a figure than former US vice president Al Gore issued a document with a recommendation that should not be dismissed out of hand as a contradiction in terms: sustainable capitalism is a new paradigm, "a framework that seeks to maximize the long-term creation of economic value, reforming the markets so that they meet real needs and take *all* costs and *all* stakeholders into account".[10] Although it expresses a minority position, it is not an isolated manifestation (the examples mentioned in Chapters 3 and 4 of this book are proof of that), but rather it is a position that is being taken by an increasing number of corporate organizations. One of the sources of enriching and revitalizing the markets themselves lies in the growing interaction between the most outstanding of those corporate organizations and expressive civil society groups.

The Rio+20 has been convened around two central issues: the green economy and governance. Contemporary societies have managed to establish governance mechanisms capable of fostering economic growth and, to a certain extent, as shown in Chapter 1, of obtaining important victories over poverty. They have been capable of carrying forward those objectives, improving eco-efficiency and reducing the amounts of material and energy used per unit value offered on the market. The governance required for sustainable development, however, is one that submits the dynamics of the economy to society's real needs and respects the ecosystems' limitations. It is the kind of governance that transforms economic growth into a means of ensuring that the purpose of development – the permanent expansion of human beings' substantive freedoms – is fulfilled. That calls for much more than renewable energy, better use of materials and the sustainable utilization of biodiversity: far more than a green economy. It requires that society shall be the central protagonist in defining the very meaning of economic activity. However incipient they may be, the signs that point to the real possibility that the twenty-first century will witness the emergence of new relations between economy and ethics, and society and nature, are nevertheless highly important, as this book has tried to show.

Notes

1 Ban Ki-moon's choice of words makes a strong impression: "what we need is a revolution" and "climate change is showing that the old model is more than obsolete" (http://www.guardian.co.uk/environment/2011/jan/28/ban-ki-moon-economic-model-environment, consulted on 26 December 2014).

2 See http://www.mma.gov.br/estruturas/182/_arquivos/rio20_propostabr_182.pdf (consulted on 26 December 2014).

3 *Bolsa familia* is an income transfer programme that reaches nowadays one-quarter of the Brazilian population.

4 In complete contrast to this appeal for visibility associated with production processes is the idea that the environmental clause could harm developing countries' exports. "Similarly care needs to be taken when adopting trade measures for environmental purposes given their potential use for protectionist ends, particularly against developing countries" (page 23).

5 See http://econ.worldbank.org/WBSITE/EXTERNAL/EXTDEC/EXTRESEARCH/EXTWDRS/EXTWDR2012/0,,menuPK:7778074~pagePK:7778278~piPK:7778320~theSitePK:7778063~contentMDK:22851055,00.html, consulted on 23 June 2015.

6 http://spectrum.ieee.org/energy/policy/cars-weigh-too-much (consulted on 26 December 2014).

7 The expression that Barak Obama used in the 2008 campaign and on other occasions afterwards was 'obscene bank bonuses'. The rhetorical power of the presidential expression had little effect in practice. In 2011 the amount of such remunerations totalled US\$ 144 billion, almost the same as the amount registered immediately before the crisis broke out (US\$ 147 billion in 2007). See http://marty4650-spincycle.blogspot.com.br/2012_01_01_archive.html (consulted on 7 April 2012).

8 Almost all of Mark Granovetter's articles can be found at https://sociology.stanford.edu/people/mark-granovetter (consulted on 26 December 2014).

9 This is the Blue Planet Prize awarded ever since the Rio 92 conference to scientific personalities with outstanding roles in contemporary socioenvironmental conflicts. The list of award winners, year by year, can be found at http://www.af-info.or.jp/blog/b-info_en (consulted on 26 December 2014).

10 See http://www.wsj.com/articles/SB10001424052970203430404577092682864215896 (consulted on 26 December 2014). 'All' is underlined in the original.

REFERENCES

ABC (2008) *Amazônia Desafio Brasileiro do século XXI: A necessidade de uma revolução científica e tecnológica.* http://www.abc.org.br/IMG/pdf/doc-20.pdf, consulted on 24 March 2012.

Abramovay, R. (2014) "Innovations to Democratize Energy Access Without Boosting Emissions". *Ambiente & Sociedade*, 17(3): 1–18. http://www.scielo.br/pdf/asoc/v17n3/en_v17n3a02.pdf, consulted on 11 November 2014.

Adeodato, S. (2010) "A batalha das embalagens". *Valor Econômico*, 19/11. http://www.valor.com.br/arquivo/858059/batalha-das-embalagens, consulted on 24 March 2012.

Alves, J. E. (undated) *O Bônus Demográfico e o Crescimento Econômico No Brasil.* Mimeo. http://www.ie.ufrj.br/aparte/pdfs/bonusdemografico.pdf, consulted on 24 June 2015.

Angang, H., H. Linlin and C. Zhixiao (undated) *China's Economic Growth and Poverty Reduction (1978–2002).* http://www.imf.org/external/np/apd/seminars/2003/newdelhi/angang.pdf, consulted on 23 March 2012.

Aston, A. (2011) "Patagonia Takes Fashion Week as a Time to Say: "Buy Less, Buy Used". *GreenBiz.com*, 8/09. http://www.greenbiz.com/blog/2011/09/08/patagonia-takes-fashion-week-time-say-buy-less-buy-used, consulted on 6 April 2011.

Ayres, R. and E. Ayres (2011) *Crossing the Energy Divide: Moving from Fossil Fuel Dependence to a Clean-Energy Future.* Philadelphia, PA. Wharton School Publishing.

Ayres, R. and U. E. Simonis (1994) *Industrial Metabolism Restructuring for Sustainable Development.* Tokyo, Japan. United Nations University Press.

Bardi, U. (2014) *Extracted: How the Quest for Mineral Wealth Is Plundering the Planet.* White River Junction, Vermont. Chelsea Green Publishing.

Bartley, T. (2007) "Institutional Emergence in an Era of Globalization: The Rise of Transnational Private Regulation of Labor and Environmental Conditions". *American Journal of Sociology*, 113(2): 297–351.

Behrens, A., S. Giljum, J. Kovanda and S. Niza (2007) "The Material Basis of the Global Economy: Worldwide Patterns of Natural Resource Extraction and Their Implications for Sustainable Resource Use Policies". *Ecological Economics*, 64(2): 444–453.

Bell, D. (undated) *O Advento da Sociedade Pós-Industrial: Uma Tentativa de Previsão Social.* São Paulo, Brazil. Cultrix.

Bellman, E. (2009) "Pobres motivam a inovação emergente". *Valor Econômico/The Wall Street Journal Americas*, 22/10, page B11.

Benkler, Y. (2006) *The Wealth of Networks: How Social Production Transforms Markets and Freedom*. New York, NY, and London, UK. Yale University Press. http://www.benkler. org/Benkler_Wealth_Of_Networks.pdf (consulted on 25 June 2015).

Benkler, Y. (2011) *The Penguin and the Leviathan: The Triumph of Cooperation Over Self-Interest*. New York, NY. The Crown Publishing Group.

Bernstein, S. and B. Cashore (2007) "Can Non-State Global Governance Be Legitimate? An Analytical Framework". *Regulation & Governance*, 1(4): 347–371.

Bibby, A. (2012) "Co-operatives in Spain – Mondragon Leads the Way". *The Guardian*, 12/03. http://www.theguardian.com/social-enterprise-network/2012/mar/12/cooperatives-spain-mondragon, consulted on 6 April 2012.

Boff, L. (2011) *A ilusão de uma economia verde*. https://leonardoboff.wordpress. com/2011/10/16/a-ilusao-de-uma-economia-verde, consulted on 24 March 2012.

Borlina Filho, V. (2011) "Veículo por habitante vai crescer 62%, planeja setor". *Folha de São Paulo*, 23/10, page B4. http://www1.folha.uol.com.br/mercado/995221-veiculo-por-habitante-vai-crescer-62-no-brasil-estima-setor.shtml, consulted on 24 March 2011.

Bortolozi, T. (2014) "Em casa, brasileiro acessa a internet pelo celular". *Valor Econômico*, 26/10, page B5.

Boyce, G. (2013) "Fuelling the Future with 21st Century Coal". *Cornerstone. The Official Journal of the World Coal Industry*, 1(2): 4–10.

Bruni, L. and S. Zamagni (2010) *Economia Civil: eficiência, equidade, felicidade pública*. São Paulo, Brazil. Cidade Nova.

Casselman, B. (2011) "Mundo árabe se defronta com o fim do "petróleo fácil". *The Wall Street Journal Americas*, 24/05. http://online.wsj.com/article/SB130627966162918763. html?mod=WSJP_inicio_section_economia, consulted on 24 March 2012.

Castro, J. de (1980) *Geografia da Fome (o dilema brasileiro: pão ou aço)*. Tenth edition. Rio de Janeiro, Brazil. Antares Achiamé.

Cechin, A. (2011) '*A natureza como limite da economia: a contribuição de Nicholas Georgescu-Roegen*'. São Paulo, Brazil. Senac/Edusp.

Cechin, A. and J. Veiga (2010) 'A economia ecológica e evolucionária de Georgescu-Roegen'. *Revista de Economia Política*, 30(3): 438–454.

CGEE (2009) *Um projeto para a Amazônia no século 21: desafios e contribuições*. http://www.google. com/search?q=Um+projeto+para+a+Amaz%C3%B4nia+no+s%C3%A9culo+21%3A+desafios +e+contribui%C7%C3%B5es&ie=utf-8&oe=utf-8&aq=t, consulted on 24 March 2012.

Clark, D. (2009) "China's Increasing Carbon Emissions Blamed on Manufacturing for West". *The Guardian*, 23/02. http://www.guardian.co.uk/environment/2009/feb/23/china-carbon-emissions, consulted on 24 March 2012.

Clay, J. (2009) *Agricultural Production from 2000 to 2050 – The Business as Usual Scenario vs. Freezing the Footprint of Food Global Harvest Initiative Symposium*. http://www.elanco. com/pdfs/Clay-Agriculture-from-2000-to-2050.pdf, consulted on 25 March 2012.

Coase, R. (1988) *The Firm, the Market, and the Law*. Chicago, IL. University of Chicago Press.

Costa, E. (2011) *Jangada Digital*. Rio de Janeiro, Brazil. Azougu.

Daly, H. and J. Farley (2004) *Ecological Economics: Principles and Applications*. Washington, DC. Island Press.

Dauvergne, P. and J. Lister (2013) *Eco-Business: A Big-Brand Takeover of Sustainability*. Cambridge, MA. MIT Press.

Deng, Q. and B. Gustafsson (2011) "A New Episode of Increased Urban Income Inequality in China". *CIBC Working Paper Series*, Working Paper 2011/16, October.

Dimantas, H. (2010) *As Zonas de Colaboração Metareciclagem: Pesquisa-Ação em Rede*. Doctoral thesis, ECA/USP. http://www.teses.usp.br/teses/disponiveis/27/27154/tde-17022011-122400/pt-br.php, consulted on 7 April 2012.

Earle, S. (2009) *The World is Blue – How Our Fate and the Ocean's Are One*. Washington, DC. National Geographic Society.

Easterlin, R., L. McVey, M. Switek, O. Sawangfa and J. Zweig (2011) *The Happiness–Income Paradox Revisited*. Institute for the Study of Labor (IZA). Discussion Paper No. 5799. http://ftp.iza.org/dp5799.pdf, consulted on 23 March 2012.

Elgin, B. (2007) "Little Green Lies". *Business Week*, 29/10. http://www.businessweek.com/magazine/content/07_44/b4056001.htm, consulted on 26 March 2012.

European Environment Agency (2010) *Chapter 7: Environmental Challenges in a Global Context*. http://www.eea.europa.eu/soer/synthesis/synthesis/chapter7.xhtml, consulted on 24 March 2015.

FAO (2009) *High Level Expert Forum – Global Agriculture Towards 2050*. Rome, 12 and 13 October.http://www.fao.org/fileadmin/templates/wsfs/docs/Issues_papers/HLEF2050_Global_Agriculture.pdf, consulted on 22 March 2012.

FAO (2010). *The State of Food Insecurity in the World: Addressing Food Insecurity in Protracted Crises*. http://www.fao.org/docrep/013/i1683e/i1683e.pdf, consulted on 24 March 2012.

Favareto, A., R. Abramovay and R. Magalhães (2007) "Direitos de propriedade, eficiência econômica e estruturas sociais em um mercado de bens culturais: o mercado de música brega no Pará". *XXXI Encontro Anual da Associação Nacional de Pós-Graduação em Ciências Sociais* – ANPOCS Caxambu-MG, 22 October, Seminário Temático 31 – Sociologia Econômica. http://ricardoabramovay.com/direitos-de-propriedade-eficiencia-economica-e-estruturas-sociais-em-um-mercado-de-bens-culturais-o-mercado-do-brega-no-para/ (consulted on 24 June 2015).

Foer, J. S. (2010) *Eating Animals*. New York, NY. Little, Brown and Co.

Fontes, S. (2010) "KM investe R\$ 42 mi para ampliar produção e lançar linha própria". *Valor Econômico*, 16/06, page B1.

Friedman, M. (1970) "The Social Responsibility of Business is to Increase Profits". *New York Times Magazine*, 13/10, pages 32–33, 122, 124, 126.

Friedman, T. (2005) *O Mundo é Plano – Uma História Breve do Século XXI*. São Paulo, Brazil. Editora Objetiva.

Friedman, T. (2010) *Quente, Plano e Lotado. Os Desafios e Oportunidades de um Mundo Novo*. São Paulo, Brazil. Editora Objetiva.

Galbraith, J. K. (2004) *The Economics of Innocent Fraud: Truth for our Time*. New York. Houghton Mifflin.

GCP (2010) *The Little Biodiversity Finance Book: A Guide to Proactive Investment in Natural Capital (PINC)*. http://www.globalcanopy.org/siteundatedefault/files/LBFB_04_C.pdf

Gerbelli, L. (2012) "Seis produtos são responsáveis por metade das exportações brasileiras". *O Estado de São Paulo*, 11/03. http://economia.estadao.com.br/noticias/economia,seis-produtos-sao-responsaveis-por-metade-das-exportacoes-brasileiras,105640,0.htm, consulted on 24 March 2012.

German Advisory Council on Global Change (2009) *Solving the Climate Dilemma: The Budget Approach (Special Report)*. http://www.wbgu.de/fileadmin/templates/dateien/veroeffentlichungen/sondergutachten/sn2009/wbgu_sn2009_en.pdf, consulted on 18 March 2012.

Goodland, R. and J. Anhang (2009) *Livestock and Climate Change: What If the Key Actors in Climate Change Are...Cows, Pigs and Chickens?* Worldwatch Institute. http://www.worldwatch.org/files/pdf/Livestock%20and%20Climate%20Change.pdf, consulted on 28 July 2010.

Goldman Sachs (2008) *The Expanding Middle: The Exploding World Middle Class and Falling Global Inequality*. http://www.ryanallis.com/wp-content/uploads/2008/07/expandingmiddle. pdf, consulted on 22 March 2012.

Graham, C. (2011) *The Pursuit of Happiness: An Economy of Well-Being*. Washington, DC. Brookings Institution Press.

Habermas, J. (1987) *Teoría de la acción comunicativa*. Madrid. Taurus.

Hagel, J. and J. Brown (2009) "Peer-to-Patent: A System for Increasing Transparency". *Business Week*, 18/03. http://www.businessweek.com/innovate/content/mar2009/ id20090318_730473.htm, consulted on 7 March 2012.

Hagel, J., J. Brown and L. Davison (2010) *The Power of Pull: How Small Moves, Smartly Made, Can Set Big Things in Motion*. Philadelphia, PA. Basic Books.

Harvey, K. (2011) *So Your Company Has a Stakeholder Team, Now What?* http://www.triplepundit. com/2011/08/company-stakeholder-team, consulted on 26 March 2011.

Hashimoto, S., M. Fischer-Kowalski, S. Suh and X. Bai (2012) "Greening Growing Giants: A Major Challenge of Our Planet". *Journal of Industrial Ecology*, Special Issue, 16(4): 459–466.

Hawken, P., A. Lovins and L. H. Lovins (1999) *Natural Capitalism: Creating the Next Industrial Revolution*. Boston, MA. Little, Brown and Co.

Hayek, F. (1945) "The Use of Knowledge in Society". *American Economic Review*, XXXV(4): 519–530. http://www.econlib.org/library/Essays/hykKnw1.html, consulted on 26 March 2011.

Hayek, F. (1967) "The Results of Human Action But Not of Human Design". In Hayek, F. (ed.) *Studies in Philosophy, Politics and Economics Philosophy*. Chicago, IL. University of Chicago Press, 96–105.

Heinberg, R. (2011) *The End of Growth: Adapting to Our New Economic Reality*. British Columbia, Canada. New Society Publishers.

Henderson, D. (2004) *The Role of Business in the Modern World: Progress, Pressures and Prospects for the Market Economy*. Washington, DC. Institute of Economic Affairs. http://www.cei.org/sites/default/files/David%20Henderson%20-%20The%20 Role%20of%20Business%20in%20the%20Modern%20World%20Progress,%20 Pressures%20and%20Prospects%20for%20the%20Market%20Economy.pdf, consulted on 26 March 2012.

Hoffman, A. (2001) *From Heresy to Dogma: An Institutional History of Corporate Environmentalism*. Stanford, CA. Stanford University Press.

Homer-Dixon, T. (2008) *The Upside of Down: Catastrophe, Creativity, and the Renewal of Civilization*. Washington, DC. Island Press.

Hommel, T. (2004) *Stratégies des firmes industrielles et contestation sociale*. Paris. INRA-Éditions.

IFPRI, Concern Worldwide and Welthungerhilfe (2010) *Global Hunger Index. The Challenge of Hunger: Focus on the Crisis of Child Undernutrition*. http://www.ifpri.org/sites/default/ files/publications/ghi10.pdf, consulted on 22 March 2012.

Imazon (2014) *Amazônia e as Eleições 2014: Oportunidades e Desafios para o Desenvolvimento Sustentável*. http://www.imazon.org.br/publicacoes/outros/amazonia-e-as-eleicoes-2014-oportunidades-e-desafios-para-o-desenvolvimento-sustentavel, consulted on 11 August 2014.

International Energy Agency (2013) *A Tale on Renewed Cities*. http://www.iea.org/ publications/freepublications/publication/Renewed_Cities_WEB.pdf, consulted on 19 November 2014.

IPCC (2011) IPCC Special Report on Renewable Energy Sources and Climate Change Mitigation. Prepared by Working Group III of the Intergovernmental Panel on

Climate Change [O. Edenhofer, R. Pichs-Madruga, Y. Sokona, K. Seyboth, P. Matschoss, S. Kadner, T. Zwickel, P. Eickemeier, G. Hansen, S. Schlömer, C. von Stechow (eds)]. Cambridge University Press, Cambridge, UK and New York, NY. http://srren.ipcc-wg3. de/report, consulted on 25 June 2015.

Jackson, T. (2009) *Prosperity without Growth: Economics for a Finite Planet.* London, UK. Earthscan. http://books.google.com/books?id=jarKLCDcePYC&printsec=frontcover&hl=pt-BR&source=gbs_ge_summary_r&cad=0#v=onepage&q&f=false, consulted on 27 November 2011.

Jacobson, M. and M. Delucchi (2009) "A Path to Sustainable Energy by 2030". *Scientific American*, 301(5): 58–65.

Kahneman, D. and A. Krueger (2006) "Developments in the Measurement of Subjective Well-Being". *Journal of Economic Perspectives*, 20(1): 3–24. http://www.krueger. princeton.edu/PDF%20of%20Kahneman%20Krueger%20paper.pdf, consulted on 23 March 2012.

Kenney, J. (2006) "Beyond Propaganda". *New York Times*, 14/08. http://www.nytimes. com/2006/08/14/opinion/14kenney.html, consulted on 6 April 2012.

Kidman, A. (2010) "75% of Linux Code Now Written by Paid Developers". *apc*, 20/1. http://apcmag.com/linux-now-75-corporate.htm, consulted on 6 April 2012.

KPMG (2012) *Expect the Unexpected: Building Business Value in a Changing World.* https:// www.kpmg.com/dutchcaribbean/en/Documents/KPMG%20Expect_the_ Unexpected_ExctveSmmry_FINAL_WebAccessible.pdf, consulted on 20 March 2012.

Kristof, N. (2010) "Our Banana Republic". *New York Times*, 6/11. http://www.nytimes. com/2010/11/07/opinion/07kristof.html, consulted on 23 March 2012.

Lakhani, K. and J. Panetta (2007) "The Principles of Distributed Innovation". *Innovations*, 97–112. http://scholar.google.com/scholar_url?hl=pt-BR&q=http://www.bic-innovation.com/ static/bic/knowledge_base/documents/OI8.pdf&sa=X&scisig=AAGBfm2ZCfCSgpvLn4Q hLnq1oWO7zi7XTQ&oi=scholarr, consulted on 6 April 2012.

Lehman, J.-P. (2010) "A grande praga da economia mundial". *Valor Econômico*, 20/09, page A15. http://www.advivo.com.br/blog/fernando-augusto-botelho-rj/desigualdade-a-grande-praga-da-economia-mundial-jean-pierre-lehmann, consulted on 23 March 2012.

Leite Jr, H., C. Alencar and V. John (2011) "Evolução do espaço destinado a automóveis em relação à área total construída dos edifícios de São Paulo". 11th International Conference of the Latin American Real Estate Society. http://www.hamiltonleite.com.br/ LARES2011.pdf, consulted on 24 March 2012.

Lemos, R. (2011) "Why Foxconn's iPad Deal is Wrong for Brazil: Brasilia's Unhealthy Obsession with High-End Technology". *Foreign Affairs*, 28/10. http://www.foreignaffairs. com/articles/136625/ronaldo-lemos/why-foxconns-ipad-deal-is-wrong-for-brazil, consulted on 6 April 2012.

Lerner, J. and J. Tirole (2002) "Some Simple Economics of Open Source". *The Journal of Industrial Economics*, L: 197–234. http://www.people.hbs.edu/jlerner/simple.pdf, consulted on 6 April 2012.

Lessig, L. (2008) *Remix: Making Art and Commerce Thrive in the Hybrid Economy.* New York, NY. The Penguin Press. http://pt.scribd.com/doc/47089238/Remix, consulted on 6 April 2012.

Lévy, P. (2011) "A esfera pública do Século XXI". In Pinto, M.V. (ed.) *Techyredes: Método para dinamizar redes sociais dedicadas a causas usando ferramentas web e protocolos de interação.* Fundação Avina. http://www.informeavina2010.org, consulted on 9 January 2012.

Little, I. (1949) "A Reformulation of the Theory of Consumer's Behaviour". *Oxford Economic Papers*, 97.

Little, P. (2014) *Megaprojects in the Amazon Region: A Geopolitical and Socio-Environmental Analysis with Proposals of Better Government for the Amazon.* Lima. Derecho, Ambiente y Recursos

Naturales – DAR. http://www.dar.org.pe/archivos/publicacion/145_megaproyectos_ingles_final.pdf, consulted on 27 August 2014.

Magalhães, R. (2010) *Lucro e Reputação: interações entre bancos e políticas na construção das políticas socioambientais.* Tese de Doutorado, Programa de Pós-Graduação em Ciência Ambiental da Universidade de São Paulo. http://www.teses.uspage br/teseundatedisponiveis/90/90131/tde-19082011-201545/pt-br.php, consulted on 26 March 2012.

Martenson, C. (2011) *The Crash Course: The Unsustainable Future of Our Economy, Energy, and Environment.* Hoboken, NJ. Wiley.

Max-Neef, M. (1991) *Human Scale Development: Conception, Applications and Further Reflections.* New York, NY, and London, UK. The Apex Press. http://www.area-net.org/fileadmin/user_upload/papers/Max-neef_Human_Scale_development.pdf, consulted on 23 March 2015.

Mayr, E. (1997) *This is Biology: The Science of the Living World.* Cambridge, MA. Harvard University Press.

McKinsey Global Institute (2011) *Resource Revolution: Meeting the World's Energy, Materials, Food, and Water Needs.* http://www.mckinsey.com/insights/energy_resources_materials/resource_revolution, consulted on 28 November 2011.

McKinsey Global Institute (2012) *Transforming Materials Management for the 21st Century.* http://www.newmoa.org/solidwaste/cwm/transformwm/pdf/McKinsey20120117RethinkingWaste.pdf, consulted on 24 June 2015.

Meadows, D. H, Meadows, D. L., Renders, J. and Behrens III (1972) *The Limits to Growth.* London. A Potomac Associates Book.

Millennium Ecosystem Assessment (2005) *Ecosystems and Human Well-Being: Synthesis.* Washington, DC. Island Press. http://www.maweb.org/en/index.aspx, consulted on 19 March 2012.

Monteiro, C. A. (2010) 'Comida rápida e obesidade'. *Folha de São Paulo,* 13 June, page A3.

New, M., D. Liverman, H. Schroder and K. Anderson (2011) "Four Degrees and Beyond: The Potential for a Global Temperature Increase of Four Degrees and Its Implications". *Philosophical Transactions of the Royal Society,* 369: 6–19. http://rsta.royalsocietypublishing.org/content/369/1934/6.full.html#ref-list-1, consulted on 20 August 2011.

Nordqvist, J. (2006) *Evaluation of Japan's Top Runner Programme.* http://www.aid-ee.org/documents/018TopRunner-Japan.PDF, consulted on 24 March 2012.

North, D. (1977) "Markets and Other Allocation Systems in History: The Challenge of Karl Polanyi". *Journal of European Economic History,* 6: 703–716.

Norton, M. and D. Ariely (2011) "Building a Better America – One Wealth Quintile at a Time". *Perspectives on Psychological Science,* 6(1): 9–12. http://www.people.hbs.edu/mnorton/norton%20ariely%20in%20press.pdf, consulted on 23 March 2012.

Novaes, W. (2010) "A trajetória do 'primo pobre' dos biomas brasileiros". *O Estado de São Paulo,* 1/09. http://www.estadao.com.br/noticias/impresso,a-trajetoria-do-primo-pobre-dos-biomas-brasileiros,603377,0.htm, consulted on 26 March 2012.

Nussbaum, M. (2011) *Creating Capabilities – The Human Development Approach.* Cambridge, MA. The Belknap Press of Harvard University Press.

OECD (2011a) *African Economic Outlook.* http://www.keepeek.com/Digital-Asset-Management/oecd/development/african-economic-outlook-2011_aeo-2011-en, consulted on 22 March 2011.

OECD (2011b) *Growing Income Inequality in OECD Countries: What Drives It and How Can Policy Tackle It?* OECD Forum on Tackling Inequality, Paris, 2 May.

Ogden, C., M. Carroll, B. Kit and K. Flegal (2012) "Prevalence of Obesity in the United States, 2009–2010". *NCHS Data Brief,* 82: 1–7. http://www.cdc.gov/nchs/data/databriefs/db82.pdf, consulted on 23 March 2012.

Olmos, M. (2009) "O futuro é verde". *Valor Econômico*, 13/12. http://www.desenvolvimentistas. com.br/desempregozero/category/todcs-nossos-autores/gustavo-santos, consulted on 23 March 2012.

Olmos, M. (2011) "Japoneses puxam debate sobre papel do carro". *Valor Econômico*, 2/12. http://www1.valoronline.com.br/empresas/1120288/japoneses-puxam-debate-sobre-papel-do-carro, consulted on 6 April 2012.

Pacala, S. (2007) "Equitable Solutions to Greenhouse Warming: On the Distribution of Wealth, Emissions and Responsibility Within and Between Nations". Conference to the IIASA [International Institute for Applied Systems Analysis]. https://vimeo. com/118433370, consulted on 25 June 2015.

Pan, J. and Y. Chen (2010) "Carbon Budget Proposal". In Pachauri, R. K. (ed.) *Dealing with Climate Change: Setting a Global Agenda for Mitigation and Adaptation*. Delhi. The Energy and Resources Institute, 13–48.

Passariallo, C. (2010) "Danone vê na baixa renda a chave para o crescimento". *Valor Econômico/The Wall Street Journal Americas*, 30/06, page B9. http://www.agenciasebrae. com.br/noticia.kmf?canal=36&cod=10276118, consulted on 22 March 2012.

Perens, B. (2005) *The Emerging Economic Paradigm of Open Source*. http://perens.com/works/ articles/Economic.html, consulted on 6 April 2012.

Peters, G., G. Marland, C. Le Quéré, T. Boden, J. Canadell and M. Raupach (2012) "Rapid Growth in CO_2 Emissions After the 2008–2009 Global Financial Crisis". *Nature Climate Change*, 2: 2–4. http://www.nature.com/nclimate/journal/v2/n1/full/nclimate1332. html, consulted on 7 April 2012.

PNUMA/Red Mercosur (2011) *Eficiéncia en el uso de lós recursos en América Latina: Perspectivas e implicaciones económicas. Estudios de caso: Mercosur, Chile y México*. http://www.pnuma.org/ reeo/Documentos/REEO%20WEB%20FINAL.pdf, consulted on 22 March 2012.

Polanyi, K. (1980) *A grande transformação: As origens da nossa época*. Third edition. Rio de Janeiro, Brazil. Campus (1st edn 1944).

Porter, M. and M. Kramer (2011) *Creating Shared Value*. Chicago, IL. Harvard Business Review, 62–77.

Prizibisczki, C. (2009) "Impactos do Desenvolvimento Tecnológico". *O ECO*, 4/06. http:// www.oeco.org.br/reportagens/21841-impactos-do-desenvolvimento-tecnologico, consulted on 6 April 2012.

Pupo, F. (2011) "Custo barra uso de asfalto ecológico". *Valor Econômico*, 31/10.

PwC (2011a) *Counting the Cost of Carbon: Low Carbon Economy Index 2011*. http://www.pwc.com/hu/ en/industries/assets/Low-Carbon-Economy-Index-2011.pdf, consulted on 12 February 2012.

PwC (2011b) *Minerals and Metals Scarcity in Manufacturing: The Ticking Timebomb. Sustainable Materials Management*. https://www.pwc.ch/user_content/editor/files/publ_indust/pwc_ impact-of-minerals-metals-scarcity-on-business_e.pdf, consulted on 18 March 2012.

Rawls, J. (1993) *A Theory of Justice*. Cambridge, MA. Harvard University Press.

Reich, R. (2008) *Supercapitalism: The Transformation of Business, Democracy, and Everyday Life*. New York. Vintage Books.

Reina, E. (2010) "SP não avança em ranking de saneamento". *O Estado de São Paulo*, 6/10, page C13.

Ribeiro, B., C. Valle and M. Capitelli (2011) "13% usam carro todos os dias em São Paulo". *O Estado de São Paulo*, 22/09. http://m.estadao.com.br/noticias/impresso,13-usam-carro-todos-os-dias-em-sao-paulo,775845.htm, consulted on 24 March 2012.

Rifkin, J. (2011) *The Third Industrial Revolution: How Lateral Power is Transforming Energy, the Economy and the World*. New York, NY. Palgrave Macmillan.

Rifkin, J. (2014) *The Zero Marginal Cost Society: The Internet of Things, the Collaborative Economy and the Eclipse of Capitalism*. New York, NY. Palgrave Macmillan.

Rockström, J. and M. Klum (2012) *The Human Quest: Prospering within Planetary Boundaries.* Stockolm. Stockolm Resilience Center. http://thehumanquest.org/the-book, consulted on 25 June 2015.

Rockström, J. *et al.* (2009) "A Safe Operating Space for Humanity", *Nature*, 461: 472–475. http://www.environment.arizona.edu/files/env/profiles/liverman/rockstrom-etc-liverman-2009-nature.pdf, consulted on 24 March 2012.

Sachs, I. (2010) *A Terceira Margem. Em Busca do Ecodesenvolvimento.* São Paulo. Cia das Letras.

Sachs, I. (2012) "De volta à mão visível: os desafios da Segunda Cúpula da Terra no Rio de Janeiro". *Estudos Avançados*, 26(74): 7–20.

Sachs, J. (2008) *Commonwealth: Economics for a Crowded Planet.* New York. The Penguin Press.

Sachs, J. (2011) "The 'Economics of Happiness'". *Project Syndicate*, 30/8. https://www.project-syndicate.org/commentary/the-economics-of-happiness, consulted on 11 August 2014.

Santos, G. and R. Medeiros (2009) "Nacionalização da GM, o carro elétrico e o futuro do Brasil". *Valor Econômico*, 12/08. http://www.desenvolvimentistas.com.br/desempregozero/2009/08/nacionalizacao-da-gm-o-carro-eletrico-e-o-futuro-do-brasil, consulted on 23 March 2012.

Sen, A. (2000) *Desenvolvimento como liberdade.* São Paulo. Companhia das Letras.

Sen, A. (2009) *The Idea of Justice.* Cambridge, MA. The Belknap Press of Harvard University Press.

Shukla, P. (1997) "Energy for Sustainable Development: A Social Engineering Perspective". *The Social Engineer*, 6(2). http://www.decisioncraft.com/energy/papers/ecc/sidc/esd.pdf, consulted on 22 March 2012.

Sieberg, D. (2011) *The Digital Diet: The 4-Step Plan to Break Your Tech Addiction and Regain Balance in Your Life.* Mississauga, ON, Canada. Three Rivers Press.

Silva, S. (2011) "Economia de água vira moda em casa e nas companhias". *Valor Econômico*, 25/08. http://www.valor.com.br/impresso/ambiente/economia-de-agua-vira-moda-em-casa-e-nas-companhias, consulted on 24 March 2011.

Skidelski, R. and E. Skidelski (2012) *How Much is Enough? Money and the Good Life.* New York, NY. Other Press.

Smelser, N. and R. Swedberg (2005) *The Handbook of Economic Sociology.* Second edition. Princeton, NJ. Princeton University Press.

Smil, V. (2011) "Global Energy: The Latest Infatuations". *American Scientist*, 99: 212–219. http://www.vaclavsmil.com/wp-content/uploads/docs/smil-article-2011-AMSCI.11.pdf, consulted on 24 March 2012.

Smil, V. (2014) *Making the Modern World: Materials and Dematerialization.* Sussex, NJ. Wiley.

Smith, P. and M. Max-Neef (2011) *Economics Unmasked: From Power and Greed to Compassion and Common Good.* Foxhole, Devon, UK. Green Books.

Sperling, D. and D. Gordon (2009) *Two Billion Cars: Driving Towards Sustainability.* Oxford, UK. Oxford University Press.

Steiner, P. (2011) *Les Rémunérations obscènes. Le scandale des hauts revenus en France.* Paris. La Découverte.

Stiglitz, J. E., A. Sen and J.-P. Fitoussi (2008) *Report by the Commission on the Measurement of Economic Performance and Social Progress.* http://www.stiglitz-sen-fitoussi.fr/documents/overview-eng.pdf, consulted on 27 November 2011.

Stuckler, D., S. Basu and M. McKee (2011) "Global Health Philanthropy and Institutional Relationships: How Should Conflicts of Interest Be Addressed?" *PLoS Medicine*, 8(4): 1–10.

Sukhdev, P. (2012) *Corporation 2020: Transforming Business for Tomorrow's World.* Washington, DC. Island Press.

Sundaram, A. and A. Inken (2004) "The Corporate Objective Revisited". *Organization Science*, 15(3): 350–363.

Thadeusz, F. (2010) "No Copyright Law: The Real Reason for Germany's Industrial Expansion?" *Spiegel On Line International*, 18/08. http://www.spiegel.de/international/zeitgeist/0,1518,710976,00.html, consulted on 7 April 2012.

Thiel, P. (2011) "O Fim do Futuro". *O Estado de São Paulo. Link*, 20/11. http://blogs.estadao.com.br/link/o-fim-do-futuro, consulted on 6 April 2012.

UN DESA (2009) *World Economic and Social Survey 2009: Promoting Development, Saving the Planet*. New York, NY. UN DESA. http://www.un.org/en/development/desa/policy/wess/wess_current/2011wess.pdf, consulted on 27 November 2011.

UN DESA (2011) *World Economic and Social Survey 2011: The Great Green Technological Transition*. New York, NY. UN DESA. http://www.un.org/en/development/desa/policy, consulted on 23 March 2012.

UNEP (2009) *Recycling: From E-Waste to Resources*. http://www.greenbiz.com/siteundatedefault/files/unep-ewaste-reoprt.pdf, consulted on 6 April 2012.

UNEP (2011a) *Decoupling Natural Resource Use and Environmental Impacts from Economic Growth*. Paris. UNEP.

UNEP (2011b) *Towards a Green Economy: Pathways to Sustainable Development and Poverty Eradication*. Paris. UNEP. http://www.unep.org/greeneconomy/Portals/88/documents/ger/GER_synthesis_en.pdf, consulted on 21 March 2012.

UNEP (2014) *Decoupling 2: Technologies, Opportunities and Policy Options*. Paris. UNEP.

Veiga, J. E. (2010) "Indicadores de sustentabilidade". *Estudos Avançados*, 24(68). http://www.scielo.br/scielo.php?pid=S0103-40142010000100006&script=sci_arttext, consulted on 19 March 2012.

Victor, N. and D. Victor (2003) *Macro Patterns in the Use of Traditional Biomass Fuels*. http://iis-db.stanford.edu/pubs/20186/macro_patterns.pdf, consulted on 22 March 2012.

Victor, P. (2008) *Managing without Growth: Slower by Design Not Disaster*. Cheltenham, UK. Edward Elgar Publishing Ltd.

Voivodic, M. (2010) *Os desafios de legitimidade em sistemas multissetoriais de governança: uma análise do Forest Stewardship Council*. Dissertação de mestrado. PROCAM/USP. http://www.teses.uspage br/teseundatedisponiveis/90/90131/tde-12082011-095921/pt-br.php, consulted on 26 March 2012.

Volans (2010) *The Biosphere Economy: Natural Limits Can Spur Creativity, Innovation and Growth*. http://www.volans.com/wp-content/uploads/2013/03/The-Biosphere-Economy.pdf, consulted on 24 March 2012.

Weber, M. (1990) *Economia e Sociedade*. Brasilia, Brazil. Editora da UnB.

Weber, M. (undated) *A Ética Protestante e o Espírito do Capitalismo*. 13ª Edição. São Paulo. Biblioteca Pioneira de Ciências Sociais.

WHO (2004) *World Report on Road Traffic Injury Prevention: Summary*. http://www.who.int/violence_injury_prevention/publications/road_traffic/world_report/summary_en_rev.pdf, consulted on 23 March 2012.

WHO (2009) *Global Health Risks: Mortality and Burden of Disease Attributable to Selected Major Risks*. http://www.who.int/healthinfo/global_burden_disease/GlobalHealthRisks_report_full.pdf, consulted on 23 March 2012.

Wiedmann, T., H. Schandl, M. Lenzen, D. Moran, S. Suh, J. West and K. Kanemoto (2013) "The Material Footprint of Nations". *PNAS*, 112(20): 6271–6276. http://www.pnas.org/content/early/2013/08/28/1220362110.full.pdf, consulted on 17 November 2014.

Wilkinson, R. and K. Pickett (2009) *The Spirit Level: Why Equality is Better for Everyone*. London, UK. The Penguin Press.

Wonacott, P. (2011) "Classe média de 313 milhões cria oportunidades na África". *Valor Econômico/The Wall Street Journal Americas*, 3/05, page B9. http://online.wsj.com/article/SB130437924244712605.html, consulted on 22 March 2012.

Woodward, D. and A. Simms (2006) "Growth is Failing the Poor: The Unbalanced Distribution of the Benefits and Costs of Global Economic Growth". *Economic and Social Affairs*, DESA Working Papers No. 20. http://www.un.org/esa/desa/papers/2006/wp20_2006.pdf, consulted on 23 March 2012.

World Bank (2007) *Growth and CO_2 Emissions: How Do Different Countries Fare?* http://siteresources.worldbank.org/INTCC/214574-1192124923600/21511758/CO2 DecompositionfinalOct2007.pdf, consulted on 12 February 2012.

World Economic Forum (2011) *The Consumption Dilemma: Leverage Point for Accelerating Sustainable Growth.* http://www3.weforum.org/docs/WEF_ConsumptionDilemma_SustainableGrowth_Report_2011.pdf, consulted on 19 November 2014.

World Economic Forum (2014) *Towards the Circular Economy: Accelerating the Scale-Up Across Global Supply Chains* (prepared in collaboration with the Ellen MacArthur Foundation and McKinsey&Co).http://www3.weforum.org/docs/WEF_ENV_TowardsCircularEconomy_Report_2014.pdf, consulted on 30 November 2014.

Worldwatch Institute (2010) *State of the World 2010: Transforming Cultures.* http://www.worldwatch.org/bookstore/publication/state-world-2010-transforming-cultures, consulted on 7 November 2014.

Zelizer, V. A. (2004) *The Purchase of Intimacy.* Princeton, NJ. Princeton University Press.

INDEX